# At the Western Front

# At the Western Front

Two Classic Accounts of the First World War by an American Correspondent

At the Front With Three Armies

and

France Bears the Burden

Granville Fortescue

*At the Western Front*
*Two Classic Accounts of the First World War by an American Correspondent*
*At the Front With Three Armies*
and
*France Bears the Burden*
by Granville Fortescue

FIRST EDITION


First published under the titles
*At the Front With Three Armies*
and
*France Bears the Burden*




Leonaur is an imprint
of Oakpast Ltd


Copyright in this form © 2013 Oakpast Ltd


ISBN: 978-1-78282-136-6 (hardcover)
ISBN: 978-1-78282-137-3 (softcover)

**http://www.leonaur.com**


Publisher's Notes

The views expressed in this book are not necessarily those of the publisher.

# Contents

At the Front With Three Armies 7

France Bears the Burden 163

# At the Front With Three Armies

German cyclists tore down the English and French flags from the Hôtel de Ville, Bruges, but left the Belgian colours flying

# Contents

| | |
|---|---|
| Preface | 15 |
| Liége | 17 |
| Brussels in Wartime | 32 |
| Namur | 41 |
| The Battle of Dinant | 46 |
| The Battle of Mons | 57 |
| Germany in Wartime | 63 |
| Germany in Wartime (continued) | 71 |
| Back With the French Army | 85 |
| The Bombardment of Rheims | 99 |
| Antwerp | 113 |
| "Annexing" Belgium | 123 |
| Through the Fighting Lines | 138 |
| King Albert of Belgium | 144 |
| Conclusions and Impressions | 150 |
| Appendix | 160 |

This book has been rigidly censored by the Press Bureau. This accounts for its publication being nearly three months belated. The object of the Press Bureau is, presumably, to prevent information from being given to the enemy. This book deals only with the first three months of the war, and in no way could some of the excised passages come under that heading.
In its uncensored form it is being published in the United States.

G. R. Fortescue.

(Much of the material used in this book appeared originally in the *Daily Telegrap*h, London, *The New York American, The Metropolitan Magazine* and other periodicals. The author makes his acknowledgments.)

Dedication
To the Hon. Harry Lawson, M.P.

# Preface

Without boasting I can say that during the first four months of the Great War I covered more mileage than any other correspondent in the different theatres of operation. When diplomatic relations were broken off between the nations which are now striving for supremacy in Europe, it was my fortune to be in Belgium. Thus I witnessed the opening of the greatest war drama the world has seen. One by one I have seen the acts of that drama pass in all their hideousness and heroism. In these pages I give a record of much that I have seen. My adventures have taken me through Belgium, France and Germany. My base was England.

The tragedy of the conflict is the annihilation of Belgium. In this book I have tried to be scrupulously just in all I say of Germany. But when the desolation of Flanders comes to my mind no phrase of condemnation seems too strong for the ruthless Teuton. There is no atonement that can blot out the Crime of Germany.

I herein state the facts as I saw them. My criticisms and impressions are based on those facts. It is possible that these criticisms may be modified when more information on certain phases of the war is available.

I wish to thank Mr. Brand Whitlock, the American Minister in Belgium, for his courtesy and aid in my work while I was in Brussels. To Mr. James Gerrard, Ambassador from the United States in Germany, and Dr. Henry Van Dyke, American Minister in Holland, I am also greatly indebted.

How I can thank Mr. Myron T. Herrick, American Ambassador in France, who twice was instrumental in having me released from imprisonment as a spy, I do not know. It was through the kindness of Mr. H. E. Johnson, American Consul at Ghent, that I saw much in Ostend. I also wish to thank Colonel M. T. Bridges, Fourth Hussars, and Captain Brandon, R.N., for their help while I was in Furnes.

I try in some way to acknowledge my debt to the Hon. Harry Lawson, of the *Daily Telegraph,* by dedicating this book to him.

Petrograd,

December 1, 1914.

CHAPTER 1

# Liége

It was the 6th of August, 1914. The clock of the Cathedral of St. Paul at Liége had struck half-past six when the first German shell fell into the city. The roar of the explosion was still in the air as I mounted the step of the refugee train, the last train out of Liége. Luckily I had a return ticket from Brussels, so I had not to wait in the terror-stricken crowd which was standing before the ticket window. I had turned the handle of the door of the third-class carriage when I heard a voice say in French: "Will you please help me, sir?" I turned to look down on a Sister of Mercy. She wore a Red Cross on her breast. Beside her stood an old lady; her hair was snow-white, her face was seamed with wrinkles and her eyes had taken on the peculiar glaze characteristic of the very old. She wore a black lace mantle over her white hair, a black silk dress, and supported herself with two black wood canes. Another woman, about thirty years old, handsome, in yellow furs, stood at her elbow.

With all care I lifted the frail figure and carried her into the coach. I placed her in a corner seat by a window. It was perhaps the first time she had travelled third class in her life. Looking around for some cushion or rug, I saw nothing but my light overcoat. This I rolled into a bundle to serve as a pillow.

"What more can I do?"

"Nothing, *monsieur, merci*," answered the Sister of Mercy.

"Thank you, sir"—the woman in the yellow furs spoke in French. She was crying softly. She sat beside the old woman and took one of the thin wrinkled hands in hers and stroked it.

"How old is madam?" I asked.

"Eighty-seven on St. Anne's Day."

"Your home is in Liége?"

"No, *monsieur*, our *château* was in Fléron. It is burned."

The coach is filling up rapidly. Opposite to me sits a pale, cadaverous looking youth with consumption written on every feature. He is talking baby-talk to a Griffon lap-dog he holds on his knee. I hear soft squeals, but they are not the cries of the dog he is petting. Catching my questioning eye, he lifts the lapels of his overcoat pockets to show me, peeping out, the heads of four puppies. Two in either pocket, they whimper softly, their eyes are not opened. When the owner shows them to me, the mother dog gently nuzzles them.

"They are but five days old, *monsieur*, the babies. I could not leave them in Liége. The Germans would eat them."

Across the narrow aisle is a Walloon peasant woman. She has the hard-bitten, cross-grained aspect of those who work fourteen hours each day in the fields, every day in the year save Sundays. She keeps talking to herself in the rough guttural Walloon *patois*. I ask my neighbour what she is saying.

"Eight sons. Five with line regiments, two with the cannon and one who rides a horse. They are all fighting the Germans."

"Where is she going?"

"To Brussels."

"She has friends there who will look after her?"

"No. She has no friends. But there is the king. She will tell him she has given eight sons for the country. He will take care of her."

The carriage is crowded now. Facing me on the front seat sit two sisters, their arms around each other's waists. One is about twenty-two and the other not more than nineteen. They might be shop-girls. Soon the younger one pillows her head on the older's shoulder and falls asleep. The older sister holds herself stiff that she may not disturb the younger one's slumber. From time to time she strokes her hair.

On the seat behind me a priest sits reading his breviary. He is short and thin, with two days' grey stubble of beard on his face. In the poor light he is straining his eyes, through a pair of iron-rimmed glasses. Two buxom, voluble, middle-class women crowd the reading priest into the corner. They are telling their experiences of the past night, interrupted by a small boy who wants to know when he is going to get his dinner.

The last to enter the car is a tall man about forty, dressed in black. He leads four small boys, each holding the other's hands. They are dressed alike—brown caps, brown overcoats with velvet collars, brown socks and shoes. The eldest is six, perhaps; the youngest three. Mentally I christen them the Brownies. The father perches them about on various pieces of luggage, and makes each one happy with a stick of chocolate. I remembered seeing them running down the Rue de Guillemins linked together as if they were playing at horses with their father. The smallest had been snapped off into the gutter in the path of a fast-running motor. But it had been stopped in time and the driver took in the father and the boys and ran them to the station.

While our carriage has been filling up, the one in front of us has been receiving a detachment of wounded. It is slow work lifting the stretchers through the narrow door, and when they are in, it is a problem how to dispose of them. Some are laid out on the floor, while others are arranged across the seats. Those of the wounded who can walk crowd into various corners of the coach and make themselves as comfortable as possible. They are remarkably cheerful. One with a bandaged head entertains the others with a stirring account of his part in the action of the night before. If his feats are but half true, the sturdy defence which the Belgian Army is putting up against the Germans is explained. This habit of vaunting oneself, which is typical of the French as well as the Belgians, is not boasting. It is nothing more than the expression of their enthusiasm. And more remarkable is the fact that most of their exploits which are so graphically described are true. They fill the Saxon writer with envy.

The wounded show the marks of the combat. The heavy coats they wear are coated with mud, their caps are all awry, and they already have that haggard look that comes from constant watchfulness; but their spirit is undaunted.

"What was your position last night?" I asked a soldier of the Fourteenth Line regiment, his arm in a sling.

"Splendid! I was the nearest man of my regiment to the Germans."

And now we get another picture. The Civil Guard, with their preposterous Derby hats trimmed with red cord and their general caricature of the military appearance, march with bayonets fixed through a side door of the station. They form in double rank, opening a lane to the car behind the one where I have a place. It is a cattle-car, a solid black box-car, with only small iron gratings near the under section of the roof. One would feel sorry for the cattle that might be condemned to travel in it. The side door is rolled back. The chief of the Civil Guard gives a signal and a score of German prisoners appear.

They are mere boys. Not one of them is more than twenty-four years old, and for the most part I judge that they have not reached the twenties. Although they have stripped their dull grey uniforms of all insignia, it is apparent that they are cavalry—the dreaded Uhlans—from the clank and jingle of their spurs.

The spike and eagle of each helmet is hidden under a grey drill covering. The buttons of the uniforms have been purposely tarnished, and it is evident that an attempt has been made to assume a service uniform as near khaki as possible. Conspicuous among them is an officer wearing the long grey German military cloak.

They are on the best of terms with their captors. Some of them are munching bread which I recognise as the Belgian ration, and when they step into the cattle-car they shake hands warmly with the Belgian soldiers who have conducted them so far. A railway attendant comes forward with a jug of water and they all swallow long draughts from it. All of them show the effects of the strain of scouting work. Their cheeks are hollow and covered with the scraggy beards of the young.

The German cavalry have been remarkably audacious. Like a pest of flies they have swarmed over the country to the north, east and south of the Meuse. Their seizure of the bridge at Visé was a daring bit of cavalry work. And I saw detachments of them working round the lines at Liége, and one squadron came into the town itself. Some hundreds of them have been captured, but if they have obtained the information that evidently the German general staff needed, the sacrifice is warranted.

When I decided that there was to be some fighting at Liége, I was in Brussels making frantic but unsuccessful efforts to rouse the American minister, Mr. Brand Whitlock, late Mayor of Toledo, to a condition of mind in which he would threaten to bring the United States into this war, unless I were given a *laissez-passer* to follow the Belgian army. In these modern days a war correspondent is about as welcome as a Catholic priest in Ulster. He is looked on as a sort of international spy. The Belgians imagine that he will give important information to the Germans if he sends out a story on the street scenes in Brussels. The English feel that he will disclose the position of the fleet if he writes about the flight of tourists from Ostend. I suppose if I were captured by the Germans I should be condemned to be hung as a spy four times—one for each country the Prussians are fighting.

As the pass was not forthcoming, I thought of doing a little travelling on my own account. I undertook to reconnoitre in a motor car. This is an automobile war. Everyone expected it to be an aeroplane

Bridge of Arches at Liége, blown up by Belgians to prevent the Germans crossing Meuse River.

war, but so far I have only seen three aircraft, two of which I am sure belonged to the Belgian Army, although they were reported as German.

It was a beautiful touring-car, limousine body painted a deep claret colour. When I stepped into it I thought that, after all, war-corresponding had its compensations. Very carefully I explained that we were to get to Liége, evading all pickets if possible.

We tried the straight road first, hoping we should be able to make a detour around Louvain. But this was not possible. The trouble with automobiling in the field is that you must stick to the roads. And every few hundred yards you run into the Civil Guards, who have the disagreeable custom of holding a fixed bayonet on your breast bone while they put you through your catechism.

After being turned back from Louvain I tried to get through by Namur. Here I did fairly well, bluffing past a number of outposts until I met Commandant Joostens of the Sixth Artillery. Now Commandant Joostens is the man who won the international cup at Olympia last year in the military jumping class. He spends most of his winters hunting in Leicestershire. He was very kind, really a most charming man, but he has strict views on the matter of passes in wartime. I offered to take any messages to friends he might have in Liége, if he would let me through. I even offered to notify all his hunting friends with the British Army of his exact whereabouts, if he could see his way to letting me pass, but, stern soldier that he is, all was in vain.

I had little more success on the north. I swear we must have violated Dutch neutrality in our efforts to evade the vigilant patrols guarding the country between Brussels and Liége. But everywhere the same thing happened; we were turned back again.

Discouraged completely, I returned to the Palace Hotel in the Place Rogier, Brussels. It is opposite the Gare du Nord. Looking up at the clock on the railway station, I had an inspiration. I would see if I could get to Liége by train. On the face of it the idea was foolish. But in war you never know your luck. Putting on a business-like air, I stepped up to the ticket window and asked briskly:

"What time does the next train leave for Liége?"

"Thirteen-sixteen. Single or return?"

"Return."

Just as easy as that. It was ten minutes to one, which is thirteen o'clock in Belgium, so I had a sandwich at the station restaurant, then stepped on board the train.

"All aboard for Liége!" the guard shouted in Flemish and French, and we were off. After all the fuss they had made along the roads, stopping me at every turn, here I was travelling to the enemies' objective as easily as if I were on a Long Island local.

That journey down was a page from Guy de Maupassant. It might have been 1870. I had the corner seat facing the engine. Opposite me there was a man with hayfever. Harvest time must be the season for hay fever. Anyway, he sneezed and blew, and sneezed again, until I thought of an awful advertisement I had once seen. It was a picture of a man sneezing and then the effect of that sneeze was painted on the atmosphere. Microbes of every genus were graphically depicted. I began to wonder if hayfever was catching. It was with relief I heard him say he was getting out at Tirlemont.

Next to Hay Fever sat a Conscript. He was not more than nineteen, and it was obvious that the red in his eyes came from much crying. He carried a few things done up in a brown paper parcel, and never said a word from start to finish of the journey.

Beside the conscript sat a jaunty man in uniform—black with silver buttons and marine blue collar and facings. It was cut in the French soldier style, and his cap was the shape used in the same army. I took him for some snappy cavalry officer. He turned out to be a veterinary surgeon.

Beside the veterinary sat a splendid looking young French priest. He was not more than twenty-two, and his light hair curled from under his *biretta* in a way to make a *matinée* idol jealous. And the way he talked about the war. He was full of enthusiasm. Let the Belgians only hold these Germans back until the French soldiers could come up, and then they would be sent scooting back to Berlin. If it were not for his vows—I am sure that a perfectly good soldier was spoiled when that boy went into the church.

Opposite the priest sat a woman with a basket. She wore a black shawl and talked about the war of 1870. She had been a young girl then living in Luxemburg. But her recollections of the Prussians were rather vague. They were all giants, she avowed. They ate like wolves. She remembered her father had said so.

"Why are you going to Liége?" I put the direct question.

"I have a little hotel in Liége—myself and my husband. I am going back to be with him."

"But don't you know that the Germans may shell Liége at any moment? You must know the danger."

"Yes, *monsieur*, I have been told often, but my husband is there."

At the side of this woman sits another priest—a dark unshaven man immersed in his *breviary*. Next is another conscript, a fair, typical Flemish type of boy. He, too, is nursing a brown paper parcel. Then we come back to where I sit.

The talk is all on the war. I find myself of special interest, for the Belgian of the people classifies all English-speaking strangers as British.

I had to give all the details of the appearance of the British troops I could remember. But when all was said they came back to the same question—"When are you coming to help us?"

The roads that parallel the railroad are jammed with troops all moving in the direction we are. When we stop we are surrounded by them and "hurrahs" are exchanged. Nothing could exceed the enthusiasm of the soldiers. Scene after scene passes, recalling those familiar pictures of the Franco-German war. In general appearance these troops look very French. The cut of their uniform is the same as the neighbouring nation, but the colours are different. Viewed at a little distance, marching through the wheat fields, they might readily be mistaken for their allies.

I have never seen a more wonderfully cultivated country than that through which we are passing. Field after field of yellow wheat meets the eye to the horizon. Already the harvest has begun. The sheaves are being gathered.

We arrive at last at the rim of a great bowl, out of which appear the steeples and roofs of Liége. Coming into the town, I can see plainly detachments of troops clearing the ground in front of the forts. Splendid bits of wooded country are being laid bare. Suddenly there is an explosion and a house that lies in the line of fire topples over in a cloud.

Stepping out into the station you might be in any one of a hundred of these continental towns. There is the same high-roofed building with primitive restaurant and newspaper stand. Pushing through you find the inevitable *fiacre* awaiting you; I hail the *cocher* and we start for the Grand Hotel—there is always a Grand Hotel. Hundreds of automobiles flying either the Red Cross or the Belgian flag are running about all over the place. It is the fashion to keep the muffler open, and horn sounding all the time, so the familiar noise of the auto is now as characteristic of war as the rattle of musketry or the booming of cannon. How the motors avoid the crowds swarming up and down the streets is a mystery. The main square in front of the city hall or, as they call it here, the *Hôtel de Ville*, is crowded as if it were election night in New York, and everybody is talking at once. If you have ever been in Paris you have often watched two Frenchmen discussing politics; well, to get an idea of what the Place du Marche, Liége, looked like the evening before the assault, imagine five or six thousand Frenchmen talking politics all at once.

The Germans have been pressing in on the town all day, the last reports place them less than six miles away; it is certain that they will attack this night.

After moving about among the crowd and hearing as much as I could, I came back to my hotel and ordered the best dinner the card offered. I have a theory that it is always best to stoke up the human engine as much as possible beforehand, when the indications are that you will not get much fuel for some time.

While eating dinner I met Lieutenant-Colonel Flibus, director-general of the personnel of the Ministry of War, and commander of the thirty-second regiment of the line; but compared to that officer, when I asked him a few simple questions about the troops, the Sphinx was loquacious.

About half-past eleven I looked out of the window to see if there was any change in the aspect of the town. Decidedly the excitement was on the increase. The motors were going as if each driver was a speed maniac immune from arrest. The crowds in the square talked louder and gesticulated more vigorously than ever. I strained my ears to listen, and over the wild hubbub of the streets I caught the distant "*boom*" of artillery. I grabbed my hat and my water-bottle and was downstairs in a minute.

From a guide-book map I had a general idea of how the city lay. Also I had settled in my mind the point from which the German attack would come. So, making myself as inconspicuous as possible, I started for the Exposition bridge to the south of the city. After I crossed that I left the roads—they were too dangerous for a man travelling without a *laissez-passer* from headquarters; in the temper of the populace any stranger might be set upon as a spy. Liége is built on coal mines; I remembered reading that in my guide-book, and it is true. When I left the main road leading to the south I soon lost myself among the coal dumps. It was a weird place in the moonlight, that section of the town; beside the smelting plants there were the city electric lighting works and a small-arms factory. A dozen chimneys towered to the moon; I felt like a regular spy as I worked my way to a high point of ground from which I knew I could get a good view of the country.

As I clambered up, now and then I caught sight of field batteries galloping along the road. I knew what this meant. Already I could distinguish the beginning of the fire of the infantry. It was plain that the German objective was the bridge over which I had just passed.

I got tied up among a lot of railway tracks as I went stumbling on across country. I lost myself three times before I finally reached the top of the clinker dump for which I was heading.

From the banks of the Meuse, which flows round the southern limits of the city, the land rises at a steep angle; the rim of hills must be all of three hundred feet higher than the river. Once you climb this ridge you get a splendid view of the whole country to the east and south. On the night of the fifth of August, 1914, that view was startling.

In the east was the fort of Fléron. Its curious outline, with the turrets above the walls, gave it the appearance of some monster Dreadnought set down here in the foothills. This likeness to a battleship was heightened by the searchlights. They swept the ground before the fort, as if it were the sea full of approaching enemies; and so it was. The shadows were lit by flashes that told the story of the desperate resistance the Belgians were making. Above the fort great greenish-white shells broke like a rain of fireworks. The guns of the turrets replied, spitting out blazing flashes that bit into the darkness. Above, the full moon shone down calmly on all.

As I was watching the distant scene at Fléron, a crash of musketry sounded almost at my feet. The Germans had been discovered coming through the woods west of the Ourthe. Already the Uhlans were tangled up in the wire and the abattis defences. With my glass I could make out ghostly horsemen among the trees. The rifle fire increased. Suddenly above the crackle of musketry I heard the long wail of a shell speeding to its mark. The shell seemed to pass directly overhead. I turned and saw that the forts west of the city had entered into action. The woods are now alight with flashes such as gigantic fireflies might make. The fort at Embourg pours down what must be a telling fire on the flank of the advancing Germans. It is almost impossible to distinguish these in the moonlight. Time and again I get glimpses of what I take for battalions advancing, but they pass like shadows. Only the flaring rifles tell the position of the troops.

For hours the fight rages in the forest. The Belgians are firing at will, while the Germans continue with volley after volley that tell of their splendid discipline. In the early hours of the morning, when the sun throws its advance guard of light above the foothills, I begin to distinguish the lines of combat. And as I watch I see a battalion of Germans advancing in close order. This is against all modern theory of tactics.

As they come on, they fall like standing corn before a hurricane. No discipline can stand before this blast of death. The line begins to waver; now it breaks. The Belgians redouble their firing. They swarm out of cover and now begins the repulse. So long have I been taught to think of the German infantry as invincible that I cannot believe my eyes. If, in our work at the Staff College at Leavenworth, I had advanced the statement that Belgium might smash the columns of the Kaiser, my brother officers would have ridiculed the idea. Whenever we had studied the problems of European wars this little nation was unconsidered. But now they were justifying what Caesar had said—"*Of all the peoples I have fought, the Belgians are the most sturdy.*"

Battalion after battalion is hurried up from the German side. But nothing can stop the Belgians now. On they drive until the firing sounds more and more distant. Boncelles Fort is literally ablaze as it rains projectiles on the retiring Prussians. As the sun shines out of a bank of clouds on a new day, that bugaboo which has frightened the world for years is laid. The vaunted German military strength has given way before Belgian fire. The claws of the Imperial eagle do not tear.

For a time during the early morning I thought that the tide of battle was against the valiant defenders of Fort Fléron. About half-past five the turret guns were silent. From the rifle fire I judged that this brought a concentrated attack at this point; and it proved to be the case as I afterwards found out. But the audacious Germans who had come to the very slope of the fort were driven back again in helter-skelter disorder by the Belgian infantry. The mechanism of the turrets had been put out of order by the splendid artillery fire of the Germans, but the infantry came gallantly to the rescue and held back the invaders until the guns could be repaired.

During the early morning, the firing slackened along the line. Both armies must be exhausted after the night's work. In this interval of calm I start back in order to get off my news.

Coming into the town I find all the roads blocked by refugees. Most of them have such of their household goods as they could collect bundled in sheets and pillow cases. One woman has a birdcage, another carries a cat in a basket. All push on with eyes filled with terror. No intelligent statement can be got out of any, they are so frightened.

"Yes, the Germans have taken Fléron.'

"The fort?"

"Yes, surely, for all night long the *obus* have dropped on the village and on the fort. Oh, our poor little Belgians."

The road is blocked with a stream of cattle that come bellowing into the town. They pour over the bridges and into the main square. The problem is where to corral them. There is a tennis-court just below the English Consulate and one herd is turned in there.

I dropped into the English Consulate in order to tell Mr. Dolphin, the cordial British representative, that a Belgian battery has taken up a position to his right and rear, about fifty yards from the consulate door.

The consul is not in, but one of his clerks gives me a glass of champagne and a sardine sandwich, so I find the world a little more cheerful. While I am eating, the consul arrives. He has been out on his motor cycle looking over things for himself. He does not believe that Fléron has fallen, and I afterwards find this to be true. Not one of the forts is in the hands of the enemy after the desperate assaults of the night. The Belgian resistance has been successful at all points.

It was not until after I got down into the town proper again that my troubles began. The first mishap was my meeting a loose lancer carrying his revolver ready for instant use. It was evidently his theory that anyone who could not speak Flemish or Walloon (I do not know which language he spoke, but I understood him perfectly) was a German spy. When I felt the point of that revolver pressing against my fifth rib, I knew exactly the answer required. The alacrity with which I produced my passport and a personal letter from the American minister in Brussels and testified to my willingness to allow any one present to search me, somewhat mollified the vigilant cavalryman.

Unfortunately, he could not read English or French, so he kept his gun handy until an obliging officer of the Ninth Line Regiment read over my papers and told the lancer not to shoot me this time. He also advised me to try and not look so much like a German; it might lead to an unfortunate mistake. That was reassuring, as the comedian would say, I don't think. This is the only face I have got, and it will have to get me through this war, even if the Belgians can't recognize its American origin.

Going down to the Grand Hotel I met a Civil Guard. He was never entitled to the designation civil in his life. I never met a more uncivil person. He bustled me down to the police-station while a surly crowd followed shouting "Lynch the German!" in their own language. I rather enjoyed getting into that station house. You would not think it possible that one should welcome the sight of a jail, but on this occasion I did. Once inside I had to wait among the homeless refugees, who had gathered there for protection. I was in need of a little of the same thing.

If anyone ever asks you, tell him, with my compliments, that the Chief of Police of Liége is all right. He can tell an American as far as he can see one. He saw this one four times that morning and recognized me every time. The last time I was brought in he called me "*vieil ami*," and asked me to stop to lunch.

I was wondering how I could acquire a flat Flemish face after my last release, when I was surrounded by another mob.

"No need to send anyone with me. I know my way to the jail," were the words on my lips, when a Flemish fist nearly broke my shoulder, and someone shouted: "*Vive l'Angleterre!*" The crowd answered with a will that would have made stage hands jealous. I was a hero. The first of the army of the English allies.

Then I went to the bazaar and found an American flag on a toy cruiser, the only flag of our country in the shop, and I nailed my colours to my Dunlop.

When I was again foot loose I went to the palace. A motor car had come in with two German officers to demand the surrender of the city and the forts. Of course I knew that the demand, as far as the forts were concerned would be refused. While the surrender talk was going on no one was allowed within a hundred yards of the palace. I suppose they were afraid we would overhear the conversation. I came close enough to get a photograph, but as there was no Dictaphone installed, no news leaked out.

Suddenly, while everyone was waiting without the palace, an explosion sounded that rattled half the city. Every heart stopped beating. Then the news ran through the crowd that the bridge of arches had been blown up to prevent the Germans crossing. As there were about seven other bridges, blowing up one seemed only an inconvenience, not a hindrance.

While I was taking a picture of the wrecked bridge, someone

AFTER DAYS OF HEROIC DEFENCE THE FORTS AT LIÈGE HAD TO SURRENDER. ALL THAT REMAINED WHEN THE GERMANS CONQUERED.

rushed up to say that the bombardment was about to commence. Another said this was not so. It was not ordered until six o'clock; it was now only a quarter past five, but the news soon spread through the city. The savage invaders were going to shell Liége. The women and children would be slaughtered.

In a wave the people moved to the station. It was a panic. Then at the station the line at the ticket window grew. No one with authority was near to override the crass stupidity of the minor official who would collect tolls while the fuses of the German cannon burned. Never shall I forget the anguished faces as the iron wheels ground on along the rails. Hope died in the eyes that watched.

The lamp in the carriage burns dimly. We have been jolting along for hours. I have just finished scratching these notes when a droning voice calls my attention. I recognise long forgotten Latin phrases: "*Absolvo te*" and then a mumbling. I search my mind for the association. Like a flash it comes,—the formula of the Last Sacrament. I catch another sentence: "*Ora pro nobis.*" Death, who marches but a pace in the rear of War has entered the coach. I turn to see the unshaven priest administering Extreme Unction to the old lady. She is anointed. The handsome woman in the furs weeps. As the voice of the priest falls, the light in the lamp flickers and goes out. We are in darkness. No one stirs. The only sound is that of soft sobbing.

Now we are approaching Brussels. With many stops and starts the train works into the city. At last we arrive in the station. It is packed with people waiting for us. They rush first to see the prisoners. There is a cheer as the grey-uniformed Germans are led between the fixed bayonets of the Civil Guard. But the cheer dies when the wounded are carried out. The Civil Guard holds open a passage, through which the line of stretcher-bearers passes. There is a solemn hush as the slow-moving column winds through the waiting throng, past the doors of the station to where the Red Cross ambulances are standing in the street. The square in front of the station is jammed with humanity. The crowd have been shouting and singing, awaiting the coming of the train.

A hush comes over them also as the line of wounded appears. Here is the visible effect of war. But the splendid spirit of the people soon asserts itself. Suddenly a voice cries "*Vivent les blessés!*" And the crowd answers with a roar: "*Vive la Belgique!*" "*Vivent les défenseurs de Liége!*"

CHAPTER 2

# Brussels in Wartime

Brussels during the first weeks of the Great War was confident and courageous. If there was ever a note of fear as to the consequences of the impending conflict, it was drowned in the great outcry of indignation with which the Belgians received the news of the invasion of their beloved country. Brussels is the heart of the nation, and during these momentous days it throbbed violently. Up to the very last the people hoped to avoid war and all its calamities, but no sooner had the news reached the city that the first of the German soldiers had crossed the frontier, than, with one accord, the whole Belgian nation rose in defence of their liberty. The first expression of patriotic fervour took the form of the display of the national colours. Not to hang out the brave black, yellow and red of the national flag would almost open one to the suspicion of being lukewarm in the cause of Belgian defence.

Looking down the *Boulevard du Nord* I saw the upper windows of every shop shadowed by the national emblem, and beneath these flags a restless throng marched all day. It seems that there is something so disturbing about the thoughts of war that it produces a restless mental condition which only finds relief in movement. All of Brussels spent most of the twenty-four hours of the day in the streets during this exciting period. With extraordinary eagerness they bought up each fresh supply of newspapers as it came from the Press. The thirst for information was unquenchable, and when the news of the first successes at Liége were published the crowds could not contain their enthusiasm. I have seen the Place Charles Rogier at night packed with a dense mob awaiting the arrival of trains from the beleaguered city, and as each batch of fugitives appeared in the portals of the Gare du Nord this throng would send up cheer after cheer. They had invested Liége with

The comic uniform of Guard Civique, Brussels

a curious personality; for the people of Brussels the city "ardent," as it had been named, typified the whole Belgian nation. It would sacrifice itself even to the point of annihilation that it might hold in check the hordes of the invader.

This enthusiasm of the populace showed itself in the untiring pursuit of spies. Germany, without doubt, had a very efficient spy system throughout the length and breadth of the Flemish nation. The centre of this system was located in Brussels. During the first weeks of war, when the Germans were beginning their now famous march through the neutral country, their spies were unceasingly active. While the Belgian authorities succeeded in running down a great many of the foreign agents, undoubtedly others kept up constant communication with the Intelligence Department of the advancing army; but the German Great General Staff must have been thoroughly informed of conditions in Belgium long before the actual outbreak of hostilities. Relying confidently upon her guaranteed neutrality, Belgium had never made any effort to conceal the actual state of conditions within her borders.

German investigators could have informed themselves of general and special conditions without let or hindrance; and as Belgium has been a great holiday ground for the German people, it may be assumed that they let no opportunity pass of picking up knowledge which might subsequently prove serviceable in war time. In their eagerness to eliminate the pest of spies, I am afraid the Belgians were led into a number of blunders. I, myself, had several disagreeable experiences, as it seems quite impossible for the Belgian people to distinguish between foreigners. The French they recognize immediately, but Englishmen and Americans were constantly being mistaken for the hated enemy.

Despite the efforts of the police, there were a number of attacks on German property in Brussels. In Europe the German beer shop has become an international institution; beer-houses owned wholly or partially by *German* citizens are found in all the cities of the Continent. In times of peace this type of *café* has always been popular. However, when the clarion note of war sounded, the people seemed to forget the many pleasant hours they had spent around the little tables of these beer shops. The very sight of the word "*brasserie*" seemed to be a challenge. At night the crowds that marched up and down the *boulevards* of Brussels would stop time and again before a beer-shop bearing a German name and vent their fury on the property of the citizen of the enemy. Popular outbreaks of this kind, I know, are difficult to control, but to me it has always seemed that such attacks are the acme of cowardice. In the first place, it is unintelligent to destroy property of this kind as the shops in themselves can have no military value; then, it can be taken for granted that the average German citizen who has established himself in a foreign city has in a measure cut the ties that bind him to the Fatherland. Under any circumstances he, individually, is in no way responsible for the course taken by the powers that be in his country. In fact, I know personally that a great many Germans established in foreign cities deplore the position of Germany in this war.

I have seen some half a dozen *cafés* practically gutted by the mobs that roam the streets. Not only were the *brasseries* attacked, but no shop known to be the property of a German was safe. A shot was fired through the window of one of the largest stores of the city and this shot in no way endangered the proprietor, but narrowly missed a Belgian employee. The municipal government quickly realised that these outbreaks should not continue, and all German property was at once put under police protection.

Of constant interest to the people of Brussels were the aeroplanes that at times hovered above the roofs of the houses. One morning the whole city was thrown into something of a panic, when at a height far beyond rifle shot, a *Taube* aeroplane was discovered. All the people watched with untiring gaze this messenger of the enemy as long as it was in sight. The German aviator turned off to the South and left Brussels without dropping a bomb.

There is one feature of these troubled weeks which stands high in the credit of Belgium; that is the manner in which the expelled Germans were sent out of the country. As I have indicated, the hatred and indignation of the populace in the capital sought expression by attacking everything German. Knowing this, the authorities had to contrive to arrange the departure of the 4,000 odd citizens with the utmost care. The American Legation had taken over the affairs of the German Legation, so the responsibility of the welfare of these aliens was placed upon Mr. Brand Whitlock, the American minister, in co-operation with the Belgian authorities. The 4,000 German men, women and children were got out of the country without suffering any hostile act. In fact, the Belgian troops guarding them acted more in the way of protectors and friends than enemies. With their own money they bought milk for the children, and bread and wine for the

GERMANY COMMANDEERED MOTORS

men and women.

All during this first week of war the people of Brussels were supremely confident. I could not help thinking at the time that they were overconfident. I had had occasion to study the military organisation of Germany and I knew that this small determined people, no matter how brave individually they might be, could not hold back the host that Germany could pour into their land. At that time it was not believed that the *Kaiser* would make his smashing blow against France through this neutral nation. After the Belgians had so courageously refused the German emperor's request to let his forces pass through their land without molestation, there were those who believed that the march of the invaders would be directed to the south. How wrong this belief was has long been proved.

Again, the Belgian people were certain that France and England would put their whole forces into the firing line of the smaller nation. The unmilitary man of the people could not comprehend the physical impossibility of doing this, and of course he had no conception of the enormous blunder this would have been from the military point of view. As I have said in another chapter, the whole nation was awaiting eagerly the arrival of the first detachments of English and French soldiers. They were certain that these soldiers would come. As day after day passed with no sign of the Allies, I heard on all sides rather acrid remarks. Even after Liége had fallen, the citizens of Brussels firmly believed their city would escape attack. It was argued that if necessary the whole Belgian Army could be concentrated in front of the capital and so turn the on-marching Germans from their course. Again, the Belgians seemed to think that Germany had no distinctive quarrel with them, and for this reason they would do as little injury to their land as possible, and reserve the fury of their fighting for France.

There were several American ladies in Brussels at the time of which I write. These ladies had been told by one of King Albert's equerries that there was no need for them to leave Brussels. They were, he said, perfectly safe in that city. It was with the greatest difficulty that, at the suggestion of Mr. Whitlock, the minister, I persuaded these ladies to leave the Belgian capital. While I knew that there was little danger of their suffering any physical violence, yet as there could be no possible reason for their remaining in the zone of operations, the quicker they left the city the better. The censor was undoubtedly responsible for the buoyant attitude which was characteristic of both the Walloon and Flemish citizens of the country at this time. To the last they denied the

German victories.

I had accurate information that German troops crossed the Belgian frontier at Visé as early as August 2. This information I telephoned direct to the *Daily Telegraph*. By using the telephone I got the news into London before any rival. However, the fact of the invasion was officially denied by the Belgian War Office the next day. On August 4, they reluctantly admitted that their neutrality had been violated. I have not yet been able to fathom the motive of the first denial. This denial was certainly a political mistake. It took off the edge of the indignation that at the moment filled the nations of the earth because of this flagrant disregard of the sanctity of treaties. How the denial could have been of any military value is not apparent. The delay in giving out the news only lulled the people into a sense of false security which made it easier for the invading Germans. The poor people in many of the frontier villages believed that they were safe, until the Uhlans came clattering down their quiet streets.

One of the bravest sights of the first week of war was the ride of the king to Parliament. At the head of a brilliant staff all mounted on splendid chargers, he rode from the palace to the Chamber of Deputies. Wearing the field uniform of a general, King Albert was in striking contrast to the officers who followed him. His uniform symbolized war. The people saw their monarch as he would take the field at the head of the army. The grave soldier-like figure aroused intense enthusiasm. Cheer after cheer greeted the little group of horsemen at whose head rode the king.

But warm as the reception of the king was, it seemed to me that the queen and the royal children who followed in an open carriage, came in for an even greater share of applause. One could not fail to notice the shadow of sorrow that already darkened the queen's brow, but the children looked on it all as an engrossing show. The charming princess Marie José, with her rebellious hair, turned her wide-open eyes from side to side as she viewed the applauding mob.

After the royal party came the different diplomatic corps. Of these the French and English representatives received the most cordial receptions. As of allied nations this was to be expected.

Though the Chamber of Deputies met under the shadow of war there was no note of apprehension in the utterances of those assembled. All took their cue from the speech of the king. That was a short strong appeal to the patriotism of the people. It was not boastful; it was in part a simple statement of what the people must do in defence of their liberty. It was a demand for sacrifice. The world has seen how Belgium has made that sacrifice. The king ended his speech with the words "*Vive la Belgique indépendente!*" The whole chamber broke into wild applause.

It must be remembered that the Belgian Chamber of Deputies has as many divisions and as many animosities as any other legislative organisation. In the first place Belgium is divided into two bitterly antagonistic races, the Flemish and the Walloons, which mix as readily as milk and lemon juice. Ever since the nation existed as such, these two races have been rivals for honour and place. Then this radical division of the people is complicated by the existence of three political parties—Socialist, Catholic and Hebrew. The disputes of these parties have kept the whole nation in a ferment for years. But with the first note of war sounding, these rivalries disappeared as mist before the summer sun. It was a nation firmly knit together that met the Germans.

The business of war preparation went on in Brussels with feverish haste. Class after class was called to the colours. To supplement these there were thousands of volunteers. Whenever anybody of troops marched through the streets traffic was at once paralysed. Even the comic *Garde Civique* came in for its share of applause. The history of the misfortunes of this force quickly turned from comedy to tragedy. Originally they were a sort of Home Guard. Their first duty was to supplement the police in the cities. Later they were given duties of a purely military nature. They built trenches, erected barricades, and I have met them doing duty as outposts. As force was not actually a part of the army, this work was out of its sphere. Finally the Civil Guard took part in several of the earlier actions. According to German standards they were civilians and not soldiers. Therefore the enemy treated them with the extreme of rigour. Captured with arms in their hands they were summarily shot.

This was a most outrageous proceeding on the part of the Germans. The Civil Guard was an organisation with uniform and officers. The uniform, I will admit, was grotesque, yet it was distinctive. It labelled the wearer as a member of a quasi-military force. The Civil Guard of Belgium was more of a military organisation than the militia regiments that form part of the armed forces of the United States. Suppose that during the war with Spain, members of the 71st Regiment, N.Y. had been captured and executed without ceremony. The case would have been similar to what has happened in Belgium. Germany had no right to deny to members of the Civil Guard the status of prisoners of war.

The truth is these civilian soldiers were a thorn in the side of the invading force. They did not understand how to cope with them. I understand the difficulty of dealing with irregular troops. It was one of the serious problems which confronted American officers in the Philippines. Yet no matter how flagrant was the violation of the laws of war, no Filipino was denied the consolation of a court martial. Under the theory by which Germany makes war, if she should come into conflict with the United States, only members of the regular army would be entitled to the rights of soldiers. Every other citizen bearing arms would be shot if captured. As part of the scheme to intimidate the people of Belgium as a whole by a military order, they legalised murder.

When the news of the constant skirmishing that was going on day after day along the frontier came to Brussels, the people still seemed confident the city would not be touched. Why they persisted in this belief remains a mystery. I think that the absurd censorship which kept the people in ignorance of the seriousness of the situation was responsible also for the panic that swept over Brussels when the facts became known. Long after Liége had been taken, the papers in the capital printed story after story about the gallant way the forts were holding out. With the greatest reluctance the press admitted the capture by the Germans of some of the outlying defences on August 15. Within three days, Brussels suddenly awoke to the truth. Then began the exodus.

There was something Biblical in the flight. They were as people fleeing before the wrath. No censor could suppress the news brought into the city by each new batch of refugees. From Liége, Tirlemont and Louvain they came, bringing stories of German savagery. Women wantonly shot, towns given over to the flames, the high men of the villages, men respected by all who knew them, given as short shrift as a mad dog. These and a hundred other cruelties were told and retold at every street corner. Then when the people realised that the authors of all this misery were now riding down on the gates of Brussels, confidence and courage died. A great fear gripped all. Were they to suffer as the people of Louvain? Haunted by the stories of the thousands who had tasted the German method of making war, the citizens of Brussels incontinently fled.

CHAPTER 3

# Namur

*Taube* aeroplanes began to make their appearance over Brussels during the second week in August. The sight of one of these air machines turned the city into a whirlpool of excitement. The crowds in the streets pointed, gesticulated, argued, while the Civil Guard commenced a fusillade which did no harm to the aviator, but accounted for many casualties in the city when the shots let off into the sky returned in a shower of lead. During this time I had been following the movements of the advancing German columns to the best of my ability, through the reports of constant skirmishing which appeared in the local press.

At that period the censorship was in no manner strict. My military training told me that the Germans were certain to come along the two main lines of communication through Belgium, and it was about this time that in Brussels we got the first news of the coming of the English troops. Stories of how hermetically-sealed railway carriages passed through certain towns in the night and how these were the English regiments were told round the tables of the *cafés*. Then the news spread that certain correspondents had stumbled on General French's army. These had been taken prisoners and only released on the solemn assurance that they would under no circumstances breathe a word of the position of the British troops.

It must be remembered that, up to this time, no one believed the Germans would make their smashing attack through Belgium. The nations of the world still had faith in the sanctity of treaties. The more I studied my maps by the light of the information which came to hand each day, the more I became convinced that where her interests were concerned Germany would stop at nothing, not even the violation of Belgium's neutrality. Every day new items appeared in the local papers telling of skirmishes taking place in various parts of the Flemish kingdom. These items could have but one interpretation. They marked the position of the advance guard of a great army pushing into Belgium.

In order to assure myself I was right in believing that the Germans were advancing in force through this region, I decided to have a look at Namur and the valley of the Meuse. It was my original intention to go as far south in Belgian territory as I could and then to return for the fighting which I had predicted in my Liége dispatches would take place before Brussels. But fate, in the person of an arbitrary French General, decreed that I should not see the fair capital of Belgium again. My belongings, I hope, are still in the Palace Hotel. I have not seen them since August 12, the day I left Brussels.

I had discovered that the easiest way from point to point in the theatre of operations was by rail, so I bought my ticket and started. No one made the least objection. The strictest orders had already been given about approaching the zone of operations, but it is certain that the Belgian staff did not believe Namur to be in the danger line. You must always bear in mind the fact that the Belgians had never made a serious study of warfare. By nature the Belge is no warrior. The great mass of soldiers, so-called, suddenly brought into being at the outbreak of war, were none the less peasants, clerks, shopkeepers, and so forth, because they wore a gaudy uniform. This uniform when donned did not suddenly endow the wearer with a complete knowledge of military duties.

With officers it was the same case. No one has to be told that you cannot make an officer capable of fulfilling his obligations to those under his command overnight. It is not in the spirit of criticism that I am saying all this; it is only to emphasise the splendid work done by the Belgian Army when pitted against the most perfect fighting machine in Europe. But this lack of training showed itself in the very aspect of the troops. I think I noticed it more among the regiments stationed round Namur than at any other place.

On my way I had noticed again the wonderful perfection of cultivation of the whole country. I think I have called Belgium the kitchen garden of Europe in another chapter. I cannot improve on the simile. The whole land through which I was passing smiled in consciousness of plenty. The neat farmhouses looked as if they had been recently gone over with scrubbing brush and cloth; they were so clean, they seemed to sparkle in the light of the setting sun.

When I arrived at the station I followed the crowd that was being herded into one corner of the building. No one could pass the gates until his passport had been scrutinized. The spy was abroad in the land. In this fortified city I found many more preparations for war than in Brussels. In the first place one could not move without a *laissez-passer.* Soldiers patrolled the streets and every few hundred yards you were held up and made to show your papers. The city presented all the grim circumstances of a siege except the actual falling of shells. Barricades were built to command all the main avenues into the city. Enormous moving vans were hauled across the roadway and turned into a sort of blockhouse. The sides were pierced for rifles and inside sand-bags were piled breast high. This improvised fort gave fair protection against rifle fire. As constructed, it was useless against guns. Trenches were dug at either side of the van. As a military effort the fortification left much to be desired.

While I was in Namur I got my first clear view of a German aeroplane. Those I had seen in Brussels had flown so high above the city that it was impossible to form any idea of their exact appearance, but here, one passed overhead not more than two thousand feet up. In shape it was distinct from any other flying machine I had seen. It recalled an insect in flight. It was what I should imagine a prehistoric scarab looked like on the wing. So striking is the appearance that you never again have any difficulty in distinguishing the *Taube*. It is painted a sparkling white with a panel of blue through the middle of. each wing.

Not only is it easy to distinguish these machines by shape and colour, but also the engine makes a characteristic sound quite distinct from that of the French or Belgian aeroplane. While I watched, this machine made a circle of the forts around the city. It was under a heavy rifle fire all the time, but apparently not a bullet came near it for it never once even trembled in flight. Even when some of the guns from the forts got into action it did not change its course.

In Namur I found the same anxious question which has been asked a thousand times by a thousand tongues in this kingdom. "Where are the French, where are the English?" There can be no doubt but that in spite of much vaunting of *"nos petits belges"* the people realised their helplessness before the German war machine. I thought at the time, and I am still of the opinion, that the Belgian Army would have been immeasurably strengthened if a few corps of either French troops or English, or both, had been rushed into the Belgian line. Of course the wisdom of such a course is doubtful from a strictly military point of view, but for its moral effect nothing could have been better. I am also sure that a leaven of French or British troops mixed in with the Belgians at this time would have increased the effectiveness of King Albert's army fifty *per cent*.

Outside of the military precautions which I have mentioned, life went on in quite the usual way in this city. The shops were opened and in the classic phrase "business was as usual." This was quite incomprehensible to me. It certainly indicated that the people of Namur knew nothing of the danger which threatened their city. It was either that, or a supreme confidence in the troops defending it. The Fourth Division which formed the garrison did not present the soldierly appearance of the troops I had seen in Liége. In view of subsequent events, appearances were not deceptive. Why Namur should have fallen as quickly as it did is to me one of the mysteries of this war. I had the opportunity of talking with some of the captured garrison when they were prisoners of war in Germany; but they could give no real explanation. From their description of events, three shots from the 42 centimetre guns was sufficient to demolish each of the forts in turn.

All my sympathies are with the Belgians—how could it be otherwise when I have seen the havoc wrought in the beautiful country?— but if what I write is to have any value I must enquire into facts that do not redound to the credit, from a military point of view, of those concerned. I have already said that the Belge is essentially non-military. This is in no way to his discredit. In fact, in these days when so many nations have sloughed off the thin veneer of civilization, it is more to the honour of Belgium that because she believed in the good faith of her neighbours she, in a fashion, disregarded military preparedness. The charge brought by Germany, in the attempt to justify her position in violating the neutrality of Belgium, that this nation had created an army for the purposes of offence is disproved by the evidence of Germany itself. A nation making ready for war would first have created trained soldiers. I have not heard who was in command at Namur. I shall read his report, if it is ever published, with much interest.

It seemed that the people of Belgium still believed that somehow the tide of advancing Germans would be turned from the country's shores.

In Namur I met M. Paul Gillan, who typifies the Belgian soldier of the improvised army. When the war broke out M. Gillan owned a very profitable preserves and sweet import business in Chatelet, near

Charleroi. His warehouse had been taken over by the military. He was, of course, given a voucher payable after the war. The provisions were to go to the sick and wounded of the Belgian Army. When his business thus disappeared overnight, M. Gillan reported with his automobile to the officer commanding at Namur the next day, "I hope the sweets are to the taste of the wounded," he said, as he presented himself, "and as my business no longer needs my supervision I have come to offer myself and my automobile for service." The offer was accepted forthwith.

When it was not required by the staff, M. Gillan put his motor at my disposal. Together we made the ride down the valley of the Meuse, which was the land between the armies at the time. My companion had the *mot d'ordre* which passed us through all the lines. As we passed swiftly along the banks of the river it was hard to believe that within a few brief weeks its waters would be stained with the blood of thousands. Uhlans had made their appearance at different points on the farther bank of the river, and as our motor was commanded by those hills we kept a sharp look out for the enemy. Every few hundred paces we were stopped by fields of barbed wire entanglements. They will be the special feature of defence in this war.

Wire cutters are part of the equipment of the German troops who have been captured, and the first inference was that they were to be used solely for cutting telephone and telegraph wires; but now we know of their more effective employment. When I motored down the left bank of the Meuse the whole country was a labyrinth of wire. Every bridge was most carefully protected in this manner, but I found out afterwards that when these bridges were actually under fire the wire was not the defence expected. In the first place the German artillery was used against it with telling effect, and during the night their scouts would creep up and cut the strands with their clippers.

Chapter 4

# The Battle of Dinant

Shortly after we left Namur we ran into the first of the French Army of the North. This was a battalion of the 148th regiment of the line which had been divided up into detachments and detailed to guard the bridges across the Meuse. For the most part they contented themselves with building a sand-bag breastwork and covering the bridge itself with a labyrinth of wire. I was informed that all the abutments were mined, but this I could not verify myself. It was curious to contrast the French and the Belgian soldier. The latter was the stolid, serious type that in no case saw anything amusing in the incidents of soldiering. But the Frenchman met every circumstance of warfare with a smile. The strain of picket duty at night, the travail of trench digging under a broiling August sun in a uniform more suitable for winter than for summer campaigning, the sleepless nights of scouting, are all subjects for joking. I conceived a great respect and affection for the French conscript during the time I had the chance to see him in the firing line. He has a great soul.

From Namur to Dinant we had constant news of encounters between the patrols of the two armies, French and German. There were only a few Belgians down in this section of their country. These were lancers who had all the burden of scouting the whole front across the Meuse. Where the French cavalry were, I have never been able to find out. The Germans were using their cavalry as a screen in the same manner as they had in the Königgrätz campaign and again in 1870. How they managed to keep the secret of their advance I shall try to explain in a later chapter. It is one of the salient points of the commencement of the war.

As we now know, there were over two hundred thousand Germans all moving across Belgium from the North, and yet the aeroplanes that circled constantly overhead seemed to be entirely unaware of their presence. When we passed Yvoir we saw the bodies of five Uhlans that had been killed there the previous day. The population of the little town gathered to see the gruesome sight. This was their first view of war at close range. They did not know how soon they were to come under the iron heel of the invader.

It is the fashion to surround the science of strategy with much mystery. As a matter of fact, the whole foundation of military success has been picturesquely summarized by General Forrest of the Confederate army, "*Getting the mostest men thar fust.*" And it was on that principle that the Germans were working. Their grey-coated *cohorts* were coming on like a tide at flood. And the most remarkable feature of it all was that neither the French nor the English seemed to realise this portentous fact.

Nearing Dinant the military activity increased. The blue coat and red breeches of the Frenchman became more and more a detail of the picture. Another battalion of the 148th regiment occupied the village immediately north of the city. They were a capable looking lot. When I first saw them, they were taking a position on the heights at the back of the town which commanded the road across the river. The men of this regiment were all of the correct military age. Not one of them, save certain non-commissioned officers, was more than thirty, and they had all the esprit for which the French are famous. Arrived in the town, I took leave of M. Gillan, who went in his motor back to Namur. I have not seen or heard from him since that day; I hope that the fortunes of war have been with him.

The first thing I noticed in Dinant was the confidence shown by the civilian population in the French troops who were guarding their homes. I went at first to the *Tête d'Or*, a famous hostelry which nestles close to the citadel. Here I met the proprietor—M. Bourgemont, I think was his name. He did not look like a hero—no—in appearance he was the typical *bonhomme*. He wore a baggy brown suit. He was fat and pasty faced with straw-coloured hair and moustache. His eyes, however, were always bright when he spoke.

"You are on the wrong side of the river, if the Germans come." I made this remark as he escorted me to my rooms.

"We are safe enough here, *monsieur*. Our French are in the citadel. They can never drive them out." He was certain the Germans were not coming by the northern route. The *commandant* had "said so."

Dinant is one of a dozen picturesque towns that dot the Meuse. It has been a Mecca of tourists for years. Here the river runs abreast of a high limestone cliff on the east, while on the west the bank slopes up to a ridge. The town itself is flat on the banks of the river. As you read later on of the fight here, remember that the limestone cliffs on the German side of the river commanded the ridge. The citadel is the pride of Dinant. It is an ancient fortress built on the cliffs with some five hundred odd steps leading up to it from the river level. These steps are cut into the solid rock.

The houses of the town sprawl on both sides of the Meuse; a fine bridge of stone and iron led at that time from one side to the other. It was this bridge that gave the town its value to the advancing Germans. The problem of the French commander was the defence of this bridge. What made this problem difficult with the small force at his disposal, was the citadel. This ancient fortress frowned down on top of the city; a force holding it would have the bridge and the road beyond at its mercy. Major Bertrand could not place his main force on the heights as the peculiar character of the cliffs made it possible to cut off the citadel from the river; also it would have been folly for him to place his troops with the river at their back.

Under these circumstances he did all he could in the matter. A half company was detailed to hold the city as long as possible, in face of attack, and then retreat across the river. As the only line of retreat was down the steps cut into the side of the cliff it was easy to foresee what was going to happen to that half company if the Germans came; but here again I was alone in my belief that the invaders were to be feared; already the French soldiers were feasting themselves on the news of the successes at Mülhausen. The 148th were wishing themselves in Lorraine where the real fighting was going on. When I told a sergeant that he would soon get all the fighting he wanted, he answered with a sceptical, "You think so, *monsieur?*"

I spent the fourteenth of August looking over the ground. I put myself in the position of the oncoming German commander and thought over how I could dispose an attacking force. I discovered that the street leading past my hotel was the main line of communication with the country outside the city to the east; it was called the Rue Sainte Jacques. That evening I decided to move to the other side of the river. I had met Captain J. A. A. F. Cuff, R.M.L.I., who was here as a sort of military observer; he had with him three or four men on motorcycles who had been scouting the country on the far side of the river, and reported Germans advancing along every road; Ciney was occupied, but what the number of the force was they could not estimate.

The most significant happening of the day was the ambush of a French dragoon squadron. One hundred of them had ridden out in the morning to reconnoitre on the German side of the river, and of the hundred, just thirteen rode in at night, and of these half were wounded. I was not allowed to hear their report, but they told their own story. The exhausted horses flecked with sweat showed how the survivors had ridden to save themselves; there was no doubt now that the Germans were coming. Major Bertrand gave the order that all who wished to leave the town should do so at once; after a certain hour no civilian would be allowed in the streets.

It was with Lieutenant Parent, who could speak English and who therefore constituted himself my especial guide, that I inspected the defences of the bridge that night. It was a picture that might well have inspired Detaille; hardly a ripple showed in the surface of the broad river, the clustering houses on the banks somehow reminded me of cattle crowding down to drink; the church with its curious minaret tower smiled at us from across the bridge. I could just distinguish the white walls of the *Tête d'Or*.

On the top of the citadel a sentinel stood out sharp against the sky line. The bridge with its field of barbed wire stretched away before us; on either side, where the winged abutments turned off at right angles, soldiers in blue and red were grouped; they had made these wall wings into a little fort, their rifles were stacked beside them, some smoked, others chatted and one sang in a low voice; it was an old Norman folk song, Parent told me, and was cast in a mournful minor key. I had seen war; many of these men—perhaps all of them—had not; they had no disquieting visions of the morrow. As we turned to the town again I caught sight of a belated fisherman a few hundred yards downstream. Why not? It was dusk now. Lieutenant Parent pointed out where the machine-guns were placed, in the upper storeys of the house bordering the stream.

"In that corner, there," he said, pointing to a window that gave on the bridge, "is my special gun. She sweeps the road."

I could hear the low voices of the men as they climbed to their posts, and at times I caught the sharp click of steel on steel. Sounds I had not heard for years set my nerves tingling, but to these men they meant nothing. Later, the sentinel on the citadel signalled with a lantern that all was well from that side. I crossed the bridge and sent a despatch of about fifty words. I tried to put a warning in that telegram, but when my French friends had censored it, it was innocuous. I looked up at the darkened windows of the *Tête d'Or* as I passed and wondered if M. Bourgemont still disbelieved in the approach of the Germans.

The next morning I was brought out of my bed with a spring by a loud explosion which seemed to come from the next room; immediately there followed the most mournful wailing I have ever heard; it was a dog in agony. While I hurried into my clothes I heard another explosion duplicating the first, and now that I was fully awake I knew the sound; it was a small shell bursting. The shell had passed directly over the *Hotel du Nord*, and smashed through the roof of the railway station within two feet of the clock which marked ten minutes past six. It did little damage except shatter a dozen windows. The third shell carried away the chimney of the hotel, leaving a great hole in the roof and incidentally spoiling the morning coffee. This seemed to worry the proprietor more than the presence of the Germans; while he was bewailing the spilt coffee, his guests scuttled to the cellar. Captain Cuff, with his escort of motorcycle scouts, made his escape in a motor. I got little satisfaction out of watching him go.

The Germans continued the shelling of the town with little effect for nearly an hour. The population had all gone under ground and only the military showed themselves in the streets. I found a good look-out position and turned my glass on the citadel across the river. Up to this time I had heard very little infantry fire. The detachment, which occupied the ancient fortress, had not been able to locate the mountain battery that was dropping the German visiting cards within the town. The enemy's infantry had not, up to the moment, put in an appearance, so at least I judged.

About seven I noticed a good deal of movement on the crest of the citadel. In a few minutes the echo of a scattering volley drifted back to me; that was the beginning of the end of the little band of defenders holding the post beyond the river. I could only judge how the fight was going from the firing of the French soldiers I could see; but it was soon evident that the Germans were attacking them on all sides. From our side there was nothing we could do. Shells continued to drop into the streets and I picked up the fuse of one of these; it was a Dopp with the fuse cut at 4,000 metres. As it was about two thousand metres across to the citadel the German guns must be another two thousand metres beyond; but the infantry was closing in on the fortress.

Now I saw that the half company, or rather what was left of it, had drawn together in one angle of the wall. But now the Germans began to make their appearance in the main street of that part of the town that lay on the other side of the river, thus they were able to take the defenders in reverse. Soon what was left of the French began to waver; first one slipped down the stone steps leading down the face of the cliff and then another followed. Most of those who came were evidently wounded, and as they crawled from step to step they were fair marks for the Germans who had occupied the outskirts of the town. Word must have passed to those still holding on to the citadel, that their retreat would be soon cut off, for suddenly the group of them fired a parting volley and dropped back to the path leading to the steps. It was then that a veritable slaughter began.

The Germans had now possession of the crest of the citadel and rained a perfect hail of death on the French; a few stumbled on the steps and lay blocking the path of those coming behind, one rolled all the way down. Now I could see half a dozen bodies, in blue and red, stretched out at intervals down the stone staircase; a few reached the street below in safety. At the foot of the stairs behind the church there is what in military terms is called a "dead angle." This means a position under a wall protected from hostile fire. The retreating French paused there a moment. Then they caught sight of M. Bourgemont, who stood in the open door of his hotel, waving to them frantically. He too was in a protected angle, safe from the enemy's fire.

What was left of the little band ran like sheep to the *Tête d'Or*, but of the number one fell. He was not dead, for in a moment he struggled up on his knees, trying to move forward. Then a rather grotesque figure in brown ran out into the shot-swept street. It was M. Bourgemont. Stooping over the limp figure in blue and red, he started dragging it to the zone of safety. He staggered a dozen paces. Then, in the absurd way fat men do, he fell. A bullet had passed through his brain.

The citadel was now completely in the hands of the Germans. For the rest of the morning they concentrated their efforts on the assault of the bridge; now the whole force on our side of the river was engaged. At once I saw how few we were, and how impossible it was for such a force to hold out against the Germans. For a time it looked as if nothing could keep the enemy from passing the bridge. I had joined Major Bertrand and Lieutenant Parent, who were with the detachment holding the abutments. Lieutenant Parent's machine-gun had been spitting a leaden stream across the bridge, and not a German dared face it. The losses among the men holding the wings of the abutments had been severe.

The Germans were firing lying down, and seemed to be men who could pick off a head as far as they could see it. The noise of the irregular explosions of rifles, the mechanical spluttering of machine-guns, punctuated by the explosion shock of shell fire, continued all through the morning hours. At eleven o'clock it began to rain, but this in no way affected the fighting. About thirty newly-wounded men were brought in. Things were at their worst just then, and I frankly admit I was choosing my own line of retreat in case the town could not be held.

At this juncture, when Commandant Bertrand was moving his men to the heights behind the town, there was a sudden increase in the volume of firing from our side of the river. It was the long expected reinforcements. The 33rd regiment of the line now deployed along the line of the ridge and some of them took position in the lower part of the town. I met a sergeant and a squad of these and sent them on to the aid of the remnant defending the bridge. Soon the French fire was smothering the German, whose attack then slackened. When this happened I went back to the hotel; the proprietor had the coffee boiling again in spite of the absent chimney, and a cup was very welcome.

The *café* of the hotel was filled with wounded, and a doctor, the local physician, was doing what he could for them. Most of the wounds were slight; one man had been hit with a bit of shell in the head, but the skull was not even cracked; others had holes through their arms, but for the most part these were little more than flesh wounds.

While I was drinking my cup of coffee, the fire having, as I have said, slackened, I saw a woman cross the open place in front of the hotel to a pillar box and drop in a letter. I would like to have asked her at what time it was written!

At one o'clock I returned to my post of observation. I saw that the Germans had hoisted their flag over the citadel. This was the signal for renewed firing. The sight of the hated colours seemed to rouse the French to renewed fury. The machine-guns barked incessantly, infantry fire exploded without ceasing. Suddenly I heard a new sound in this infernal chorus, eight loud detonations, followed by hissing whistles, drowned the minor explosions; it was the French field artillery. Ask any soldier his sensations when he hears the welcome notes of his own guns; no music is more pleasant. This was the first time I had heard the French artillery, and instantly I recognized that experts were handling the pieces. They found the range at the first salvo; in less than five minutes they were dropping projectiles into the citadel so fast that the Germans went out helter-skelter; one shell cut right across the flag ripping the red from the black. Another infantry regiment comes up now, the 73rd, and these add the din of their rifles to the chorus. Curiously enough it was only about this time that I began to realise that troops, up and down the river from where I was, had been also engaged all the morning.

Now the action quickly turned in favour of the French. Those of the Germans who had come down into the streets of the part of the town which stood on the right bank of the river, were compelled to withdraw. After a most careful scrutiny I could not see the head of a German on the ramparts of the citadel. The shells of the mountain battery suddenly ceased to fall in Dinant, and before the station clock, which had marked the last hours of so many, stood again at six, the first day's fighting at Dinant was ended. Another regiment came into the town, the 84th, but these were too late for the fighting. They knew what had been going forward, for the road behind the bridge is dotted with the dead; they lie in all sorts of contorted positions, their blue coats are splashed with red, the red trousers are dyed a deeper crimson. The cheers of the troops arriving sink down as they pass this grim evidence of war.

Such was the first day's fighting for Dinant. The French had repulsed the German attack, but it was easy to see that they were not in a strong position. Their artillery had saved the day. At that time the Germans had not a single piece of field artillery in action here and the mountain battery was only a one-pounder. As a matter of fact, the action from the German side looked to me more like a reconnaissance in force than a serious attempt to carry the bridge. Of course, carried away by their first successes they naturally thought that they could carry the bridge with a rush, and had not the French reinforcement arrived just at the moment it did, there is every chance that the enemy would have taken the town that day. As it was, this was only a feat deferred.

I have heard that the French crossed the Dinant bridge and took the offensive against the Germans advancing from the east; this I have not been able to verify. If it was so, it was a grave error, which can only be put down to the fact that the French still persisted in the idea that no great force of the enemy was coming across the Meuse here.

It may not be amiss to record a few impressions from a military point of view. It was the intention of the French to hold the Dinant bridge at all hazards, and with this aim they posted their strongest force behind the wings that sprang from the abutments. These were built of limestone blocks and in themselves offered good cover; but as they were only three feet high they could have been vastly improved by the use of sand-bags for head cover. The German sharpshooters picked these men off like experts in a shooting gallery. This was a minor oversight compared with the mistake made by not constructing covered approaches to the advanced positions. The citadel, as I have already said, commanded the whole town. It was impossible for the French with the troops available, to attempt to hold that point, therefore it was all the more important to protect such positions as would come under its fire.

Actually when the men behind the bridge wall were picked off and it became necessary to bring forward reinforcements, the men had to be rushed to an open field of fire where they suffered unnecessary losses. Again, when it became imperative to change the position of the French to the ridge behind the town, they had to be marched under fire all the distance. The road over which they passed was lined with dead. They were piled in two lines at either side as close as if they had been dominoes tumbled over in a row; there they lay in all the grotesque attitudes which men shot in action take, the first sacrifice of the French nation to Mars.

As I had seen two years' active service in the Philippines, where concealment was the first essential in all fighting, it is natural that the red breeches of the French infantryman struck me as the most incongruous uniform conceivable. This matter of conspicuous uniform is not a question of opinion as some of my French friends seem to think, it is a question of fact; red is a more visible colour than grey or drab green, therefore it makes a better mark at which to shoot, and men in groups wearing this colour are more easily seen. The French had covered their red-topped caps but the trousers stood out as striking as claret stains on a clean tablecloth. I know that at two thousand yards it is difficult to distinguish troops wearing uniforms of any colour, but short of that distance red is the most conspicuous colour one could choose.

I had an unusual chance to compare the visibility of the French and the German uniforms, and the superiority of the grey is incontestable. I found it difficult to pick up the individual men lined out along the crest of the citadel with the aid of a twelve-power glass; whereas the French troops I could pick up with the naked eye.

The night of the fight I started back towards French headquarters with the intention of reporting my presence to the staff. While I was in Belgium and had passes from the Belgian authorities, I knew it was necessary to have these *viséd* by the French. On the way back I passed five regiments of the line all being hurried to Dinant. What struck me immediately was the seriousness of the men; they were young and I felt sure that the Gallic temperament had not changed, yet these men wore expressions of seriousness unusual with the French; not that their spirit was extinguished, but they exhibited a solemnity only equalled by Scottish regiments. This solemnity was particularly noticeable in the officers, who were as grave as schoolmasters.

What struck me most on this walk against the tide of war was the total absence of cavalry. I had been a cavalry officer, and as such, could not conceive how troops could move without a sufficient complement of the mounted army. Later I discovered the reason for the absence of cavalry, and I place it as one of the contributory causes of the defeat of Charleroi and Mons. What was lacking in horse-soldiers was made up for in artillery, and I state without hesitation that the French artillery is the best in the world. This opinion, which I expressed at the very outbreak of hostilities, has been confirmed on every battlefield where the French gunners have had chance to show their mettle. I had the opportunity of seeing the two batteries that drove the Germans off the citadel at Dinant, in action; from the moment the officer commanding chose his position, every manoeuvre was carried out with machine-like promptitude. Not a pound of lost power.

One of the thrilling sights of war is to see a battery gallop into position. I had seen Grimes' battery take its place on the side of El Pozo Hill in Cuba, and have always since measured others against the American gunners. Not until I had seen the French did I find their superiors. Like the United States artillery officer, the Frenchman is wholly professional. It needs but a glance to see that he belongs to a *corps d'élite*. The two batteries at Dinant galloped up, unlimbered, took the range, loaded and fired in such a splendid manner that I almost applauded, and I am convinced that the French system of a smothering fire is the correct theory for the use of field artillery. Here I saw eight projectiles all dropped in a radius of fifty yards and the Germans in sight were driven helter-skelter. In the moral effect this system of firing is also superior. There is no more comforting sound than the whistle of the French shell passing over your head in the direction of the enemy. That I can testify to, personally.

That night I passed in a so-called inn which boasted only four rooms. All were crowded to suffocation with soldiers. I slept for a time in the corner of the room surrounded by them. A division general and his staff occupied the adjoining room. Earlier in the night, officer and soldier mixed in what might be called easy familiarity. Such demarcation as exists in our army does not seem to exist with the French. I heard a major of artillery in violent argument with the division general on a point of tactics, and he won the argument.

Motorbus after motorbus rolled up to the little village all through the night. They had journeyed all the way from the *boulevards* of Paris. A detachment of red-trousered troops would tumble out and the bus would lumber off into the darkness. About midnight it rained. The troops who had not been able to crowd into the little inn now made a last effort to push into its shelter. A few bedraggled infantrymen got past the door. On the rough cloth of their blue coats the raindrops stood out in the faint light like crystals. In vain they looked for a yard of space in which to stretch themselves. Finally they lean up against the wall and soon nod in overpowering sleep. All night long the road without echoed with the rumble of passing cannon.

CHAPTER 5

# The Battle of Mons

In this chapter I am going to criticise freely. I know I lay myself open to the charge of squaring a grudge, but I must take that chance.

To make my position clear it must be remembered that I had traversed the Belgian-French advanced posts from Wavre Gembleaux, Namur, down the valley of the Meuse to Dinant. As I have stated elsewhere I have had ten years' service in the United States, and I think I may say that I am not an untrained observer.

From the first I had been astounded at the smallness of the French force in this zone. I knew that from a strategical point of view the military occupation of Belgium by the French had its drawback, but as long as the occupation was a fact I could not understand why it was not complete. Coming down the Meuse all the signs pointed to a strong force of Germans advancing from the east. I surmise that they crossed the Meuse near Huy; but more than this, it was evident, at date of which I write, that an overwhelming German army was moving across central Belgium. The German cavalry was everywhere brushing aside the small groups of Belgian cavalry which attempted to oppose it.

It cannot be said that after Liége the Belgian Army offered any serious objection to the advancing Germans before they reached Louvain. Not that the home troops could be expected to do much in face of the enormous numerical superiority which the enemy had developed in their country. The Belgian line was too extended. Either the Belgian forces should have been brought back to the positions selected by the French to offer battle—Charleroi, Mons—or enough troops should have been sent forward from the allied armies to check at least the German advance through Belgium. As it was, the Belgian Army was driven off the line it had selected without having caused any serious inconvenience to the advancing Germans. It was at this time that the crime against Louvain was committed.

The Belgian Army having been eliminated, the enemy could now devote his whole attention to the other armies. By the way, I may mention that the fact that an English Army had arrived in Belgium was not known in Germany until the news was published in the English papers. This I have on high German authority. When it was known that the Expeditionary Force was in their front it became the ambition of the Germans to capture or annihilate it.

General French found himself opposed by an enormously superior force. When the Germans heard that the English were in front, they had determined to concentrate their main attack against them. There are three splendid ways of coming down on Mons from the north. Grey-coated columns were soon marching at full speed along these roads.

After spending the night at Onhaye, as described in my last chapter, I marched back to Athénée, where I was told I should find French headquarters. I had been up to that time scrupulously careful in all my moving from point to point with the advance troops, to comply strictly with the rules governing correspondents. I had my passes stamped at every post I passed, and in the expectation that I should eventually meet the French forces, I had been careful to provide myself with a special letter from the French minister in Brussels, recommending me to the courteous treatment of the officers of the French Army.

Besides this letter I had first my passport as an American citizen. Second, I had a personal letter from the American minister, Mr. Brand Whitlock, which he had given me in Brussels as an extra certificate of identification to the Belgian staff. I had next the pass issued by the Belgian Minister of War. This had my portrait in the corner and had so far taken me safely all over Belgium. Next I had my *laissez-pa*sser from the commandant at Namur permitting me to go to Dinant; and last, I had a pass to the Belgian General Staff at Louvain. Despite all these papers of identification General P—— made me a prisoner. The French have a most exaggerated fear of correspondents. They attribute their defeat by the Germans in 1870 to a correspondent. It was, they say, the correspondent of the *Standard* who made known the position of General MacMahon's army in one of his dispatches, a piece of information which permitted the Germans to cut this general and his army off from Bazaine, who was besieged. I think the story is told in von Moltke's memoirs. If I have heard that story once, I have heard it a dozen times in my wanderings in the war zone. General P——, in his order for my arrest, said I was held because I had seen operations of his army of an important character.

I will not go into the indignities incident to my detention. I am a great admirer of the French people as a whole, and I have many friends in France.

My place of confinement was Givet. I must say that my jailers treated me with the greatest consideration as far as their orders permitted. M. Lefort was my favourite sentry; he was a notary from Revin, which is on the line to Rheims. As for the hostess of the hotel of *Le Cheval Blanc*, whose name I have not in my notebook, her rum omelettes almost made me ask to have my prison period lengthened.

At last I was released and sent back to Paris. All during my confinement I had been wondering what had happened to the army of the British at Mons. The thought of their position was still with me when I crossed the Channel on my way to London. When I arrived in that city I was so astonished at the apparent indifference, or at any rate ignorance of the real condition of affairs in the war zone, that I wrote the following:—

> Solemnly I warn the people of England that this is the beginning of a time of great trial. For Englishmen must be the bone of the army of the Allies. We have a *corps d'élite* here ready for the word of fire, but more must come. The enemy is advancing like a tidal wave towards the valley of the Meuse. Many lives must be sacrificed to dam this engulfing flood. A gigantic battle may open on the morrow. Whatever its result, let England be ready.

This appeared in the *Daily Telegraph* of August 22, 1914. Wherever I told the story of what I had seen along the front of the contending armies I was greeted with surprised protests. I must exaggerate. The French must know where the main German blow was coming. They must be preparing for it. Mr. Harry Lawson, the Proprietor Manager of the *Daily Telegraph*, however, understood at once the seriousness of the situation.

It was the policy of the English newspapers at that time—a policy dictated by the War Office—to avoid publishing disquieting news. The facts of the Battle of Mons were not entirely known to the public until the publication of General French's stinging report. Personally I think that this concealing the facts in the earlier days of the war has had a prejudicial effect on the present state of England's preparedness. If the whole story of the fighting at Mons had been made public, if the stories of the heroism of the different regiments had been written, recruits would not have been so slow in coming forward at the beginning of the war. It seems that England needs the stimulus of defeat to arouse her real fighting blood. In the beginning this stimulus was suppressed. The volunteer army would be far more advanced today, (as at time of first publication)—I write in the first weeks of November—in numbers and effectiveness, if the story of Mons had been read in the homes of the British the day after it occurred.

I understand perfectly the necessity for the suppression of news which will give information to the enemy. Incidentally, why was the news of the wonderful transportation of the British troops across the Channel ever published at all until after the war? What I contend is that the description of feats of bravery, even with heavy loss, instead of hurting a cause, helps it. The matter is beyond argument.

In accordance with this policy some papers went so far as to make statements which were not in accordance with the facts. It was at the time of the fall of Namur. This news came from an independent source that was reliable. While first admitted, it was afterwards vigorously denied. I was especially interested in the capture of this important point, as I had considered it as the real *point d'appui* of the best line of defence the war zone offered. It was the key of the situation. It stands at the junction of the Meuse and Sambre Rivers. It was on one of the most important lines of communication of the enemy. The actual fighting lasted hardly more than two hours, when the place capitulated. After the tremendous struggle which the Belgians had given the Germans at Liége, I must say I was disappointed in their showing here. I had no opportunity of making a detailed inspection of the forts at the time of my visit, but on paper they were stronger even than those at Liége. But I have since come to the conclusion that any fortress constructed over ten years ago is outdated in a military sense.

The railway led directly into the city and the Germans had no difficulty in bringing as many men and as many guns to Namur as they wished. Here it was that the famous seventeen inch howitzers first made their appearance. It is certain that no gun in any of the Namur forts could approach the German mastodon pieces. What force the enemy had here is not yet certain. At least, it was two corps, perhaps more. Under the circumstances there seems, after all, some reason for the Belgian defeat. What would have been the issue if a corps of

French troops had been thrown into this region, can now only be a matter of academic discussion. Yet I think the triumphal march of the Germans might have been halted again, at least as long as it had been at Liége, if this plan had been adopted. When Namur fell, the carefully chosen battle-ground of the French and English became untenable. If the Allies had not already been in full retreat, they would have been compelled to retire as soon as Namur was in the hands of the enemy.

Wherever he met the Allies he was numerically superior. Add to this the high standard of *morale* created among his troops by their first victories, and you have an army that nothing could stop. Kluck, the victorious, was coming down on Paris like an invading Juggernaut. He crushed all before him.

It is said that General Joffre plays the game of war as if it were chess. A contoured map of the whole war zone, some five metres square, has been modelled in *papier mâché*, and on this map the corps and divisions of friend and foe are represented by wooden blocks. Every feature of the terrain, hills, valleys, railroads, rivers, wagon road, forest and plain is marked to scale on the model. Thus the master sees at a glance the disposition of his own and the enemies' forces. In an adjoining room sits an adjutant who receives an average of five hundred telegrams a day. These all bear on the movements of the troops. Each new bit of information as it is received is at once communicated to the *generalissimo*. He reflects alone in the map-room. He moves the blocks. The order is given, and the change is immediately effected in the theatre of operations.

On the other hand, the Germans were confident and settled in their plan. No historical record can show anything superior to the marching of the Germans during the first weeks of the war; at that time their organisation was working without a hitch. As a united force, a homogeneous military establishment, the world has never seen its equal. Do not think I am partial to the Germans. I hope I shall write with an unprejudiced mind; but from a military point of view I cannot help admiring the German machine.

Out of the gloom of the first weeks of war the retreat of the English army shines resplendent.... The greatest test of generalship is a retreat. In comparison a victory is simply organised. Remember that the plans for a retreat must be drawn up under the most difficult circumstances. Decision must be prompt, orders are immediate, and every precaution must be taken to prevent the retreat becoming a rout. For officer and private it is the most nerve-testing experience of war. I think when the scores are all added, the withdrawal of General French from Mons will count more than the victory of Kluck. With the German superiority of numbers it was no extraordinary feat to drive the English back, especially as this superiority of force was quite unexpected. General French had made no error in the disposal of his command. His cavalry which was covering his front as far forward as Waterloo sent back reports. It was only when he was in danger of being completely surrounded that he gave the command for retreat. All during this struggle the British soldier hung on with national tenacity. As usual he did not realise when he was licked.

The British Expeditionary Force, for its size, was perhaps the finest army the world has seen. Man for man no other organisation could produce their physical superiors. In training they were all veterans. They were enthusiastic marksmen. The infantry was of the famous English brand which sticks till the last round. The cavalry was the best that hunting officers could make it. The artillery, while hardly up to the French standard, fulfilled its difficult rôle. The officers were the best type of English gentleman. From Mons to Le Cateau they contested every inch of the ground. The Germans were on all sides.

One officer has told me that for hours his battalion marched parallel with a force of Germans. They were so far within the lines that by chance they were sometimes mistaken for friends. From Le Cateau to St. Quentin and beyond, the retirement was even more difficult. It seemed to be without end, no reinforcements appeared, and all day and night they were harried by their pursuers, yet panic never appeared in their ranks. The great retreat was a masterly performance.

CHAPTER 6

# Germany in Wartime

After my return from the Belgian and French theatres of war *The New York American*, a newspaper which was anxious to get an accurate account of conditions in Germany, suggested to the *Daily Telegraph* that I might be sent to that country. It was arranged that my services should be transferred direct to the allied newspaper. It was as the military correspondent of *The New York American* that I made my journey to Berlin.

There were current in England at that time all sorts of rumours on the supposed state of affairs in Germany. It was said that the poorer classes were starving; that the country was on the verge of a revolution and that the war was highly unpopular. It was my mission to verify these rumours and incidentally get to the front if such a thing were possible.

I know there are partisans who will take exception to my simple statement of the facts as I found them, but it must be remembered that I am a neutral and try to see with an impartial eye. In Germany I found conditions during the first weeks of September almost normal. I say almost normal, because the railroad service was to some extent interrupted both by the supply trains moving to the front, and trains of wounded returning. Also, the population as a whole was responding to the electrifying stimulus of a popular war. The sentiments of the people are epitomized in the two German mottoes, "*God, King and Fatherland*," and "*Deutschland über alles.*" From prince to pauper, the triumph of Germany was the thought of all.

On my way to Berlin I travelled in a train loaded with wounded. They had been sent back from Namur and Mons. All were cases which are classified as slightly wounded, although it was apparent that some of them were grievously injured. One young soldier who could not have been more than twenty-two had been struck at an angle through the left eye. It may be said that he was lucky not to have had the bullet come straight at him, yet it seemed to me that this man at least had given his share of himself to his country. But the only thing which occupied him at the moment was the question whether he would be allowed to rejoin with only one eye. He was only a second lieutenant, and one rose quickly in time of war. He told me when he discovered my nationality, that he was one of the German Olympic Games' Team, and that he had been training under the American athletes who had been imported to Germany as instructors.

Several others of the men had head wounds of minor importance, and one had been unfortunate enough to be shot through the jaw. More than fifty *per cent*, of the wounded, however, carried an arm in a sling. The few who had been hit in the leg sat with their limbs stretched out on the carriage seats, and it was plain that the jolting of the car was exquisite agony. But they had no complaints. All seemed to take their wounds as a matter of course. It was part of the business of war.

The plan of sending back the slightly wounded is a new departure in the German Army. Sending the lightly hurt to recover in the care of their families has proved a great success. The men recover more quickly under congenial surroundings, and the government is relieved of considerable expense.

From the first I saw that in Germany war was a business proposition. Every detail was as carefully considered as it is by the American Car and Foundry Company. Nothing was too small not to be done well. I studied the bandages of these wounded, and saw that they were as skilfully applied as if the work had been done in a quiet hospital far removed from the conditions of warfare. To me the condition of those bandages told the story of an efficient field hospital: and an efficient field hospital is one of the tests of a well-organised army.

On the journey to Berlin what impressed me most was the matter-of-fact way in which the situation was accepted. There were no curious, cheering throngs at the different stations, no indulgence in cheap sentimentality. A few people stood gathered on the platform as the train stopped, but these were all volunteer nurses. The work was to render assistance to such of the wounded as needed it. They distributed hot soup, sandwiches, and even beer, to some of those *hors de combat*. But it was all done in a quiet way that suggested method and efficiency. I have journeyed extensively in three war areas, and from what I have seen I do not hesitate to say that in the matter of the evacuation of the wounded, no other organisation can approach the German.

At one of the junction stops—Wunstorf—our train passed a contingent of Belgian prisoners. There were three train-loads of box cars filled with them. As the captives were penned in the cars, which were solid, save for a grating which was open for a few inches under the roof, they were not travelling in comfort. The cars were doors with their wicked-looking bayonets pointing inward, joked with the men of our train as we passed.

I could only get fleeting glimpses of the faces of the prisoners. Here and there I looked into a pair of hungry eyes staring from the blackness of the box car. But I could not distinguish the numbers on their caps to see if I had any old friend among the captives. I estimated the number of prisoners at a thousand, and heard that they were part of the army which defended Namur. The German papers were constantly boasting of the number of English prisoners they had captured, so I was on the constant lookout for captives in khaki; but I saw none.

When our train approached Berlin, one got a picture of another side of war. Many little pathetic scenes were enacted at the different stops. The news of the coming of the wounded had been wired ahead. Mothers, wives and daughters gathered to meet their loved ones. I remember one girl—she had the air of still being a bride—almost smothering her husband with kisses. Talking like a runaway phonograph, her eyes never left his face. Her own were lit with pride and love, yet while I watched she never let her glance wander to the shattered arm her husband covered in a sling. As the train pulled out I saw her still smiling up at him in rapture, oblivious to the world. At other stations, women with searching eyes hurried from window to window of the train. They have come to look for those dear to them; some are disappointed. Slowly despair creeps into the searching eyes as the train moves onward. They turn, the saddened women, the world shall not see their tears.

The first symptom I noticed of the war in Berlin was that the people were newspaper mad. The local sheets were selling like extras on election night; and this went on every hour in the day up till eleven o'clock at night. Not only did the newspapers sell like hot cakes, but a pushing mob stood all day and after the electric lights were lit, outside the offices of the local papers waiting for the latest bulletins.

Every bulletin was greeted with cheers. It was the time of the Russian disaster in East Prussia. First it would be stated that thirty thousand prisoners were taken, then sixty thousand, and finally ninety thousand. This feverish thirst for news went on unabated all during my stay in the German capital.

After the newspaper mania, the next symptom of conflict was the change of names of certain hotels and shops. Every English and French name disappeared in one night. The Hotel Bristol which has a name that is a considerable asset, became the Conrad Uhl, after the manager. The Westminster Hotel became the Station House and the Piccadilly Café did a thriving business under the title *Vaterland*; as perhaps more beer is consumed here than in any other beer-hall in Berlin, the name was justified. One of the amusing sides of this frantic effort to eliminate everything foreign comes to the surface, when a local jeweller who had the time of the world showing on several clocks proceeded to paste out the faces of the timepieces registering the hour in London, Paris, Petrograd and Brussels. Rather significant was the broad sea-map in the window of the North German Lloyd Office. Not a miniature vessel floated on the seascape.

In the confusion that has engulfed commerce, trade secrets are being stripped of their petty deceptions. It now comes to light that "Sheffield steel" has been for years manufactured and exported from Germany, and all the famous makes of English gloves are put together in Bavaria. It is the business man of Germany who feels the situation most. To him the war is a simple matter of economics. The more he reflects on this the more gloomy he becomes. Yet I cannot say that there was anything abnormal in the aspect of Berlin at the time of my visit. The streets were crowded, but it was with a holiday mob. Confidence was the note of all. In fact I may say of all the capitals, Berlin was easily the gayest I visited.

The *cafés* were open till midnight, and some even later. They were filled most of the time, and among those crowding round the little tables sipping their beer, I could not find one with an anxious face. Even the famous night life of the German capital went on as usual. The only exception was that the branch of Maxim's was closed as well as the *Palais de Glace*, the notorious dancing-hall. As for any shortage of supplies, it existed only in the imagination of certain writers. I lived better at the Adlon Hotel than I did in Paris. What is more, the prices for rooms and food were more reasonable. At the Bristol the management were still serving an excellent luncheon for three marks. They could not possibly have done this if there had been any considerable advance in the price of eatables.

I have been told that great misery existed among the submerged tenth. This is not peculiar, admitting that it is a fact. I cannot say that I noticed any striking lack of men in the crowds that marched up and down the *Unter den Linden*. There was one feature of life in Berlin that existed nowhere else; that was the continual passing of troops preceded by their bands. Why the band should have been suppressed in England in this war, is something I shall never pretend to understand. If the idea is to divorce soldiering from music, I can tell those who plan it that they will never succeed; not if they want to keep up the supply of soldiers. I noticed at once in Germany what a difference the notes of a playing band made both to the men marching and those gathered to cheer them on. Why I felt the thrill of the thing whenever I marched a few paces with the columns myself, and soldiering is no treat to me. In London the troops might be marching to their own funerals. In Berlin they were going to a fete.

Even as early as September the story was circulated in England that Germany had called out her last man. It was said that the cities were denuded of males. This was not the fact. I saw plenty of men of the military age in the streets of the capital, too many in fact. It seemed to me that many of them might be better off in the army. Of course preparation and training was going on everywhere. One had only to take a trip out into the environs to see "cannon fodder" in the making on all sides. Potsdam was the great recruiting centre. Here the training of the embryo soldier went on from morning to night. From what little I was allowed to see, it was a very thorough process. Even their enemies must grant that the Germans know that art of the preparation for war better than any other people.

The mobilisation of the German force has been the theme of military epics. The striking feature of this almost magical summoning of the strength of the empire was the appearance of every soldier with a complete new equipment. From helmet to boot he wore an outfit straight from the quartermaster's *depôt*. Even the equipment for the artillery was replaced. Harness, shoes, extra wheels were all fresh from the Ordnance depot. No army the world has seen could boast such perfection of detail. In the matter of uniform the Germans sprang their first surprise. The invisible grey was a change of which the French and English knew nothing. Personally I think it the best colour for campaigning I have ever seen. Every professional soldier

Sedan Day, 1914, in Berlin. Guns captured from the Russians paraded down Unter den Linden.

will enlarge on the few sentences I give to the military organisation of the Germans. Without going into technicalities it is admittedly the best in the world.

Although I made diligent effort I was never permitted to see one of the famous 17-inch howitzers. It was always said that they were all in the field. I did see a photograph of one. I do not believe that there were many of these Brobdingnagian guns ready when hostilities opened. Even now, I doubt if more than six are being used against the Allies. A great deal of capital has been made out of these cannon. . . . I do not believe it is yet proved that they justify themselves. Used against forts they are invaluable, but beyond this their value is problematical. To move them is a matter of immense effort of an incidental nature. Every bridge over which they pass has to be specially strengthened, every road specially prepared. In siege operations no weapon designed by man is more formidable, but sieges will be rare incidents in future wars.

I was in Berlin on the anniversary of the battle of Sedan. It was made the occasion for a tremendous celebration and display of cannon captured from the enemy. I have never seen a greater concourse of people in a given area. From the Brandenburg Gate to the emperor's palace the sidewalks and the two outside roadways of *Unter den Linden* were jammed with people as thick as caviar. From an upper window of my hotel, which was near the gate, as far as I could see, this river of humanity stretched. They had come to see some eighteen field pieces taken from the enemy. All Berlin was surely there. On this day what ordinarily would be called confidence became arrogance. The Fall of Sedan is a proud day in German history. The Fall of Paris would be a prouder one. You must remember that at that time the army of von Kluck was marching relentlessly and swiftly towards the capital of France.

It was even hoped that the celebration would be made a joint event. When the first of the captured artillery appeared under the Gate the cheer that rose was the sound of the sea in a storm. Two long, slender, grey French guns were given the place of honour in the procession. German soldiers mounted the horses, German soldiers sat on the caissons. After the French came some of the Bull-dog Belgian pieces. I wondered if any of my friends had manned them. Then came some machine-guns that had been taken in the fighting in East Prussia. As each new type of cannon came into view the cheering broke out anew. Soon this enormous concourse could no longer voice their emotion in mere shouting, so they burst into song. A few voices took up the words at first, then others, until the notes of *"Deutschland über Alles"* swelled to a wave of sound that seemed to rock the walls of the houses. From the human point of view this was the most impressive thing of the war. Here I heard literally the voice of the people. They cried that their enemies should be trampled in the dust; they gloated over the mute evidence of their enemies' downfall.

The most significant bit of information on the hopes of the military party came to my knowledge about this time. With some other correspondents, I was discussing the probable duration of the war with Lieutenant von L——, of the King's Hussars attached to the general staff.

Lieutenant von L—— had put the question—"How long do you think the war will last?" Remember this conversation took place the first week in September. Guesses were ventured ranging in time from three months to three years. Lieutenant von L——'s surprise increased at every answer. Finally, when three years seemed to be the limit, he smiled and said, "I will let you into a secret. The war will be over in two weeks. I do not say that there may not be some guerilla fighting along different frontiers after that time, but hostilities between great armies will end within two weeks." Obviously he believed that Germany was going to repeat the campaign of 1870. When several of the correspondents tried to argue that this was too much to hope for, and pointed out pregnant reasons for thinking that France and England were not so nearly beaten, the lieutenant relapsed into moody silence.

CHAPTER 7

# Germany in Wartime (continued)

Perhaps the most interesting personality I met in Germany was Lieutenant Werner. He is the man who was the first to fly over Paris and drop bombs on the defenceless inhabitants. Yet he is not a ferocious-looking character, quite otherwise. His gaze as he looks at you through his monocle is mild; he is almost fat. I was told that he was something of a tennis player, but he must have been a bit out of condition when I saw him. Never have I seen a more harmless-looking pirate, for no doubt he is a pirate.

Lieutenant Werner—I am sorry to say he forgot to write his initials for me—of the Imperial Flying Corps, comes from Hanover, where he is well known in sporting circles, and at the outbreak of the war he had taken up flying as an amateur. At this time he had been running his machine about six months. He was immediately enrolled in the ranks of the German aviators and began his duties at once. He followed the first army to Brussels and saw his first action at the Battle of Mons. His description of the pictures one got of the fighting from a height of two thousand feet was fascinating. It must be the ideal position for a war correspondent. He hovered over the contending armies throughout the day, watching every phase of the fighting.

"The English fight very well; they have held their positions until I could no longer see them because of the smoke of the shells of the heavy German artillery." (Lieutenant Werner speaks with considerable accent.) "Our soldiers came on them from three sides. I hoped they would be all captured; but at last they began to go, slowly, very slowly."

The aviator followed the retreating armies to Le Cateau, sending back messages of their every move. Here he says the English were again attacked, and when taken in the flank by heavy German fire they were compelled to retire in haste.

His very extraordinary story was of his flight over Paris. Attached to the army of General von Kluck, Lieutenant Werner was directed to fly over the French capital and drop bombs where they would do the most damage. The Eiffel Tower with its wireless apparatus was to be an especial objective.

In flights of this character, safety requires that the aviator maintains a height of from five to six thousand feet. Werner says that at that height it is impossible to distinguish buildings. Also the smoke which always accumulates in a haze above cities adds to the difficulty of locating fixed points. But there is no trouble in distinguishing the crowds that always gather in the streets when an aviator makes his appearance over a hostile city.

"To these people I dropped many papers saying that the report that the Russian army was at the gates of Berlin was a lie. This story many French papers had published at that time. Then when I find my little machine going over the Eiffel Tower, I drop two bombs."

"Did the bombs fall near the Tower?"

"No, I think not. I could not stay to see. Two other flying-machines were approaching, one a Bleriot and one a double-decker Bristol. I go up at once. I know I can beat the Bristol, but the Bleriot may catch me. He is coming at an angle across the course to my lines. When I am on a higher plane I make straight for home. I must pass that Frenchman; it is a blood-hot race, but I win. We are so close though, that we fire at one another with our Brownings; but neither hits. It is difficult to shoot when you are flying. Soon I am well back in my own lines. The Frenchman turns. The next day I go back to Paris and drop more bombs."

There is the story that comes as near being a realisation of Mr. Wells' *War in the Air* as anything that has happened in modern conflict.

What was in my mind during this conversation was, "Does this man know the cowardice of his deeds?" The dropping of a mangling, death-dealing projectile on defenceless women and children was not my idea of soldiering.

"Do you not sometimes drop your bombs on non-combatants?" I was trying to phrase the question diplomatically, when my pirate was called away peremptorily.

To me it was an extraordinary revelation of what discipline would do. Here was a mild-mannered, blue-eyed, fat Teuton, the type you expect to see drinking beer and rearing a large family, doing the most bloodthirsty deeds all at the call of the *Kaiser*. There was nothing in the outward aspect of Lieutenant Werner to make you suspect that he was the murderer of women and children, yet reduced to plain words, that is what he was. Germany is trying to hide too many crimes under the name of war; she cannot succeed in this case. How she can get her sons to do such things I cannot explain.

During the first week of my stay in Berlin, the "magnificent" plan of campaign of the *Kaiser* was made known to me. It was not told me in confidence, so I have no hesitation in repeating it here. I think my informant, who held an official position, was trying to impress me.

Germany was preparing to invade England with a Zeppelin armada. As many as sixteen of the monsters of the air were at that moment ready tugging at their moorings like hounds in leash. When the French army was disposed of, which was only a matter of a week or so (this conversation took place in September, 1914), a strong German force would be sent to take Calais. This accomplished, a new "Krupp surprise" surpassing the 17-inch howitzer would then appear. This is a gun of a longer range than any in existence. It is also 17-inch calibre; but while the howitzer can throw a shell only five miles, it is solemnly affirmed that the new "surprise" can hurl a ton of explosive from Calais to Dover.

Six of them mounted at the French port would play havoc with the English Fleet in those waters, and permit the aerial armada to approach the English coast undisturbed. In the consternation that would ensue the German Fleet would emerge. Here another surprise was in store for the foe. All the ships of the Hamburg American Line and the North German Lloyd Line carried guns and were protected with armour plate. This was to be expected; but they had been altered in outline so that at a distance it was impossible to distinguish them from super-Dreadnoughts of the German type. Thus when this enormous fleet appeared the English would not know on what ships to concentrate their fire. In the confusion, the Germans would have the British warships completely at their mercy. The fleet destroyed, the German Army would then invade England at its leisure. If I may be permitted the phrase, it was "some plan."

While in Berlin, I visited the prison camp at Alten Grabow. There were in captivity about three thousand French soldiers, two thousand Belgians and some English civilians. Alten Grabow is one of the permanent practice manoeuvre grounds for the different army corps scattered all over Germany.

The prisoners of war were housed in long stables. There were sixteen of these, and in each not more than three hundred prisoners were confined. Stalls divide the stables, and each stall is floored, carpeted with two sacks of straw which serve the captives as beds. In the mangers at the heads of the stalls were ranged such few knickknacks as the soldiers still possessed.

The sixteen long stable buildings are surrounded by a barbed-wire fence 8 feet high. Every few yards along this wall of wire stands a sentry, his bayonet glittering in the sun. Inside the barbed-wire fence the prisoners are free to wander as they will, but they hardly ever move a dozen yards from the particular stable to which they are assigned. For the most part they sit in little groups, spiritless and dejected.

I first visited the Belgian captives. They were the men of the Fourth Division who had been taken at Namur. The German officer with me, Lieutenant von Leusner, King of Prussia's Hussars, had been stationed in Washington, and only returned to Germany in time for the war. He made no objection to my questioning the prisoners.

"How long had the fight at Namur lasted?" I asked a corporal of the 13th Line Regiment. "Not more than two hours," he replied.

"Why did you put up such a feeble resistance?"

"We were too few; outnumbered three or four to one, we were alone. The Germans overran us from three sides."

"Were there no French troops in Namur?"

"No, *monsieur*, not one."

"And the forts, why did they fall so quickly?"

"They were old. Three shots from the great German guns and they were finished. The Germans were too many for us and their guns were too great."

This last sentence summarised all the explanations of the feeble defence of Namur.

I crossed to the French, and in the first stables I entered saw the slightly wounded. All told, there were about seven hundred hit, but none here showed a severe hurt. They lay stretched on their straw sacks staring straight before them with unseeing eyes. All were gaunt and yellow with privation. Not one moved as I passed down the aisle. Only their glittering eyes showed that they were alive. One remarkable feature of all the wounds was the absence of infection. In all great wars of the past, previous to the Japanese-Russian War, it was rare that wounds would heal cleanly. Gangrene appeared almost immediately, and this infection so complicated the original hurt that a bullet wound in the leg or arm meant the loss of the limb. In the thorax the appearance of gangrene meant death. Today a man may be struck as often as five times—I have seen such cases—and yet not be classed as dangerously wounded. With ordinary care the bullet-holes heal rapidly.

Here I had a chance to contrast the uniforms. Not only does the German soldier fade into the dust, but his uniform is well adapted to the needs of his work. The French soldier is not only as conspicuous as a windmill on the sky line, but his long coat and baggy trousers make the lightest work around camp a heavy, physical strain.

I questioned a soldier of the Hundred and Ninetieth French Infantry about the fighting at Mons and Charleroi; here is his description.

> It was Saturday, August 22nd, and very foggy. We did not know we were being attacked until the shells began falling from the sky. We took our places in the trenches, but could see nothing, for the fog surrounded us. Out of this invisibility bullets began to come. We could see nothing, but we knew the Germans were in front; so we too, fired.
>
> For a time the fire slackened, and we were confident we had driven them back, then, like ghosts, there came thundering down on our flank a squadron of Hussars. On their hats were the skull and cross-bones of Death. They stumbled on our trenches, and our guns drove them back. Then the artillery commenced again. We could hear the shells singing overhead.
>
> All day long the fighting lasted. We shot and shot until I no longer had any feeling in my shoulder. Still the Germans came. We knew there were more and more of them from the downpour of their bullets; yet even when the fog lifted we saw only a very few. It was fighting the unseen. Then came the order to fall back, but before we could move they had surrounded us. Then they brought us here.

When I questioned him as to his treatment as a prisoner, he had but one complaint—the ration of bread was short. He had soup and coffee, all that soldiers could expect, but not enough bread. Lieutenant von Leusner overheard this. It was explained that the bakery had broken down for the day. A full allowance was promised shortly.

Conspicuous among the French prisoners were the "*Turcos.*" The Germans made little secret that they hated the black soldiers. I had been told that they were shewn no quarter; but here was evidence to

The single British prisoner at Alten Grabow, Germany, September, 1914.

the contrary. The prison officer stated that they made more trouble than all the other prisoners combined. Among the captives were a number of alleged *franc-tireurs*. They were caught not actually firing—in that case there would have been short shrift for them—but under circumstances that pointed to their having aided the French. Some of these were wounded.

The sanitary arrangements of the camp were primitive but safe. Down the central open space between the stables were placed a number of washing troughs supplied with running water. Here the men could bathe if they wished, and under certain restrictions, wash their clothes.

By mistake, a number of severely wounded prisoners were sent to Alten Grabow. These were housed in little *lazarettos* near the entrance to the camp. Their plight was pitiful. They lay very quiet. One does not move when a cruel bit of iron has torn its jagged way across your chest. While everything possible was being done for them, yet their wounds demanded all the conveniences of a modern hospital.

Despondency—that was the dominant note of these prisoners of war. They sat about in listless groups hardly talking, each one busy with his own thoughts. A few played cards, but the game went on perfunctorily. Time and again they would turn their eyes to the high fence of barbed-wire and the helmeted Prussian with his gun, pacing behind it. Then, hopelessly, their glances would come back. Escape was not to be dreamed of, and they had no news; only story after story of French defeats with which their captors fed them. This was the true refinement of cruelty.

It seems curious that with all the improvement in the general conditions of warfare, the prisoner is still as badly off as he was during the Civil War. Once captured he becomes something of an outcast. His own people take almost no further interest in him. It is simpler to enlist new men than to exchange captives. Then there is always a stigma attached to a surrender. So the position of the prisoners of war does not excite the sympathy it should. This is not fair. From what I have seen of them they are entitled at least to a square deal. Their existence should not be forgotten. The machinery of an exchange is, I know, complicated and slow, but that is an evil which could be cured. The intervention of neutrals is always possible. In justice to the men that fill the war prisons on all sides, a simpler and quicker method of exchange should be devised.

In Germany I found the same prejudice against allowing correspondents in the zone of operations as existed in France. I cannot leave the prisoners without mentioning an incident which might have brought me into uncomfortable complications. While I was inspecting the different French quarters I soon found myself among troops with the familiar 148 on their collars. This told me that things had gone badly with my friends after I had left Dinant. I was talking with Lieutenant von Leusner when I noticed that two of the French soldiers were regarding me fixedly. Suddenly I heard one of them whisper to the other.

"*C'est le journaliste qui était avec nous, n'est-ce pas?*"

The soldier addressed studied me for a minute—luckily I was dressed differently—then after a pause he replied:

"*Non, pas possible.*"

I have often wondered what would have been the effect on my German officer guide if these former comrades had openly greeted me. Yet the officials in Berlin were infinitely more considerate and courteous in their treatment of the newspaper man than the officials of the other nations. I will not discuss the general attitude of the military towards the correspondent here. I reserve that for a later chapter. I take this occasion to thank Baron von Mumm for the invariably polite reception he gave me at the time of my visits. While I never reached the actual "front" from the German side I was allowed to visit the forts of Liége. As I had seen the German assaults on the famous Belgian city, I was delighted with this chance of seeing the ground from the German side.

Eight of the correspondents who were in Berlin at the time made up the party bound for Liége, and in the stock phrase everything was done for our comfort. It was during this trip that I met Mr. Irwin Cobb of the *Saturday Evening Post,* Mr. Louis of the "Associated Press," and Mr. John McCutcheon of the *Chicago Tribune.* These gentlemen, under the advice of a German military doctor, were taking the waters at Aix-la-Chapelle. Not that they were prisoners. No, even when they were in the guardhouse with a sentry standing over them, they were assured that they were nothing so low as prisoners, they were guests. Mr. Cobb told the story of their chase after an elusive battle, and it is the only bit of humour the war has yet afforded. I see in his published article that he suppresses much that was amusing in his adventures. After all, war is not a joking matter.

We went by motor from Aix to Liége. That motor trip told me more than all the stories of atrocities I had read in the Brussels papers.

Here was the evidence of a crime that still cries to heaven for vengeance. Whole villages given to the flames. Towns once sheltering ten thousand peaceful people, now no more than blackened walls and rubble. God knows what had become of the inhabitants.

What proved to me more than anything else that the accusation made by Germany that Belgium was preparing for war was false, was the evidence of the feeble resistance put up by the Belgian troops along the line of the frontier. They did destroy sections of the railroads and dynamite certain tunnels, but this is not actively holding the invader in check. The country hereabouts is full of splendid defensive positions. Every road is commanded by higher ground that would have been favourable to the defenders, and every ford and bridge offers the same chance. For some reason I am not able to understand, the Belgians preferred to make their stands in the towns along the roads. Perhaps they thought the walls of the houses preferable protection to the positions that might easily have been fortified in the open country. It was unfortunate both from a military point of view and a civil one, that the towns were made the rallying points of defence.

Naturally the enemy turned his artillery against the houses where the Belgians were posted. Then when they had gained a town, they utterly destroyed it on the ground that it had sheltered fighting soldiers. It did not matter to the Germans that a citizen might have his home occupied by the soldiery through *force majeure* and that he himself wished only to avoid the actual conflict. Now, in their policy of spreading terror through the peace-loving population of the country they were going to over-ride, they put all to fire and sword. If there is a just God, Germany must pay heavily for this crime.

As Germany has been the chief war-like power she has had the making of the rules of the game. From a military point of view I see the course of German reasoning in this matter. Brutally, it is that in order to advance through an enemy's country with the minimum of loss, the civil population must be terrorized. In Germany I heard circumstantial stories of the attacks made by civilian men and even women on the German detachments advancing through Belgium. I do not know whether the stories were true or untrue. I think some of them were true; but what did the Germans expect when they threw two hundred thousand of the most brutal soldiers the world has seen, into what was at the time the most peace-loving nation of Europe. It was the most conspicuous example of Might overriding Right that history records. When one reflects on the course of Germany in this war, how trivial the tomes of platitudes published from the Hague Peace Bureau seem.

Coming on Liége from the east, I realised that the difficulties of the attack were not as great as I had imagined them to be. There were plenty of gun positions, and what surprised me, a good deal of cover for troops advancing against the forts. As I have said here the country is higher than along the valley of the river. It forms a sort of table-land.

Our inspection was confined to the Forts Pontisse and Loncin. In this last fort General Leman had his headquarters during the fighting. The forts in Belgium are nothing like the popular conception of such defences. At a little distance they look like hills dotted here and there with Brobdingnagian mushrooms. The hills are the forts proper, actually subterranean chambers where the main garrison live, and from which the turrets, the mushrooms referred to above, protrude. Of course the outline of the fort is cut with trench and sap where infantry can be placed in order to repel assaulting infantry, but all the artillery operations take place underground. Tunnels lead from one section to the other, reminding one of the cross section of an ant-heap, while faint incandescent lights show the path ahead. I had the same feeling, not altogether a pleasant one, that I had when I visited the Catacombs in going through these forts. The thought of the Catacombs came back to me more vividly at Loncin. Here, about six hundred of the garrison had been trapped underground.

Our guides took us through the magazines, and I saw that the Belgians had plenty of ammunition when they were compelled to surrender. The German officers, however, pointed out that the forts were not in a proper condition for effective defence. One of the most important features of forts of this character is the system of fire control. A telephone connexion is established leading to all the different points—offensive and defensive—of the periphery. Without this the commander is in the dark. At Pontisse the telephone system was being arranged while the attack was going on.

The turrets are the unique feature of this type of forts. From the outside they resemble a huge iron mushroom! From the inside they almost duplicate the gun chamber of a battleship. Here are all the mechanical devices used on shipboard—the ammunition hoist, the sighting mechanism, a bewildering battery of levers and screws and electrical switches. Right beside the position of the gun-pointer hangs a telephone receiver. Through this receiver he gets his orders and

Fort Pontisse, Liége.
Notice mushroom turret where men standing. Guns there.

clamps his piece accordingly. Projectile and powder come up out of the darkness below. One follows the other into the breech. It is closed and locked, then the turret-turning and lifting mechanism is put into operation. The iron mushroom revolves—pushes out from the side of the hill—comes to a stop: a bursting explosion, and it sinks back like a turtle withdrawing his head.

All of the turrets I saw contained two six-inch guns. I did not see any piece of larger calibre. I do not think that there are any guns of larger size at Liége. If this is so it makes the resistance put up by the Belgians all the more praiseworthy. When we were surveying the country from the tops of the fort, the German major of artillery who was in charge of the party pointed out the different positions occupied by their gun batteries. The emplacement of their seventeen-inch howitzers was not more than five miles distant. The whole hillside which composed the face of the fort was peppered with huge craters marking where the attackers' shell had struck. At Pontisse I did not see any evidence of extraordinary damage done. The dents made in the turret covers were of no importance, while projectiles landing on the hillside must have exploded harmlessly.

At Fort Loncin one got a very different picture of the effect of German artillery fire. Here a shell had penetrated to the magazine, and wrecked the fort more thoroughly than an earthquake could have done. Nothing now remains but a mass of iron and rubble. The cement walls of the underground passages were reduced to so much slag. The conning towers were tossed about like old stove-pipes. The face of the hill looked as if it had suffered a landslide. As I made my way cautiously over the debris I recognised a smell I have come to know too well—the odour of corruption. Under ruins over which I climbed were the bodies of the entrapped garrison. Here and there I saw a bit of uniform—a cap, a torn coat, a shoe—mute evidence of the human side of this struggle. For the six hundred brave soldiers of Belgium who lie here entombed, Fort Loncin is a glorious monument. I have not been able to reconcile the differences in the date given by the Belgian staff and that given by the Germans for the fall of Liége. The Germans told me that they were in full possession on the eighth of August. The Belgians insisted that the forts were still holding out as late as the fifteenth.

The amount of damage done to the city of Liége was inconsiderable. A number of shells had fallen into the central portion of the town, but as they were from the smaller German field guns they left little mark. A few houses had been destroyed. These, our guide told us, had belonged to a band of Russian students who had defied German authority. One saw the burnt houses; one could picture what had happened to the students.

It was easy to see that the people here were a conquered race. Sullen looks followed the grey motors of the Germans everywhere. The women did not attempt to disguise their glances of hate and rancour. Woe betide the Germans if this civil population gets the chance to pay off old scores.

In Liége I saw the arrogance of the German to his enemy. The attitude of the swaggering *junkers* must have been particularly galling to these people. Not only had they been compelled to pay an enormous ransom, but now they must harbour the enemy who had made the city an advanced base, and watch in impotence the many preparations going forward for the making of war against their own kin and their allies.

Here it was that the German major showed his brutality by violently upbraiding the waiter who served us at lunch for misunderstanding his order given in German. He stormed and swore in the proverbial fashion of the trooper, insisting that the poor Fleming knew German perfectly and only pretended ignorance in order to show his hatred of the conquerors. In fairness I cannot say that I saw many similar incidents.

The two things which met the visitor on all sides at this time in Germany was first the supreme confidence of the whole population in their ultimate success, and next the virulent hatred of the English. Nothing was too vile to say of the British people, no adjective too contemptible for the little army from England which had checked them. This hatred showed itself in the ridicule heaped on the prisoners of the Scottish regiments, and distinction in the treatment given to the English captives and that given to the French and Belgians.

The last two days of my stay in Berlin saw a startling change in the aspect of the city. The singing, shouting, enthusiastic mob that had thronged the streets during the previous fortnight suddenly divided into hundreds of little groups that stood about discussing the news of the day in low, concerned voices. The stream of humanity that nightly coursed up and down *Unter den Linden* had changed its character. It had lost its boisterousness. Some subtle alchemy was at work.

The change came about slowly. It began with the news of the Battle of Lemberg. Despite the claims of the bulletins from Austria, it was soon whispered about that the army of Franz Josef had been smashed. The bulletin which stated that "for strategic and humane reasons the Austrian forces had been withdrawn to a stronger position in the rear," told its own story. Why they should withdraw for "humane" reasons except through concern for the lives of their own soldiers, was not explained.

Shortly after the Battle of Lemberg the Austrian cavalry officers, General von Uexhel, and General Paar, an *aide-de-camp* of the emperor, passed through Berlin on their way to the Great General Staff. They carried the Austrian cry for help against the Russians, and it was the answer to this call, the transposition of certain army corps from the West to the Eastern theatre of operations, that ruined the German campaign in France. Immediately there followed a change in the dispositions of the armies of the North. Two corps from General von Bülow's army entrained and were hurried across the empire. Every other railroad in Germany stood still while this movement was carried out. The depleting of the forces in France at this time was a vital error. It is said that it saved Vienna. This is doubtful, as Vienna was not in imminent danger, but it surely lost the Germans Paris.

The news of von Kluck's reverse came at the very moment when the Berliners were expecting to read of the capture of the French capital. The wording of the bulletin from the General Staff on the subject, while not alarming, was significant. But it came as a shock. The people had been told that von Kluck's cavalry patrols were under the walls of Paris. Why then had it not fallen? Accustomed as the populace were to the accounts of success following success, the news of a check was doubly disquieting. Bulletins stating the total number of prisoners of war—some two hundred and twenty thousand—brought no cheers from the crowds outside the newspaper offices. They wanted Paris.

There is another side to the picture of life in Berlin. Mourning is more and more in evidence, and I noticed each day more and more death-cards "For King and Fatherland" among the advertisements in the newspapers. A son, a husband, a brother was lamented. These cards appeared in the journals throughout the empire. I saw them in newspapers published in Hanover, Cologne, and Aix-la-Chapelle, all using almost the same phraseology. The Germans had a rather cruel way of sending news of a soldier's death. One morning a mother, a wife, or a sister would receive back a letter she had sent to the loved one in the firing line. In red ink across the face of the envelope was written the one pregnant word, "*Gefallen.*"

CHAPTER 8

# Back With the French Army

As there seemed little chance of my being allowed to witness the operations of the German army for some considerable period, I was recalled to London. It would not be just if I did not record the fact that all the time I was on German soil I met only with courtesy and civility from the authorities. I also feel sure that the gentlemen of the Foreign Office made every endeavour to have me attached to the headquarters in the field. But the military who were in the saddle in German affairs could not be bothered with correspondents at that moment. I regret that I had not the opportunity of seeing the German going into action from his own side. It might have thrown some light on certain of his tactics which seemed entirely unsound.

I did have the chance of making some study of the German supply organisation, and their system for the evacuation of the wounded. In general terms these two important factors in an army's success could not be improved upon. In fact the whole German military organisation seemed to me to justify all that I have heard our enthusiastic *attachés* say in praise of the marvellous war machine. If the Prussian fails the fault will not lie here.

When I got back into France I found the whole situation changed. The Battle of the Marne had been fought and the victorious onslaught of the Germans checked. If it were not for the fact that one of the most difficult of military feats is to turn a losing army into a winning one at a moment's notice, I think General Fuchs, when he pierced the German line, might almost have fought his way clean through.

The mix-up along the enemies' front at this time, makes it impossible to come to definite conclusions as to what might have happened if the initial success of the Allies could have been pressed home. At any rate Paris was for the time safe, and the Germans could be defeated.

These were the important facts.

I hope I may never see Paris again under the same circumstances. I could not have believed that the light-hearted capital of the French could have been so transformed. It was a veritable *morgue*. It might have been a city suffering a terrible pestilence. All the shops were closed, the heavy iron windows never being lifted during the twenty-four hours of the day. The few people who passed on the streets hurried by as if they were afraid someone might accost them. The effects of the panic that ensued when the government deserted the capital, were visible everywhere. Yet behind the despair that showed in the faces of the people was an invincible courage. The French were a people with their backs to the wall.

Such a thing as getting a pass to follow the French armies being entirely out of the question, correspondents had to take all sorts, of chances in order to do their duty by their papers. My original *modus operandi*, which was to place myself where I expected the "front" to come and there await developments, had become more and more difficult. The Germans were no longer advancing. And the French troops had monopolized all the means of communication. When I finally managed to get near the field of operations, I found that the modern battle had two distinct drawbacks. It was too long in time, and too long in space.

The Battle of the Aisne[1] was still going strong after twelve days of uninterrupted fighting, and it was being fought along a front of one hundred miles. This was fairly early in the combat. How long it finally lasted, and how much ground it covered, I have never been able correctly to decide—and the authorities differ. If a correspondent attempted to tell the story of such a battle completely he would fill a large volume. Unfortunately he can only see a limited section of the field, and what he reports is merely of local interest, one might say. If I were a censor I would let all the correspondents get right into the trenches with the troops. That is, if I wanted them to send back news that could not be of the slightest use to the enemy. The man who attempts to paint word scenes of modern-day battles can only produce miniatures.

After twelve days of continuous fighting, it is not to be expected

---

1. *1914: the Marne and the Aisne* by H. W. Carless-Davis and A. Neville Hilditch - Two Accounts of the Early Battles of the First Year of the First World War - *The Battles of the Marne and the Aisne* by H. W. Carless-Davis and *Troyon—an Engagement in the Battle of the Aisne* by A. Neville Hilditch also published by Leonaur.

French soldier with proclamation of capture of Rheims issued by German general.

that infantry will advance with dash. In battle formation they crawl forward. On the Aisne it was approximately five miles from the German gun positions to the French emplacements. The French infantry took a full day to cover half that distance. This was about the rate of progress of the whole French Army. During the later operations, when the infantry was in contact all along the front from Belfort to Nieuport, an advance of less than this meant a prolonged battle wherever it was attempted. The armies were like tired wrestlers struggling for each inch of advantage without apparently moving, while they are making the most violent efforts. Seen apart, the engagement one day at Soissons would in any other age have been classed as a considerable battle. Today it is only an incident in a series.

Under the present conditions of modern warfare, military movements are carried on at a snail's pace. The cavalry soon loses its snap. Luckily, as the lines close it is no longer needed to develop infantry positions. The work of scouting is somewhat relaxed as the general position of the enemy is known. Then soldiers become veterans after a month's fighting of this nature. Everything becomes a matter of dull routine. The man becomes accustomed to warfare. The artillery loses the feverish haste which marked its operations during the earlier days of campaigning. Batteries take their stand to cover infantry advances with deliberation. Pieces are loaded, sighted, fired, and loaded again slowly and mechanically. With the artillery the matter of range-finding has been greatly simplified since the era of the aeroplane.

Whenever a battery commander takes position, he turns his glasses skyward to see if he can discover any of his air scouts to spot for him. It is the duty of aviators to hover over the gun position of the enemy, and so disclose the point of fire for their own artillery. When an artilleryman sees one of his own flyers cutting figure eights off on the horizon, he trains his guns below him. Then in a manner most leisurely he opens fire. As with the old system, while the friendly artillery attempts to silence the guns of the enemy, the infantry forms its line of battle. The men go to their positions with just as much hurry as labourers going to work. Once under the protecting salvoes of the artillery, they go forward, but not as the charging mass pictured in the illustrated papers. Rather do they give one the impression of weary men who have a difficult and disagreeable task before them and who are determined to carry it through. These are the impressions of war as one sees it waged today.

I found nearly all the doors closed to the writer in France. That

German prisoners in street in Sézanne September 19.

is, the writer of the news of the war. How the French Government was able to forbid not only the foreign correspondents but their own journalists in the war zone is beyond understanding. The French are a nation of writers, and here, day by day, material was being produced which would give men with but a modicum of talent the chance to shine as bright lights of literature, yet the French newspapers carried less war news than any in the world, I dare say. Personally I look on this as a great loss. I do not believe that the suppression of the little information which under the censorship in vogue might leak out, would make up to France for what she has lost to literature by forbidding her writers the fields of battle.

In my own case I decided to make myself as inconspicuous as an ant. Yet I fear I hold the record for arrests. Three times have I been held in *durance vile*, as the phrase goes, and those two words describe the situation accurately.

Remarkable as it seems, I found in all countries where the war was in progress, that the easiest way of getting from place to place was by train. Invariably when I travelled by motor I was stopped. But when I decided on the point which promised the most favourable field, and then bought a ticket to the nearest town on the railroad to that point, I always got there. The train service was kept up as well as could be under the circumstances, which was certainly a godsend to the correspondents. At the time of which I write, the second week in September, much space had been devoted to the battles directly in front of Paris, but little had been written concerning the operations in the East beyond Châlons-sur-Marne. These were grouped together under the title the Battle of the Marne, but they were distinct in result and bearing on the future plan of the Germans. As this had been the country where Napoleon had fought a very interesting campaign, the field was doubly interesting. With the object of covering this field I bought my ticket to Sézanne, and started early one morning for as near the front as circumstances would permit.

I remember when I arrived in the unpretentious French town that the landlady said luckily I could have a room. The officer who had occupied it had died the day before, and as the *Hôtel du Boule d'Or* seemed to suit me, I occupied the unfortunate officer's bed, but I don't think I had any bad dreams. The hotel was a sort of unofficial hospital, and I was continually meeting orderlies carrying meals to the upper rooms.

From all sides I heard rumours of the doings of the German crown prince, who commanded the invading armies in this section, and for a brief time he, with his staff, had occupied the Château de Mondemont. I motored out to the *château*, which is about ten miles north of Sézanne, and there I was able to compile the story of the repulse of the army of the crown prince.

The Château of Mondemont was a tornado centre of attack and defence during the battle. When the fighting began it sheltered the staff of the German Army. In the next three days it was taken and retaken four times. Bullet-spattered walls, the shell-rent roof, great craters of fresh-turned earth that peppered the lawn, trees split and shivered across the road, testify to the smothering of shot and shell it had suffered, and gaping round holes four feet in diameter had been opened by the giant projectiles in the *château* garden walls.

When I was there, bloodstained uniforms—the blue and red of the French and the grey of the German—still littered the lawn. Piles of empty cartridge-cases, rifles broken at the stock, bits of leather, and here and there an unexploded projectile, tell a story of fighting more fierce than that which raged around the farm of Hougoumont at Waterloo.

Mounds of newly-turned earth spot the roadside. Crosses, from which a *képi* or a *casqué* hang, mark these graves of friend and foe. Such is the grim testimony of their heroism.

Inside the *château* is evidence of another kind. In every room, amid the debris of fallen plaster and shattered woodwork are dozens of empty champagne bottles. The old concierge who leads me from room to room tells of the nights of revelry enjoyed by the German staff. He describes the dinner of the night before the French attack. The countryside was ravaged to furnish the table of the Germans. I tried to get the old man to describe the crown prince, whom he served so often, but he could say no more than that he was very young and very proud.

While the Allied Armies were carrying through the splendid offensive movement at Meaux and Soissons on the left and left centre, the right centre was also advancing irresistibly against the enemy. Roughly, the army of the crown prince occupied the front from Fère-Champenoise to a point east of Epernay. The advance guard was on the road Sézanne-Epernay, and the crown prince is supposed himself to have slept in the Château de Mondemont the night before the French took the offensive. The German Army is estimated at five *corps d'armée*.

The country between Sézanne and Epernay presents problems that would tax the ingenuity of the most astute strategist. Rolling with a few wood-covered hills, here and there villages joined by fair roads, it looks on the surface entirely practicable for all operations. But it is a death-trap. The valleys are wide swamps. And into these swamps the enemy was finally driven. While I was at the *château* a dozen starving German soldiers—some of whom were wounded, came out of hiding in the marshland and gave themselves up. They had been concealed for days; in the *moraines*, as the swamps are called, are sunk some forty pieces of German artillery.

According to a copy of the order of battle issued by the commander of the French army corps, the "*Division du Maroc*" had the honour of the assault on Mondemont. The soldier who was my guide over the battlefield ran short of adjectives in describing their bravery. The savagery of war is pure joy to the "*Turco*."

When the order to assault came, like a pack of wolves they struggled up to the German position. On they pushed, smashed by the rifle fire, but always advancing. As they drew nearer many threw away their guns and rushed at the foe, armed only with the vicious French bayonet. Nothing human could stand before them. Fighting stubbornly the Germans fell back. But no sooner had the French entered the *château* than they in turn came under the German shell fire. With this protection the enemy came closer and closer. The infantry crept from the bottom to the top of the hill, and slowly the French retired.

Every square yard of the walls of Mondemont shows a dozen bullet scars. The wooden shutters of the windows are starred with holes, and these marks of battle are almost equal on the east and west faces of the building. The Germans held the place but an hour, when the French retook it. Then an annihilating gunfire drove them out. But they would not be baulked of their prey. Reforming in sheltered ground, they took up the counter charge. Now the 75 centimetre guns of the French play havoc with Mondemont. With a yell the gallant "*Division du Maroc*" charge and retake it. Troops of the second line are rushed to their support. For the second time that day the *château* is in the hands of the rightful owners.

There is a pause in the fighting. Both armies are literally panting from their labours. The headquarters of the French corps begins work among the debris of torn papers left behind by the German staff. A new order of battle is issued. Its final words are "*Résister à l'outrance!*" Such is the spirit of the French in their fighting. But like gluttons for war the enemy comes back to the attack next morning. Under a superbly gauged gunfire the grey-coated light infantry move forward on Mondemont. They outnumber the French. Bit by bit the latter give way. For the third time the enemy holds this key of the battleground.

Then the whole story is repeated. Again the "*Turcos*" dash into the murderous fire coming from the *château*. The supports from the line regiments follow on their heels. The Germans fall back, the Château de Mondemont again flies the tricolour of France.

With this break in the centre the whole line of the enemy wavers. The French press forward at every point. The Germans gradually withdraw, converging on the road Châlons-sur-Marne-Verdun. In this withdrawal they stumble into the swamps.

The artillery dashing across country for the roads in the rear first fall into the quagmires. The horses flounder about in the mud up to their cinches, while caisson follows gun into the marsh. The retreating infantry comes to the assistance of the gunners. They manage to bring a little order out of the chaos. Fighting a rear-guard action, the proud army of the crown prince makes good its escape. It had been within sixty miles of Paris when it was defeated.

I have put together this story of the defeat of the crown prince from the testimony of eyewitnesses. Soldiers who were in the fighting, peasants who viewed it from afar, an intelligent curate and the veteran keeper of the *château* have contributed parts of the picture. The rest I have seen for myself. When there I still saw the debris of battle. Piles of brass cartridge cases marked the artillery positions, empty small-arms shells told where the infantry had fought. In itself, the ruin of the *château* spoke more vividly of ruthless war than anything I had heretofore seen, except the newly-filled-in trenches marked at both ends with rude crosses. As I stood before one of these reflecting, my soldier guide said in a low voice—

"Sixty of us lie there, *monsieur*," and this was but one of hundreds of these graves that marked the countryside.

I made a special study of the terrain in this part of the war zone, as the attack here seemed to me of special significance. If the French had not stopped the army of the crown prince, Paris would today have been in the hands of the Germans as Brussels is. I do not say that the French would have given up the fight. I think they would have retired to Bordeaux, and kept up the struggle just as Belgium is doing. General Joffre, while the Germans were coming through France like

A LITTLE CHURCH NEAR SÉZANNE

a plague of locusts, said, "I shall await them on the Seine." He is supposed to have decided that as his enemy was advancing in an arc, he would wait until that arc was sufficiently extended before giving his decisive counter attack.

According to his view the enemy would not be spread enough until his forces had reached the Seine. I think it was a lucky thing for France they were checked at the Marne. In my opinion the first army to be thoroughly whipped on French soil was that of the crown prince. This saved Paris. At the time of the victory of Sézanne, the French did not know the extent of the damage they had inflicted on the enemy. In fact they did not make claim to a decisive victory. In the official communication the most they claimed was a drawn battle. Actually they had smashed the flower of the German military power. Of course the Germans have enormous recuperative powers, and with their superb organisation they soon recovered from the blow.

I think, contrary to the general impression, that the great battles round Paris did not begin with the defeat of General von Kluck. That commander's misfortunes were due directly to the retirement of the German left wing on the night of September 6-7. The mystery which has surrounded the movements of the German armies disappears when we know that the main body of the crown prince's army retired nearly forty kilometres during that night, and the following day. Such a retreat almost amounts to a rout.

In the plan of the German operations the path that promised the greatest glory was reserved for the crown prince. This was in accordance with the policy of bolstering the fast-fading popularity of the House of Hohenzollern. Throughout Germany he had been acclaimed as the Hero of Longwy. His futile demonstration against Verdun[2] had been magnified into a series of glorious assaults. In the official bulletins he was declared to have inflicted a serious defeat on the French here. I had read this in the papers while I was in Berlin. As a matter of fact the French army opposed to him had been carrying out a splendid defensive retirement. Opposed by superior numbers they had contested with stubbornness every inch of the ground lost; and in the end they assumed the offensive in a most effective manner.

The Germans after the taking of Longwy—an obsolete fort—advanced on the line Verdun-Ste. Ménéhould-Châlons-sur-Marne. There progress was exceedingly rapid. When the Uhlans of von

---

2. *'Neath Verdun* by Maurice Genevoix - The Experiences of a French Soldier During the Early Months of the First World War also published by Leonaur.

Kluck's forces were in Chantilly the main body of the crown prince's army was yet two hundred kilometres away. Then this army was ordered to push on with all speed. The order of march up the Champs Elysées was being drawn up, and as the crown prince was to head this historic march, undoubtedly dressed in the uniform of his pet regiment, the Death's Head Hussars, the French troops opposing him must be brushed aside.

The left wing of the Germans gave battle on Sunday, September 6. The fighting began at daybreak and continued with unprecedented fury until dark. The artillery fire went beyond anything the history of warfare has hitherto recorded. Shells were timed to be falling at the rate of thirty in thirty seconds. I have this record from a trustworthy source. In this day's fighting the French guns were served with undeniable superiority. The loss they inflicted on the Germans can never be approximately estimated, but I hardly credit the figures of one hundred thousand as the total German casualties. Great as the French victory was, this loss was not sustained. It is said that twenty thousand were killed in this action round Sézanne, but this probably includes the loss on both sides.

It must be remembered that the German army was advancing on a front nearly forty miles in extent, and the country north-east of Sézanne is the most treacherous in all France. Acres upon acres of marshlands line the valleys. Here, as I have already described, the enemy suffered the most.

But the French also made severe sacrifices. The famous —— Corps was almost wiped out of existence. Spurred by the knowledge that they were fighting for the very existence of Paris, each French soldier was as three in this battle line. Against such desperation the Germans could do nothing. After the first day's fighting neither army could claim much advantage in position gained. The French had made certain advances, but also they had fallen back at other points. An enormous quantity of ammunition had been used up. The total French expenditure is put at four thousand shells—hundreds of caissons were empty.

Then on the night of September 6-7 began the mysterious German retirement. The fighting still went on along the whole front, but the main forces were withdrawing.

From the information at hand there are but two ways of explaining this retreat. First, there may have been a sortie from Verdun. Such an operation put through while the main force was engaged, would have wrought havoc in the German Army.

The second theory is that for some unknown reason the German transport service broke down completely. Granting this to have been the case, after the enormous expenditure of ammunition during the first day's action, unless this supply could be immediately replenished, the crown prince's army must fall back, or be captured.

The circumstances of their precipitate flight incline me to the last explanation. Of course the fighting on this wing continued for several days, but the Germans were only trying to save what was left of a badly crippled army from complete destruction.

With the crown prince retreating, there was nothing else for von Kluck and von Bülow to do but execute the same manoeuvre. This brought about the Battle of the Oise, and all the subsequent fighting along the Marne. From that time the French began to achieve certain successes.

It is remarkable to note that from the moment the French took the offensive against the German left wing, that army almost disappeared from the theatre of operations. It is said that it was moved in a body to the extreme right when General Joffre began his extraordinary flanking movement. At any rate this army, which at one time was headed straight for the *Avenue de l'Opéra* with the purpose of following the footsteps of their fathers in the march of 1870, no longer appears as a factor in the German attack.

While I was at Sézanne I heard constantly the rumour that the crown prince had been wounded. I did not believe this. When I questioned the keeper of the *château* closely about this (he was responsible for the story), I found that his tale did not fit well with the facts. I think he endowed the heir of the Hohenzollerns with a mysterious hurt in order to please popular demand. From the papers published in Berlin the crown prince was removed to the Russian theatre of operations shortly after his failure before Paris. It is surmised that he was sent to a field that was supposed to offer better opportunities for potential heroes. But from what happened in Poland it seems that the unfortunate heir-apparent again failed in his ambition.

With the Battle of the Marne the tide of German success began to turn. After General von Kluck's first retirement they were never able to regain the ground lost. Corps upon corps was jammed into the angle of the Allies' line at Ribécourt in a desperate attempt to pierce it. But it was a vain effort. Grey-coated soldiers were fed into the French field of fire like corn into a hopper. They were ground to dust.

It was about this time that what I shall call the Siege of Germany began. Many had already marvelled that modern battles could last two weeks without cessation. As a fact fighting continued in the same area for months. It was not the same battle, although some writers delighted to head their stories "the fortieth day of the Battle of the Aisne." This conveys a wrong impression to the untechnical. Infantry and cavalry do not advance during such time. What happens is that the troops of the contending armies "dig themselves in "whilst the artillery continues an uninterrupted fire. The men in the trenches are relieved as often as circumstances permit, but this kind of fighting, as one officer described it to me, is "living in hell."

The German field fortifications in the rear of their original line of battle were splendidly planned and painstakingly constructed. Their trenches not only give shelter from the enemy's projectiles but from the elements. Their bombproofs deflect shells and keep out rain and cold. And the weather played an active part in the campaign.

I think the fact that winter was approaching influenced the Germans in attempting the suicidal counter-attacks which characterized the second stage of their operations. Nothing short of the most decisive victory could bring the war to an end, and Germany was willing to make any sacrifice to achieve such a victory. In the beginning of October, despite their genius for organisation, the lines of communication began to be seriously congested. The evacuation of the wounded and the return of "empties" interfered with the replenishment of the ammunition supply, and as blood is to man so is ammunition to an army. Then, in addition, the situation was complicated by the necessity of providing the troops with winter kit. When it became imperative to tax an already over-burdened transport with a million blankets for distribution throughout the German front in addition to an uninterrupted ammunition supply, the greatest military advance the world has ever seen, and let us hope ever will see, came to an end.

At this time I saw a vast improvement in the French soldier. The recruit whom I had seen on the Meuse was a veteran on the Marne. When I compared the regiments I met beyond Sézanne with the troops I had seen in Dinant I was astounded. The men were bronzed and looked hardened to a degree. Not only were they physically fit, but they worked smoothly in the grooves of military routine. The improvement in *morale* was marvellous. The dread of the German military bogey was dead.

CHAPTER 9

# The Bombardment of Rheims

How any commander could have trained his guns on the Cathedral of Rheims passes human understanding. If it had been in Bible times that such wanton sacrilege took place a plague would have overtaken the guilty people. The gun-pointer would have been struck blind as he took aim. Since the days of Divine retribution are past, it remains for human agencies to punish the sacrilegious offender. But what punishment will suffice? It is one of those crimes which are so great that they stand outside the human catalogue. For this scandalous sacrilege there is no atonement.

I reached Rheims while the city was still being bombarded. When I had climbed to the highest window of the north-east tower two shells aimed at that tower fell not twenty yards away in the street below. The Germans were not satisfied with the damage they had already accomplished. It seemed as if their fury could not be appeased while the noble towers of the revered "poem in stone" still rose above the blackened ruins of the cathedral walls.

Fortunately for the world and future generations, the damage as first reported proved on careful examination to have been exaggerated. The grand church is not a pile of smouldering rubble. Irreparable as is the hurt to the detail of the structure—no hand of modern times could restore the broken statues of the *façade*,—yet the four walls, the roof and the towers stand. The damage to them is great but not beyond repair.

During the first bombardment the cathedral was under fire for an hour. How often it has been fired on since I cannot say, but it was during this first chastisement that the building suffered most. It was not that the shells in themselves did very much damage, but they set the woodwork of the building on fire and thus indirectly brought about serious destruction. A complication which played an important part in the conflagration was a scaffolding which had been built up against the face of the structure on the tower in the north-west angle. Repairs were in progress at the time of the outbreak of the war, and this scaffolding served in the work. Although the Abbé Chinot, who is the rector of the cathedral, made all possible effort to check the fire at the outset, he failed, and soon sparks which had fallen in the building on the straw which served as bedding for the wounded, set all in flames.

The church being considered sanctuary, harboured the wounded that had been found in the city when the French had retaken it. A red cross flag floated from an improvised flag-pole on the north-east tower, but this emblem did not prevent the Germans firing directly among the disabled. It is difficult to write of the scene that ensued in the cathedral when its walls burst into a sheet of flame. As I stood before the charred bodies of those unfortunates who, broken in body, were caught in this holocaust, it seemed that these Germans had paid the price for all the harm their comrades had done. Singed and blackened bodies lay in odd corners of the towering nave. Other bodies also charred are stretched in the ashes of some out-houses. Think of the moments of agony suffered by these men as they lay helpless with blazing timbers falling about them.

These prisoners were in the cathedral. The archbishop, aided by the Abbé Chinot, broke through a door on the north of the edifice to find some fifty of the German wounded gathered in the centre of the nave. They looked about with bewildered eyes as if deciding which end were preferable, the flames or a bullet. The priests, making those who could walk bear the badly wounded, led the way to a place of safety. But hardly had this pitiable procession appeared outside the cathedral when "Death to the Barbarians!" shouted some. "You must kill us first," quietly said the men in holy orders. Some of the prisoners in mortal fear rushed back into the veritable furnace the building now was. The others, under the protection of the archbishop, were led to a printing-shop nearby. When they were there, the mattresses on which the badly hurt were lying were found to be smouldering.

All during this scene the shells from the German howitzers sailed screaming overhead. Remarkably few of them hit the mark. One landed fair on the roof of the structure, and soon that part of the cathedral was in flames. Another struck one of the flying buttresses on the north-east and tore it from the wall. Some of the beautiful windows were completely destroyed by shrapnel. Here was the irreparable

RHEIMS CATHEDRAL.
NOTICE BROKEN GLASS WINDOWS.

loss. These windows were of stained glass which had been placed by the hands that built the cathedral in the twelfth century. They were an artistic inheritance beyond price. Now shattered and torn from its leaded setting, the wonderfully tinted old glass litters the stone floor. Can Germany repay for these?

Another artistic loss that can never be repaired is the destroyed figures that were originally carved in the walls of the cathedral. These figures were unique in architecture. Now they are charred and blackened stone.

It was in fact the fire which caused the most damage to the building. As in all such edifices the stone roof was surmounted by a wooden one. When the fire spread to this, falling sparks caught all other inflammable matter in or about the cathedral, thus adding fuel to the fire. The galleries under the eaves of the roof were still burning when I climbed over them.

But all this damage was little compared with the destruction of the beautiful *façade*. Nothing more wonderful than the front of the Cathedral of Rheims existed in ecclesiastical architecture. Students from every quarter of the globe had been here to admire its magnificence of conception, and the skill with which it had been executed. It was an elaborate carving of groups of the holy saints of the church all gathered round a carved descent from the Cross. The figures of the saints were cut into the detail of the doors and windows of the cathedral, making an *ensemble* without parallel for its beauty of design.

The havoc among these carvings beggars description. Here stands a nun with her head broken off—another shows not only the head gone but the breast and upper part of the body wholly destroyed. Other figures have lost an arm, a leg, or have in some manner been hurt so that no hand can restore them. The figures that surround the scene of the Crucifixion are split and, when I last saw them, ready to fall from their place. The columns that framed the windows were broken. And the wonderful rose window that makes the main feature of the facade was partly shattered. It made one's heart sick to see such wanton outrage. When I climbed to the bell towers I found they had been melted by the great heat. While the noble building stood it had suffered much.

I have been witness of much of the savagery of the Germans in war, yet with all that I have seen I cannot bring myself to believe that they fired on the Cathedral of Rheims through pure maliciousness. Whenever I have found other outrages, there has always been present

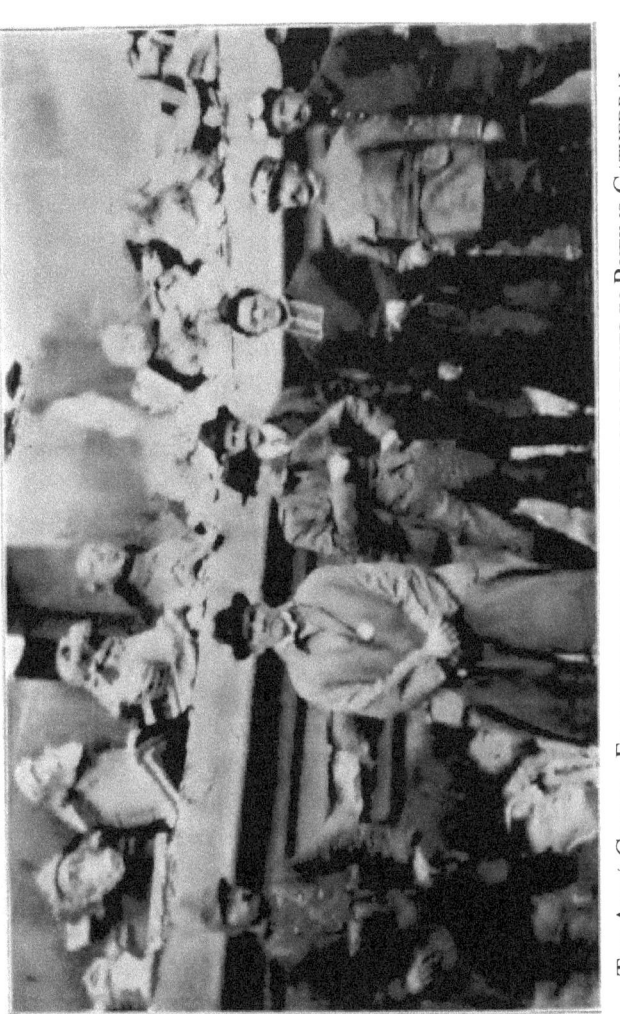

THE ABBÉ CHINOT, FRENCH SOLDIERS AND CORRESPONDENTS IN RHEIMS CATHEDRAL DURING SECOND BOMBARDMENT.

THE GERMANS CLAIMED THAT THESE SOLDIERS WERE USING CATHEDRAL AS OBSERVATION POST.

the cloak of military necessity to cover the multitude of their sins. It is my aim to be fair in all I write, so I give here an incident of my stay in Rheims and my explanation of the outrage.

While I was in the window of the highest tower of the cathedral two shells, evidently fired at that tower, missed it luckily, and fell twenty yards away in the street below. These were the only two shells that fell in that part of the city that day. Of course the tower was the one nearest the German lines, and an artillery duel had been in progress all morning. Needless to say I came down from the tower in a hurry. When I thought the matter over it seemed to me that it was very curious that all during the day only two shells should have fallen near the cathedral. Although the incident made splendid copy and I looked on it as a unique experience, yet I felt that the shells had not been fired with the object of giving me copy and a sensation. When I began to try to reason out cause and effect, I remembered that of our party who were inspecting the ruins, my colleague, Mr. Ashmead-Bartlett, who was formerly an officer in the Guards, wore his old service uniform, and I also brought to mind the fact that two French officers of the Aviation Corps, in uniform of course, stood with us in the window while the *abbé* pointed out the German positions. There were thus, at the time the shells fell, three uniforms framed in the window. It may be only coincidence, but to me it seems that the uniforms were the reason for the shells.

I could picture the German artillery officer with a powerful glass trained exactly on the tower, and two of his guns aimed at the window. It is a fact that the French were supposed to have used the towers as posts of observation that brought the first projectiles in this direction. Could it not have been possible that, seeing what he supposed to be a party of officers studying his positions, the German fired again? If this were so, I can believe that they saw uniforms on the tower in the first place. I can readily believe that the French soldiers or officers who climbed to the highest point within their lines during the early days of their occupation of Rheims, were merely sightseers; but of this the distant German artilleryman could not be certain.

The fact that Rheims lies in a hollow and that there is no available bit of high ground in the vicinity from which the defenders could watch the effect of their shells, would always make German gunners think French officers seen on the tower were more than idly curious visitors. An agreement had been reached by the French and German staffs which placed the cathedral in a neutral zone, so long as it was not

View of damage, main entrance, Rheims Cathedral.

used for military purposes.

In the first week of the French return to Rheims they had placed a searchlight and a machine gun on the highest angles of the tower, in order to fight off the aeroplanes that constantly hovered over the town. On condition that these war implements were taken down the Germans promised not to shell Notre Dame de Rheims. The case has only been fought out in the newspapers and the most important witnesses have never been summoned, so judgment must be reserved until the war is over. The Germans have enough on their consciences without this crime. Let us hope they can clear themselves.

At the time of my visit, September 21, although the city had been under fire all the previous day, and intermittently, before that time, it was the section in the vicinity of the cathedral that seemed to have suffered. Here I saw houses that had been set afire by German projectiles, and where the houses were not entirely destroyed, great gaping holes in the walls showed where shell had smashed through. In this bombardment over one hundred non-combatants (among them women and children) had been killed. Rheims had been taken by the Germans on September 5, the anniversary of the day it had been entered in 1870.

On that day I sat talking with Baron Mumm in the Foreign Office in Berlin. He himself told me the "good news." As a member of the famous champagne family he was delighted that his countrymen held the Mumm plant. Although it has thrived in France for years, the organisation was entirely under German control, and nearly all of the stock was held in Germany. When the German army in this theatre of operations assaulted the city and its environs, the House of Mumm was immune.

The war year will be famous as a champagne vintage. All the vine culturists classed the grapes as the best in quality grown for many years. But who would gather the grapes under shell fire? Unless the Prussians are driven off, one of the finest harvests Champagne has seen must rot on the vines.

No great harm had come to the champagne which was already bottled in the cellars of the planters. While the Germans were in possession of Rheims they paid for all that they drank and as an answer to the many accusations of their intemperance, left fifty million bottles untouched in the caves of the six most renowned houses in the world.

I am writing of Rheims and the cathedral as I found them in Sep-

RHEIMS CATHEDRAL.
THE ROOF OF THE CATHEDRAL WAS BURNED OFF.

tember. Since I was there the city has been under fire almost without cessation. What its present condition is I cannot say. More damage to Notre Dame is reported, but the details have not yet been made public.

It is the condition of the women and children in a city under bombardment that always makes the strongest appeal to me. I have so often seen them crushed between the grinding wheels of the war machines, that to my mind their case needs a strong advocate before future peace conferences.

Every road leading from Rheims was crowded with old men, women and children. They were fleeing in mortal terror from the fire and iron that rained upon the city. The distress brought upon them innocent victims of men's savagery beggars description. Only those who have heard the terrifying shriek of the shell, and seen the havoc projectiles make when they crash through the walls of houses, can understand the fear that racked the souls of the women and children of Rheims. Many of them were plainly the victims of hysteria. At every sharp sound they would crouch and tremble. Thousands trudged along the roads not knowing where they were going, or how they were to live during the days that followed. Their only thought was to escape the hurtling iron.

For days and nights these fugitives lived in the open fields, dividing carefully the little hoard of food they had been able to carry with them. When this food was gone they starved or begged from others, but what had others to give? In such an extremity each must fend alone. The plight of the old, the young, the tenderly nurtured, was pitiable. Some sat by the roadside staring straight before them with unseeing eyes. Fear and grief had hypnotised them. Despair had darkened their minds.

One is so helpless in the face of such misery. I have heard that since this war began an organisation has been founded with the object of caring for non-combatant sufferers. In France and Belgium such an organisation is an urgent necessity. The distress of the unfortunates who live in the theatre of operations calls for practical relief. Hundreds are today dying from exposure and lack of food.

Coming away from Rheims I was, for the second time in France, arrested as a spy. Our motor, which was large, handsome and conspicuous, got caught in the columns of the *corps d'armée*, which was changing front. We were not interested in the manoeuvres of this corps and only chafed at the delay. We wanted to get the story of Rheims back to the waiting world. I say "we," for my friends Richard Harding Davis,[1] Gerald Morgan and Ellis Ashmead-Bartlett, were my co-adventurers. When the motor was held up we tried to convince a very smart general officer, first, that we were not spies, and second, that it was mostly for the sake of France that the story of the ravage of Rheims should be cabled to the fifty million people who got their news from the papers we represented. His only reply was that there were plenty of well-dressed spies travelling through the French lines in motors. When we asked to go on to Paris, under guard if he wished, that we might be identified by the American Ambassador he only answered that it was impossible.

When our motor was confiscated and we were turned over to the *gendarmerie*, we could only wait for the next turn of events.

In the meantime my friend "Dick" Davis provided a picnic lunch. Davis is the best man in the world to go campaigning with. Not so much for his charming personality, his fund of reminiscences, which are many, as he has reported every reputable war—and some disreputable ones—since he was twenty-one, but because in the field he is always the generous provider. Davis starts out with a bigger pack than anybody else. It is necessary. Everybody else lives on him. This time he produced a bottle of champagne. Under the circumstances could anything be more fortunate? Also some tinned herrings, cheese, biscuits and sandwiches. I contributed a splendid appetite and a generous appreciation. Assuming attitudes of indifference and ostentatiously drinking the champagne, we disdained our captors. After lunch we went to the "guardhouse," a villainous stable. Here three other correspondents had been in confinement for three days.

For some reason it was suddenly decided to send us back to Paris. General A—— must have realised that the case was one which could not be handled there. So in three motors, under guard, we started back for the capital. We had to show the way to our guards.

When we arrived in Paris after some delay at General Headquarters, we were ordered to the Cherche-Midi prison. This is the prison that figured so prominently in the Dreyfus Case. I refused point blank to go, insisting on my right to see the American Ambassador. Then Major —— called a couple of *gendarmes*. I executed a "strategic retirement." The Cherche-Midi prison is as gloomy as the Bastille. I feel sure that never before did three motor loads of prisoners drive so

---

1. *Richard Harding Davis' Great War* by Richard Harding Davis also published by Leonaur.

RHEIMS CATHEDRAL.

noisily up to its doors. Once in the prison we took possession of it like a lot of political delegates arriving at a Chicago hotel. Most firmly did we object to the cells. The poor gaoler was most apologetic. They were the best cells in the house. Some very high French officers had occupied them. No, they did not suit. And dinner? We wanted dinner. He was very sorry, but he must send out for it. At this Ashmead-Bartlett drew out about three thousand *francs* in paper, and selecting a bill said, "Send for the best dinner in Paris." At this the whole prison staff got busy.

I did not stay for that dinner. But it was historic. Even now the warden of the Cherche-Midi and the underwardens tell and retell the tale. They were all invited. The prisoners were waiters—that is the regular prisoners, not my companions. No German banquet in a captured *château* could have surpassed it. The gaoler of the Cherche-Midi longs for some more American prisoners I believe.

My protest had done some good, for shortly after we arrived at the gaol, two officers of the general staff came and took me to the American Embassy. We arrived after the ambassador had gone to bed, so we went around to the apartment of the military *attaché*. He identified us and asked for our immediate release. After a good deal of quibbling, the staff officers agreed to hold us under guard in the building of the general staff that night and decide if we could be released in the morning. We had been ordered under arrest for eight days, as we had seen movements of troops of great importance. Just because his old army corps got in our way on the road from Rheims to Paris! The next day Mr. Herrick procured our release, but not until we had been sentenced not to leave Paris for eight days. It was not an arduous sentence.

THE EFFECT OF SHELL FIRE ON A PRIVATE HOUSE IN RHEIMS

CHAPTER 10

# Antwerp

All passes having been refused to military correspondents in France, and the French making themselves daily more disagreeable to the journalists whom they picked up in the war zone, my paper, the *Daily Telegraph*, determined to send me to Russia. But before I could make arrangements for going to this new field, events took a definite turn at Antwerp, so I was hastily ordered to cover that beleaguered city.

When I arrived in Flushing it already harboured several thousand refugees. Pale, haggard, and many of them still with nerves vibrating from the sound of the shells, they crowded into the little Dutch port, hoping to find there a haven of safety. Every train from Roosendal brought more of the refugees. All day, boat after boat had steamed down the river crowded to the rails with those who wanted to escape from Antwerp.

As yet the city had not fallen, but the Germans had brought guns that had a range of five miles up to their advanced positions, and with these they could reach well into the centre of the city with deadly projectiles. Somehow the news that the English and Belgian forces that were defending Antwerp were about to evacuate the city, leaked out, and the citizens thinking themselves abandoned to the enemy, became the victims of their own terror. Escape was their only thought. When the bombardment began it was the signal for such an exodus as before seemed impossible outside some sensational book of fiction.

Men and women fled before a fear of death in frightful form. That fear was plainly written in the face of every citizen of Antwerp. I remember seeing a young, pale, but rather pretty woman who sat alone in the station refreshment-room. This room had been the centre of a clamouring throng for hours. I noticed her sitting alone, and as I entered the refreshment-room for the first time, a solicitous waiter

Ships were full to overflowing with Antwerp refugees

placed coffee, a sandwich and some scrambled eggs on the table before her. She did not seem to notice the food—her dark eyes looked steadily off into space as if picturing some vivid terrifying scene of the bombardment. After getting something to eat myself, writing a dispatch and taking it to the local telegraph office, all of which occupied a couple of hours' time, I again returned to the refreshment-room. There was the girl (she was in the early twenties), sitting as I had first seen her, the food untouched, her unseeing eyes turned back on the scene of the night before.

From the moment the first shell fell in Antwerp the whole population was seized with panic. The streets leading to the railroad station were crowded with a frightened struggling mob, pressing onward to escape the hail of iron and fire. Actually, the shells reached only the southern section of the city, and did little damage there. The great oil tanks which stood in the danger zone had been emptied, the petroleum being turned into the River Scheldt. They had been set on fire, however, and what remained of the petrol was burning murkily. A few houses had caught fire from the hail of projectiles.

One of the most pathetic among the many little groups of refugees was a woman with two small children, girls, four and three years old. In the flight from Antwerp the rule that holds on a sinking steamer was put into effect—"*Women and children first!*" Because of this rule a number of women found themselves without male protection, stranded in a foreign country. The woman to whom I refer had been, with the two children, pushed on an already overcrowded lighter as it was towed away from the wharf. With a voice of anguish she asked advice of me as how she might again find her husband. I could only suggest that she should advertise in the local papers. While she told me the tale of the bombardment as she had witnessed it, she spoke of the soul-piercing shriek of the shells and the never-ceasing boom of the cannon. When she said cannon, the elder girl looked up, tears sprang to her eyes, and she said piteously, "*Pas plus de canon, maman, pas plus de canon.*"

When I arrived in Flushing the information I gathered from the refugees led me to believe that Antwerp would not be evacuated for two or three days. Therefore I arranged with an old Dutch tug master to take me up the river to the besieged city the next morning. It was arranged that we should start at daybreak. It was still night when I stumbled down to the wharf-side and clambered over two other crafts to the deck of that tug *John Bull*. Mysterious and ghost-like, the crafts crowded into the little harbour looked in this hour. Not a star showed, and where I knew the river flowed, was abysmal blackness. I was still sleepy, so using my dress-suit case for a pillow I lay down in the stern-sheets of the tug.

Soon I saw a sturdy short figure emerge from the bowels of the tug, looking for all the world like a gnome. I recognized Captain Hermans. With the first streaks of grey dawn the tug churned its way out into the broad mouth of the Scheldt. Steaming up the river under a leaden sky, the bow of the tug cutting through the waters like a knife, I witnessed a panorama of history. As far as the eye could see a stream of vessels rushed down upon me. In the distance they looked like a ghostly armada. Every type of craft was there—transport, tender, lighter, trawler, collier, coaster, yacht and hulk, followed in a procession that lost itself where the sky met the waters. All the ships followed the same course. Over the quiet waters came the distant boom of cannon. The ships were fleeing from that sound. With my glass I was soon able to make out the human freight the vessels carried. They swarmed over the decks. Some even climbed into the rigging. Soon the *John Bull* was among them. I could see the faces of haggard women. I could hear the cries of frightened children. All stared in wonder as we passed. Some shouted the question where we were going.

"To Antwerp," answered Captain Hermans.

"Turn back! it's burning! The Germans are there! Turn back!"

The words carried over the water a wailing note of alarm. Without heeding this warning we kept on. I had hopes of reaching the city before it fell. When the *John Bull* arrived at Lillo, hardly seven miles as the crow flies from our goal, we heard that Antwerp had fallen. A captain of a Belgian river patrol boat stopped us to give us this unwelcome news and forbade us to go further. As the spire of the famous cathedral of Antwerp was in sight, to turn back was indeed a disappointment.

From Belgian soldiers I learned that the British and Belgian forces which had been holding the city began their evacuation the previous night. In the confusion of this night march, part of the English force wandered over into Holland and were there interned. The main body of the defenders retired in a most orderly manner, reluctant to leave this city which they had so gallantly defended. Among the very last to depart was the king commander.

In my opinion the holding of Antwerp was a strategic error.

When the Belgian Army retired to Antwerp it was supposed to be

THE FIRST GERMAN TO ENTER BRUGES.
WHEN WE MOTORED INTO THE TOWN THE CITIZENS WERE CRYING IN TERROR, "THE GERMANS WILL KILL YOU," BUT HE IS A HARMLESS-LOOKING FELLOW.

falling back on an impregnable position, from which it could threaten the enemy's lines of communication. In fact, Antwerp was not impregnable, as was conclusively proved, and the Belgian forces made only two sorties against the German communications. Thus during the period when it would have been a factor of importance if joined with other French or English corps, because it was isolated, its influence on the development of the early campaign was almost negligible. This is a lamentable fact. Not for one moment did this considerable force check the onrush of von Kluck, or weaken the blow aimed by the German advance against any part of the French line. This inactivity, however, is forgotten in the splendid righting of the Antwerp Army in the defence of the Yser.

As a further reason for the abandoning of Antwerp, I advance the theory that a fortified city is a military weakness. This has been proved time and again in the present war, (1914). Liége, Namur, Maubeuge, and Antwerp indicate the truth of my contention. Since the extraordinary range of modern artillery has made it possible for siege batteries to pour shell down upon a defenceless populace from positions far beyond the outer ring of defending forts, all fortified cities have become hopelessly vulnerable. Now that the homes of inhabitants may be inflamed by fire bombs, what is gained by surrounding any city with walls and ramparts?

The engineers who planned the defences of cities twenty years ago, failed to reckon on the genius of Krupp. They could not foresee the devilish ingenuity of the German. In fortification we have a modification of the armour-plate and projectile penetration problem. Ramparts erected a score of years ago were proof against any shell that artillerymen could then conceive of. They never dreamed that it would one day be possible to hurl a ton of iron and explosives a distance of ten miles. Yet this is what is claimed for the German 17-inch mortar. And what is the value of any fort when aircraft of every sort can fly over them and drop bombs at will?

Another handicap of the fortified city is the fixed line of defence. This line it is certain is well-known to the enemy. The German gunners' map of Antwerp have ranges accurately scaled off from the forts to every possible gun position before them. This makes for a fight between the seen and the unseen. When the turret of Fort Waelham was destroyed, not a German had been seen by the men in it—that is if we except one in a *Taube*. The Belgians there first knew they were under fire when two or three random shells fell in the vicinity. Then the aircraft circled over their heads. Down came a naphtha bomb, fair in the wall of the fort. A cloud of stinking smoke marked the spot. This made a perfect target. In five minutes the turret cracked under a rain of iron. The shells fell like meteors from a cloudless sky. Such is the effect of indirect fire. It is difficult even for the trained eye to discover the positions of howitzer or mortar battery using high angle fire. Under it a novice artilleryman is helpless.

Again, the one-time advantage in calibre and range which fortress artillery possessed has disappeared. In fact, the siege artillery brought into action by the Germans has nearly always been superior to the defenders' cannon. This is another strong argument against fortification, at least against fortification that has not kept pace with gun improvements: and no fort I have seen in Belgium can be classified as modern. A great deal of misinformation has been published on the strength of the fortified cities that have been so easily taken by the Germans. It may have been policy to overrate these forts in order to deceive the enemy, but the misinformation had the effect of creating confidence in the impregnability of the defended cities that events did not justify.

When this confidence has been destroyed by German success, the moral effect on our people and even on our troops has been bad. The impression among the Belgians and French is even worse. Since Antwerp fell, the unthinking will consider German artillery as more destructive than an earthquake.

Is it not better to admit that the turret and concrete fort, as conceived and built by General Brialmont has proved to be a complete failure? Concrete, even when reinforced, cannot stand against modern shells of large calibre; and in the peculiar type of fort that defends Antwerp, once the concrete is cracked, it becomes impossible to operate turret machinery. Thus one well-placed shot will put two guns completely out of commission. There are two guns in each turret. The concrete chips get into the groove in which the steel semi-spherical hood revolves, and jam until it is no longer possible to turn it. This one defect should be sufficient to condemn this kind of construction.

But the concrete fort has two other fatal weaknesses—the first is the mistake of making the fire-control and observation tower serve also as the searchlight station. What better target could one want at night than the glittering disc of a searchlight? and if your light is hit, your observation station is destroyed. This error in fortification building is nothing compared with the final fault of the Brialmont turret

All that I saw of Antwerp.

fort. This is the light shaft. After devising an intricate system of subterranean tunnelling in his fort, and covering it with a heavy wall of concrete, Brialmont leaves a sort of chimney 2 feet square opening into the very heart of the defence. The light shaft opens directly over the ammunition cell. I saw Fort Loncin at Liége after a shell had dropped down the light shaft. It could not have been more disrupted by an earthquake. Nothing remains but a heap of rubble. Both turrets were torn from their foundations and upended. The concrete walls were so much slag; perhaps this was a lucky hit. Even so, other lucky hits will find the same vulnerable mark. A soldier of the Namur garrison told me that much the same thing happened in the fort he was in.

Again, no gun I have seen in a turret fort was larger than 15 cm. calibre. I understand that larger guns were ordered for the forts at Antwerp, but as war opened before they were delivered, Herr Krupp has kept them for home use. Also the concrete for many of the Antwerp forts had not arrived before the city was invested. The turret at Fort Waelham and Fort Wavre, Ste. Catherine were defended by sand-bags only. Under the circumstances it was brilliant work that they held out as they did. At Fort Waelham a copper brewing vat was set up as an imitation turret, and it drew considerable German fire.

But leaving the special defects and getting back to the general question of fortified cities, the fatal defect in the whole theory is that it leaves the garrison exposed to capture. The war of 1870 demonstrated this, time and again, and in this war many good soldiers were made prisoners when Maubeuge fell. Luckily the handful of English and Belgians holding Antwerp found a safe line of retreat when the forts crumpled beneath the enemy's fire. Those interned in Holland are but a small part of the defending force.

I have already mentioned the weakness of the civil population in a fortified city. Since the Germans have degraded the noble profession of arms by throwing shell and shrapnel among women and children, the inhabitants of the city open to bombardment are doubly unfortunate. It is hard to keep the terror that spreads among them from lowering the *morale* of the defending garrison. Very rightly General Paris directed that all civilians should leave Antwerp.

In the taking of Antwerp, the Germans achieved more of a moral than a material victory. Under the present circumstances the city has only a limited strategic value. The neutrality of Holland destroys the city's military worth, but how long will Germans respect that neutrality?

A SQUAD OF GERMAN CYCLISTS TOOK POSSESSION OF BRUGES ON OCTOBER 14.

CHAPTER 11

# "Annexing" Belgium

Reluctantly I turned my back on Antwerp. It was my good fortune to have been in the vicinity of all the eventful scenes of the war up to this time, and being barred from seeing the bombardment was a disappointment. In this war the correspondent works under so many difficulties. It is not a question of getting to the front—the best we can do is to place ourselves in a certain position, and wait for the front to come to us. In the early days of the war this was easy. As the German inundation advanced this became more and more difficult. Soon the whole continent was crowded up with soldiers. However, working on this principle, I trans-shipped to a refugee boat bound for Ostend. It was one of the mail boats that ordinarily run from Folkestone to Ostend. It had made two trips to Antwerp, carrying off fleeing citizens.

On these two voyages its larders had been emptied. For twenty-four hours I suffered all the physical anguish of the refugee. His mental anguish I escaped. Two apples and a stick of chocolate was all I had to eat during these twenty-four hours. My bed was the softest place I could find on the deck. There were not enough cabins for the women and children. In the middle of the night it rained, but when I felt sorry for myself I thought of the plight of those around me, then I would forget my own troubles. Picture yourself in an overcrowded steerage, then fill the minds of the passengers with haunting fear and you can imagine what it was like on that refugee ship.

From talk with some of the passengers I learned that the Belgian government was already in Ostend, so I knew the army would eventually come to that city. When after many delays our ship did arrive at the popular seaside resort I made a curious discovery. Although I had eaten almost nothing for twenty-four hours I was not hungry. I had no inclination to make up for my lost meals, a new and curious

Belgian dog transports in Ostend

experience for me.

Ostend presented a most inspiring picture of military activity. Motors filled with Belgian, French or English soldiers flashed back and forth along the Digue. Men in every type of uniform from the Highlander's kilt to the Frenchman's red pantaloons hurried up and down the narrow streets. Detachments of Belgian dog artillery were packed in the main square. It was a picture to gladden the heart of any war correspondent.

As I walked along the Digue to my hotel I saw that the Kursaal, the great gambling casino, had been turned into a hospital. The roulette table had been replaced by the operating table, and instead of the continuous call of the croupier one sometimes heard the low moan of the suffering wounded.

When I arrived in Ostend I found enough troops here to hold back a German Army; at least from their unceasing activity one got this impression. My hope was that they would decide to hold Ostend. This seemed a remote chance, however, for an acquaintance with that part of the coast convinced me that there were no defensive positions worthy of the name.

The Belgian Army which had evacuated Antwerp was still wending its way into the town. Artillery columns clanged through the streets and all day long I heard the uneven tramp of tired infantry. Carefully watching the indications, I soon saw that no stand was to be made here. I kept watch on certain British transport columns that were camped just over the canal bridge and when one night it "*folded its tents like the Arab, and silently stole away*," I began to suspect that no fight would be made here.

The rumour that Ostend was to be abandoned to the Germans spread in the mysterious way that such news does. British and Belgian troops were still as far beyond the town as Ghent, when the Ostend populace began to make its preparations for flight. When I found there was to be no conflict I decided that the only "story"—as newspaper men call it—the situation offered, was from the German side. I had been to Ghent with Mr. H. E. Johnson, the American Consul, who had temporarily removed to Ostend and on the road there I saw an English division moving out of Eccloo and still long columns of Belgian troops marching tiredly westward.

In Ghent I talked with some officers of the Belgian armoured motor detachment, who I discovered were acting as rearguard. They had captured a motor belonging to the German Aviation Corps and were

The London 'bus, a long way from home.
Cathedral Square, Ostend.

proudly putting it in order for their own service. There had been a rearguard skirmish that morning.

It was apparent that the Germans were to be allowed to sweep across Belgium with no opposition. Two days I motored into Bruges to meet them.

I found the inhabitants fleeing in terror. "They'll shoot you! They'll shoot you! The Germans are here!" Here was proof indeed that Germany had succeeded only too well in putting the fear of her wrath into the hearts of the simple Belgian people.

I had placed an American flag above the windshield of my motor and confident in this protection, I drove into the central square of the old city, and drew up before the famous restaurant Panier d'Or. In little groups many of the people of the town hurried across the square flying before the invaders.

Soon, however, it was realised that the Germans were entering peacefully, assuring the populace that so long as they showed no hostility they would not be molested. I watched a detachment of about forty cyclists in grey with long guns slung over their shoulders ride in and take possession of the town. They were not the arrogant type of Teuton soldier I had seen in other fields—mostly they appeared to be older, more settled men. All were smoking. Some drew deep draughts of blue vapour from china bowl pipes, while others puffed at long black cigars. Their first act on entering Bruges was to tear down the English and French flags that were flying from the *Hôtel de Ville*. The Belgian black, yellow and red colours they did not touch. By some sort of military magic, posters in four languages, German, French, Flemish and Walloon, suddenly appeared on all the hoarding of the town. These told that Bruges was now a German city and called on the citizens to obey strictly the orders of their new masters. These posters were signed by General von Beseler.

By this time the advance-guard had scattered to take positions on the different roads leading out of the town, and certain of the city fathers there had been taken as hostages.

I was very much impressed with the business-like manner in which the German soldiers went about their work. I knew the duties of an advance-guard entering an enemy's city and could appreciate the difficulties of this manoeuvre. But these men went through with the task in that systematic thorough manner characteristic of the whole German military organisation.

I went around the town in my motor without let or hindrance,

BELGIAN SOLDIERS SPYING BRITISH MONITORS, OSTEND, OCTOBER 11.

some of the soldiers even saluting my American flag. They even posed for their photographs and showed a most friendly spirit in every way.

It is the fashion to represent the German soldier as an ogre. I know that as a class he has done some unforgivable things in this war. Yet the individuals whom I met on many occasions were far from being awe-inspiring monsters. The troops that came into Bruges that afternoon were all the steady father-of-family type.

After an hour in the town during German occupation I turned my motor back towards Ostend. I went unquestioned, and hardly two miles outside Bruges I ran into the last stragglers of the fast retreating Belgians. Late that night I was once more in Ostend.

In the seaside town I found the preparations for departure far more advanced than when I had left. I saw outside English head-quarters motor after motor, loaded with impedimenta, snort off down the Digue and disappear in a cloud of dust. I lived at the *Hôtel de Phare* where it was possible to watch the departing staffs without difficulty.

When on the following morning I saw the French general having breakfast in the hotel, while his motor with baggage strapped behind stood waiting at the curb, I knew that the final chapter of the evacuation of Ostend was about to begin. That day the city began to empty itself as a theatre where someone has shouted "Fire!" The roads to Holland and France were soon dense with the fleeing multitude. On they trudged, each carrying some bundle with all that the war had left them. The exodus continued for three days. During this time there was the greatest confusion among the crowd that struggled in the boat station and on the quay.

Here thousands stood close packed waiting their chance to board departing steamers. Many of these were women and children. They waited here from daylight to dark, to daylight again, without food or drink. Several children died. Vessel after vessel was loaded far beyond the danger-mark with human freight, and left for the hospitable shores of England. But still the crowd thronging on the wharf never seemed to dwindle. When the last ship cast off, those despairing ones in the rear who saw their last chance of escape slipping away, pressed forward frantically. The scenes of this flight now come back to me as the vision of some frightful nightmare. The dread in the faces of the fleeing women, and the pathetic helplessness of the children are haunting memories.

Out of the confused impressions one picture is clear. By the roadside I see the body of an old man. His dead fingers still clutch the little bundle of his belongings. Unheeding the crowd rushes by.

Since I have left Belgium I have sometimes heard the question as to what indemnity the people of the ravished kingdom will ask when war loosens its grip on their beloved country. To me the question is absurd. There is no money, not all the wealth of the world, that can wipe out the misery or efface the memory of those terrible days and nights. Three English women stayed in Ostend doing their best to help the stricken people. Two of these were members of the English Red Cross. Almost alone they transferred more than two hundred gravely wounded Belgian soldiers to a waiting train, and started them to the French base hospitals. These two women worked without stop for twenty-four hours to empty the improvised hospital. When the Germans entered they found it bare.

Another work of distinct merit was that carried on by the Double White Cross Society, under the direction of Mr. Batonyi, Secretary of the American Consul, and Mrs. Coster. The broad aim of this Society is to aid all non-combatants in the war zone, irrespective of nationality. From daylight to dark Mrs. Coster laboured, distributing food and clothing to the peasants who paused here in their flight from the oncoming Germans.

Ostend was now held by but a handful of the Belgian rearguard. In aspect it was a city of the dead. Every house showed a blank face of close-drawn shutters. Every shop had lowered its iron window. As I tramped the deserted streets my footsteps echoed at every corner. A little beyond the circle of the centre of the town, house after house stood empty. Some stood wide open just as the owners had left them. The city brought to mind a visit to Pompeii. I looked in one house. A pot of jam with half a tin of biscuits stood on the table. A vase of dead flowers graced the mantel. The floor was littered with bits of twine and brown paper, the debris of hasty packing. Another that had been empty was occupied by a newly-arrived family of refugees.

I came back to the fish market. Here two days before a German aviator had dropped three bombs, and I stood making careful study of the little damage done. Suddenly I heard the clatter of hoofs on stone, and turned to see a Belgian cavalryman galloping down the Digue shouting "The Germans are here! The Germans are here!" Beating his tired mount with the full length of his rifle he disappeared down the coast shouting the hoarse-voiced warning. Within five minutes a lieutenant and six Uhlans trotted into the square in front of the *Hôtel de Ville*, and took possession of Ostend. These were followed by about

THE FIRST GERMAN TO ENTER OSTEND.
HE KNEW THE WAY WELL, AS HE SPENT EVERY SUMMER FOR THE LAST SEVEN YEARS THERE. OCTOBER, 1914.

twenty men of the Cyclist Corps, who rode up and down the streets exploring the town. As is usual in war, the horses of the cavalry had been used up and the cyclists made a very good substitute for horse soldiers. Nearly all the Germans smoked long black cigars. The few people left in Ostend watched in ill-concealed alarm as if expecting momentarily an outbreak of savagery. The startling feature of the performance was the absolute silence that reigned. The shouting of the exploring soldiers was the only sound in the streets.

It was evident from the first that these invaders had no intention of harming any of the inhabitants. One or two made friendly advances and the Belgians were soon clustering about them in questioning groups. After a time they even joked together. The whole attitude of the conquerors had changed. No longer did they want to plant fear in the hearts of the Belgians. Conciliation was in their very word and act. I later found out in a talk with one of the junior officers, that the order had come from headquarters that stern measures were no longer to be used against the people of Belgium. That this was a policy dictated by the expectation of annexation there can be no doubt.

Within half an hour General von der Goltz motored into Ostend and entered the *Hôtel de Ville*. He is still straight after fifty odd years of soldiering. He held a conference with the Burgomaster, the Chief of Police and the American Consul. Very briefly he stated what he expected of the citizens of the town, and directed the Burgomaster and the Chief of Police to see that no German soldier was hindered in the performance of his duty. The American Consul was to serve the interests of the many neutrals and non-combatant enemies still in Ostend. In this difficult task Mr. Johnson acquitted himself admirably.

The first excitement of the occupation ended, I returned to my hotel for breakfast. The breakfast-room looks out on the sea, and while here I witnessed a thrilling drama in two acts.

A low mist, as fleecy as steam, hung over the water. German cyclist soldiers in soiled grey uniforms and helmets awry rode silently up and down the Digue, as the brick road on the seashore is called. After the confusion of the last three days the city was for the first time peaceful. Suddenly out of the mist appeared a vessel flying the French flag. As she came straight on towards the long pier I made her out to be a destroyer. Slowly she steamed into the unknown danger. She was well on the long pier before any of the German cyclists saw her. A crowd stood on the Digue watching tensely. Suddenly a man ran out to meet the destroyer. We could see him waving his arms. Now he is abreast

Before the Germans had been in Ostend more than a few hours, they were the centre of interest to the Belgian populace.

of the French war vessel. But two grey-coated cyclists are pedalling after him.

We can see the gallant citizen haranguing the captain of the destroyer. Slowly she comes to a stop. In a moment the water in her wake is churned to white foam and she is running full speed astern. The German soldiers pedal swiftly along the pier, but when they arrive at the end, the destroyer has put a hundred yards of green water between them. The soldiers waved and shouted, but the low hull of the French war vessel soon disappeared in the mist from which it had so mysteriously come. Here I expected to be an eyewitness of a "German atrocity." The citizen who had warned the captain of the destroyer was now walking calmly back the length of the pier.

More German cyclists, with long guns slung across their backs, were approaching. As the man had openly aided an enemy, according to the German laws of war he should be shot. I expected to see him made to stand with his back to the sea on the edge of the pier, while a squad of soldiers fired at his breast, but to my surprise the Germans never noticed him. I think he must have had a thrilling moment when they passed. In my opinion this unknown citizen of Ostend deserves the highest rank of the Legion of Honour. He unquestionably saved the French destroyer and took his life in his hands in doing it. Under the circumstances I consider his act one of the "nerviest" I have ever witnessed. It will ever remain a mystery to me why he was not summarily executed.

Half an hour later a ship's launch appeared out of the mist, but this boat turned before it came within a thousand yards of the pier. Watching German soldiers waved to it to come on, but as the invitation was declined they opened fire. After firing some fifty rounds they gave up hope of a naval victory.

Hardly more than a company of Germans occupied Ostend the first day. But as rooms were engaged for forty officers at the *Hôtel Royal Phare* it was evident that a considerable force would enter on the morrow.

In justice to the German officer and soldier against whom so many charges have been brought I must put down the fact that in Ostend I found him to be civil, courteous and even friendly. Most of the men—it was a reserve corps—looked like middle aged fathers of families. Sentries on post were often surrounded by children to whom they were showing all the delightful mysteries of their equipment. The officers were all willing to talk with me and never resented my questioning, which was sometimes rather direct. Of course they boasted of the prowess of Germany, and of what they were going to do to the English, but that was natural. On the whole they were just like the same class in any other land. Certainly there was nothing to stamp them as the monsters certain members of the press made them out to be. It was hard for me to believe that these were men of the army that had sown such desolation throughout Belgium.

In my conversation with some of the Hussar officers, I found out that heavy columns of troops were expected at Ostend. "We have a hundred thousand men on the way to open the road to Calais, and if they are not enough another hundred thousand will follow."

While I was not advertising the fact that I was a war correspondent, the statement of this officer was an indiscretion, even to a casual neutral. His companion remonstrated strongly. In view of the future developments of the campaign along the coast my protesting Hussar knew what he was talking about.

The next morning I watched the columns of the Third Reserve Corps march into the town. As has been always the case whenever I have seen the German Army I was strongly impressed. These were undeniably efficient fighting men, and being a reserve corps most of the men were over thirty. My own experience has convinced me that the soldier between thirty and forty-five is more reliable on a long campaign than the younger man. As they marched across the canal bridge these bearded grizzled Germans impressed an onlooker as tried veterans.

The only point I could find to criticize with this corps was that it seemed not to have its complement of artillery. I saw only certain batteries of machine guns with the column of the main body. It is quite possible, however, that the field artillery did not enter the town.

The occupation of north-western Belgium by the Germans was a skilful political and military move. From the political point of view, holding practically the whole of the country gave Germany a splendid advantage in any trading that might take place during peace negotiations. For this reason the kingdom was to all intents and purposes annexed. I noticed, however, one significant fact, which only future developments can explain. In almost every instance of German occupation there was no substitution of flags. The Belgian colours always floated from the official quarters, even though Germans were handling all the administrative machinery.

It was the German hope that they would be able to fortify this

German officers have their first look at the sea. Ostende digue, October 16, 1914.

part of the coast without being molested. They hoped that as Ostend, Blankenberg and Zeebrugge were the towns of an ally, they would be immune from bombardment from the sea. As long as it was possible, England respected the property of her Belgian friends. But when stern military necessity compelled it, the British ships turned their batteries on these seaside towns.

CHAPTER 12

# Through the Fighting Lines

In Ostend my wife had joined me and she shared my subsequent adventures. The seaside town had again taken on all the bustle of war preparations. The scene was much the same as it had been two days ago, except that German officers filled the hotels, German soldiers crowded the streets, and the musical note of the German automobile horn had taken the place of the raucous call of the English and Belgian cars.

Although Americans were popular with the Germans, I knew that according to their regulations I should not be allowed to remain long in the firing line. I knew that I could get a pass to Brussels without difficulty. What I wanted, however, was to rejoin the Belgian Army. I determined to ask openly for a pass to Dunkirk. The idea was perhaps rather presumptuous.

When I came to make the request, I found some forty officers of the staff enjoying a royal breakfast at my hotel. If there was any truth in the old adage that a man is more approachable after he has eaten, surely this was my opportunity. The best of fish and fowl that Ostend afforded was being served. Magnums of Irroy and quarts of Burgundy lined the centre of the long table. When I made my simple request to the German adjutant, he was certainly taken aback.

"Dunkirk is not yet in our lines. If you wish to go there, I shall have to ask the general."

I had, of course, explained that I was an American seeking to escape from the battle area. I watched the adjutant as he interrupted General von Beseler just as he was drinking a toast. Without a moment's hesitation he replied:

"*Ach!* let them go."

While the adjutant was scribbling my pass, I noticed that every other one of the officers assembled wore the coveted iron cross.

We lost no time in getting into the motor. Our baggage was already strapped on, and with a farewell blast of my horn we started on our dash through the lines.

My only worry at the time was gasoline. This precious fuel had become so scarce that it was impossible to purchase any. Every gallon had been commandeered by the military authorities. Only the generosity of a Belgian ambulance chauffeur made it possible for me to move the car I was running.

It was a damp, hazy day, and twice before I had reached the outskirts of the town, ghostly detachments in grey came out of the fog and halted me. The first time it was a cavalry patrol that examined my papers. Our second challengers were a platoon of infantry, carrying their rifles at the ready. The officer who stopped me had his revolver drawn. These men showed that they expected to meet their enemies at any moment.

Speeding along the road that runs parallel with the sea, we passed the last German outpost at Middlekirk. After scrutinizing our pass, they cheered us on our way. Two miles beyond, on the Ostend-Nieuport road, we were halted. My wife prepared confidently to present our pass.

"For God's sake, not that one," I whispered. "He's a Belgian!"

With skilful sleight of hand she got rid of the incriminating German paper, while I produced my tattered permit signed by M. de Broqueville, the Belgian Minister of War. The lone sentry nodded. He signalled me to pass.

"The Germans are coming," I told him.

"Let them come," he answered.

That is the spirit of the whole Belgian Army. This soldier, who stood alone facing the might of Germany, typifies Belgium. Searching his eyes, I saw there that he had already determined upon his sacrifice. He made nothing dramatic out of this dogged devotion to duty. That he should give his life for his country was as inevitable as it was right. The shot that struck him would be the warning to his friends.

Two hundred yards farther down the road, at Westende, our way was blocked by a Belgian machine gun detachment. A trench had been dug across the macadam, out of which emerged the blue barrel and brass stock of the rapid fire gun. This was just an advance position held in defence of the road. I studied the faces of the men holding the post. Each soldier had that look of grim determination which told that they had looked on death and despised its terrors.

The pluck of the Belgian Army must pass into proverb. For over three months they have borne the brunt of the German advance through their own country. Harried from point to point by an enemy infinitely stronger and better organised, they have given way only when it was not humanly possible to resist longer. It must be remembered that within their own boundaries heretofore the Belgians have received little or no support from the English or French. Few Belgians took part in the battles of Mons or Charleroi. At Liége, Namur, Louvain, Termonde, they have met the enemy single-handed.

In Nieuport the motor stopped. Mentally I pictured the neat little town after the German attack. I had seen so many of these villages in the wake of the Prussian. Nothing but blackened walls and rubble remained.

Leaving Nieuport, we found the road blocked by a stream of refugees. In this crowd there were those who had walked from distant Antwerp. Before arriving at Furnes, we met on the road a detachment of sappers returning from having blown up an innocent-looking villa with a concrete foundation. So elaborate was this foundation, that it would have served admirably as a gun emplacement for artillery attacking Dunkirk.

Arriving at Furnes, we found there the headquarters of the Belgian army. The little town was the scene of unceasing military activity. An unending stream of transports crossed the square diagonally. Every conceivable kind of motor, from the rakish armoured car to the runabout, had been pressed into service and now served the constant demands of the Belgian Army. Smart town cars with elaborate limousines were filled with loads of bread. Trucks with the name of some well-known Brussels brewery carried consignments of ammunition to the trenches. All day and night without interruption this stream of supply ebbed and flowed. In the darkness I watched the unending procession of head-lights which made one think of fabulous, fiery-eyed monsters of fairy tales. Companies of infantry changing position marched in and out of the town. Cavalrymen tended their sore backed mounts in every stable. In the centre of the square the transports of the staff took part.

Among the confusion of Belgian uniforms I had noticed certain officers in khaki. Afterwards I met two officers who had been attached to Belgian headquarters. They were at this time planning the attack which developed into the Battle of the Yser.

While in Ostend I had seen British warships, cruisers, destroyers and monitors hovering off the coast. With my glass I had studied the guns that poked out of the turrets of the monitors. Seconding these was a battery of bulldog howitzers. My thought at the time was that these ships were to be used in bombarding the coast if the Germans should take possession. I now found that my guess was only partly right. In Furnes the British officers I had noticed and a young, light-haired lieutenant from one of the destroyers, held several councils of war. I was fortunate to be there at the time. Here the plan of bringing the monitors and destroyers to the aid of the land troops was worked out.

King Albert was informed of the plan of attack, and he entered into it with enthusiasm. And when the word got about among the Belgian troops that they were to attack the enemy under the protection of the British naval guns, there was a sudden change in the atmosphere of Furnes.

I was at Furnes only during what might be called the prelude to the Battle of the Yser. At this time I had been received in audience by King Albert, and it was imperative that I should get that interview back to the office of the *Daily Telegraph* in London. To do this I had to go myself.

It was a clear Sunday morning when ammunition motors, loaded with their deadly missiles, one by one left the square for the front. The men on the armoured motors which looked so formidable, began polishing up their cars with that care and affection supposed to be the exclusive characteristic of sailors. Shortly these motor-cruisers lumbered out on the road marked "To Ostend." After these followed the cavalry. They rode as jauntily as if bound for their first engagement. Hardly had the clatter of the hoofs of the cavalry died out across the bridge, when the field artillery rumbled through the town. The horses, a bit tired and jaded, moved slowly. But the men seated on the caissons looked fit and fresh.

The heart of all the Belgian soldiers in the trenches thrilled when they received the order that they were to take the offensive. They knew that beyond them, scarce two kilometres distant, they should meet the grey-coated enemy. It was a clear, sunshiny day. Suddenly a deep boom sounded across the water. Then a ball of white smoke rose and hovered a moment above the decks of one of the monitors. The whistle of a shell cut through the air. Another boom came as an echo of the first, and a shell burst right among the enemy. Lovie and Slype were the targets of the gunners. There is a sort of blockhouse near the first village that the enemy occupied. This point received special attention.

After the ships' batteries had searched the country south of Middlekirk for some time, the order was given for the Belgian infantry to move forward. As with one impulse the men sprang from the trenches and crept forward on the invader. The rattle of the machine gun supplemented the noise of the naval Long Toms. Then the field artillery added to the chorus. But all this noise could not drown the irregular *rat-tat-tat* of the infantry.

The country here is flat and criss-crossed by a most complicated system of canals. The river itself is a magnified canal. The Belgians of course knew every foot of the country and were seen moving in a long line straight on the enemy's position. The news had arrived early in the morning, telling of a splendid British fight on the right; it was known that they had forced the Germans back far east of Dixmude. With this in mind it seemed to be the ambition of the Belgians to outdo the achievements of their ally. It was plain to be seen that the Germans did not relish the shells of the warships dropping in their rear.

Now actually caught between two fires, their line began to waver. As the determined Belgian infantry pressed onward, slowly the enemy gave way. It became apparent that they were not present in as great numbers as had been first reported. The cannonading from the sea increased, the infantry fire redoubled. The whole German line resting on the sea was now in full retreat. The Belgians pressed home their advantage, and when night fell they found themselves well in advance of the positions they had occupied in the morning.

The Battle of the Yser marked a crisis in the war. As the Battle of the Marne proved the turning-point of German success in the first stage of the campaign, so this contest for the canal through the north of Belgium signalled the failure of the second German offensive plan. The figures are not yet available, but I think when the cost is counted, it will be found to have been the bloodiest battle of the war. Perhaps in the Russian theatre of operations there will be battles in which the losses are greater, but up to the present I think the Battle of the Yser holds the record. The credit of holding the Germans back at this most vital point belongs in the first place to the remnant of the Belgian Army.

I have followed that army from Ghent to Bruges, from Bruges to

Ostend, from Ostend to Nieuport. Though they were retiring from Antwerp, there was nothing about them to suggest a defeated army. I must again record my admiration of the rank and file of this valiant little force. I have been fortunate in having unusual opportunities of observing it on the march and in the field of battle. Against the heaviest odds it has fought with extraordinary tenacity, but nowhere did it show more spirited courage than when defending this last angle of Belgium. There is no higher degree of courage than that shown by the army of the Yser.

On the right of the Belgians, along this line of defence, was the famous British Expeditionary Force. I did not have the chance of seeing the splendid fighting they put up at Dixmude. But in Furnes I heard many details of the struggles going on in that district. And it must be said that the example of the Allies spurred the Belgians to the limits of bravery. The two almost unconsidered armies held back the might of Prussia.

It was imperative that I should return with my copy of the interview with the King of the Belgians to London. My paper, the *Daily Telegraph*, had been collecting funds for the relief of the needy in Belgium, and this fund was to be placed at the disposal of the king. The plan had greatly pleased His Majesty. He had sent his thanks for this work to the proprietors of the *Daily Telegraph* through me. It was with the greatest reluctance that I left Furnes.

Hardly had I crossed the French frontier, than I was again arrested as a spy. Twenty-nine of them, by actual count, surrounded me, presenting their bayonets at my chest.

How I was released after a short arrest, which was shared by my wife, is a matter of detail. A complete apology was offered by the French officials.

CHAPTER 13

# King Albert of Belgium

While I was in Furnes I determined at all costs to get an interview with the king who leads his own army. As a man and a soldier he had won the admiration of the world, and he was a personality of extraordinary interest. Through the intercession of a friend an audience was arranged for me. I was to be received after luncheon. During that luncheon I drank a silent toast to my luck.

Escorted by two officers of the crack Belgian cavalry regiment, I was ushered into the long oak hall of the *Hôtel de Ville*. It was a moment before my eyes were accustomed to the dim light that filtered through the leaded windows. Then I saw standing before me, his hand extended, the King of Belgium. As we shook hands I noticed that he wore the regulation blue general's uniform. I looked in vain for ribbon or glittering order. Standing before the great open fireplace of the hall, the light threw the grave lines of his face into deep relief.

My interview was concerned first of all with the Christmas Fund for the Belgian refugees which is being collected by the *Daily Telegraph* of London. King Albert speaks English perfectly but slowly.

"I have been deeply touched by this other proof of the generosity of the English people. Again they give substantial evidence of their great sympathy." The king paused. When he spoke again his voice was lower. "Poor Belgium, now merely the edge of a nation, appreciates most sincerely all that her generous ally is doing."

The practical side of the sovereign showed itself as he continued:

"I know already how hospitably my people have been received in England. In this respect I hope the Belgian men who are there will be given work. This is the first requisite, for I do not wish that any ablebodied citizen of my country should become a charge upon a friendly people. Let them not be pauperized. It has been the misfortune of these men that they were compelled to leave their country that they might lead those dependent upon them into safety. In England I know the unfortunate women and children of my country are safe."

"Has Your Majesty any suggestion as to how the Belgian refugees can best be helped?"

"The need of the present is food and clothing for those who have been driven from their homes. In the future it will be necessary to rebuild those homes. Then we shall want every aid to repair the havoc wrought by the enemy."

At these words, spoken so feelingly by the king of these stricken people, there flashed into my mind the many scenes of desolation and ruin I had witnessed. The burnt homes, the devastation of the battlefields, the fleeing multitudes clutching their bundles, all seemed to pass in review in the dim light of this improvised audience chamber. Even now the distant guns of Dixmude made a low accompaniment to our talk.

"Has not your Majesty a message for the American people?"

For a minute the king was thoughtful.

"I hope that the American people will remember that Belgium has been scrupulously exact in carrying out its obligations as a neutral country. It has never been our policy to interfere in international politics. Like the United States, we have been concerned only with our own problems. Belgium is fighting to defend her neutrality, and she will fight as long as that neutrality is invaded.'"

This was the answer to the calumnies I had read in certain papers which tried to justify the invasion of Belgium. I remember the charge that Belgium was undertaking war-like preparations. This charge I knew to be false. I had lived in the country for two months before the fighting began. I knew that the army was not on a war footing. More than that, I had seen that it was concentrated in the centre of the country far from any frontier. This was not the position of an army expecting invasion. I remembered that Belgium was accused of making secret treaties with certain neighbouring nations. The frank, blue eyes of the man before me was enough assurance that this accusation was baseless. He continued speaking.

"No nation has more hospitably entertained foreigners than Belgium. Year after year we have received them, always treating them as the best of friends. Our greatest boast in Belgium is our liberty, and this liberty extends to all who live within our borders. The Germans who have lived with us in Antwerp, Brussels, Ostend, have enjoyed this liberty to the fullest." Once His Majesty hesitated, as if weighing his words. "Even after the war began, the German citizens found within our borders were treated with kindness and care. The American Minister, Mr. Brand Whitlock, and the Secretary of the Legation, Mr. Gibson, can testify how, when the four thousand German men, women and children were waiting at the Gare du Nord on their way to Germany, it was my Belgian soldiers who went and bought milk for the children and bread for the men and women.

"I hope that the American nation as a neutral will not forget how the neutrality of Belgium has been violated. When the war is ended, this fact should bear heavily on the terms of peace."

When our talk was about ended, a questioning look came into the king's eyes. With an aspect of sadness deepening on his features, he asked: "Is it true that Belgium has been annexed?" I was glad to be able to respond "No!" For the first time King Albert smiled.

★★★★★★

As before the blast of pestilence, the peaceful people of Belgium fled from the invader. The women, the children, the old and the afflicted saw the serried grey ranks approaching, and their hearts chilled with terror. Some instinct told of the afflictions that were to come. But these afflictions have proved greater than any could have pictured.

Imagine the emotions of the villagers of Visé when they heard the wail of the first shell. Think of their terror when this ball of fire and iron crashed through the roof of a house and the first home was given over to the flames. When that happened, in a flash all understood the scourge of war.

In July no country in Europe gave a more composite picture of peace than Belgium. I have watched the men and women toiling in the fields, and have marvelled at their industry. From before sunrise until dark they laboured. I have even seen them at work by moonlight. These were the people of the few contented acres. And they had tilled every available inch of soil, until the whole country seemed a vast market garden. The industry the Belgians showed in farming was duplicated in the mills and the lace factories. No nation was more devoted to the arts of peace.

Having seen this side of the picture, the contrast that came with war was all the more appalling. I remember standing on the Fragnoe Bridge in Liége, the morning after the first German night assault. Women with fear written in their eyes hurried past me. Each carried a bulging sheet slung over the shoulder. That sheet contained all that war had left them. With the women came children, pale girls who trembled as they walked, and small boys who sobbed unheeded as they stumbled onward. These had been caught between the fighting armies. Their homes lay in the path of the invaders. For this they suffered. A house that stood in the line of fire was ruthlessly razed. It did not matter how innocent the owner may have been of any active part in war; it was a crime that his property should impede the killing that was going forward.

The human stream I watched crossing the bridge had lain all night under the shower of shell and shot of both armies. Many of those in the crowd had seen a vagrant bullet kill or maim someone dear to them. One woman had her grey-haired mother struck down at her side. All had heard the terrifying screech of missiles overhead. The night they had passed left them filled with the fear that is born of some mighty cataclysm.

After the stream of frightened non-combatants—yes, among them—came a herd of lowing cattle. These were driven forward into the ranks of the refugees. They knocked against carts that some of the more fortunate were trundling. The carts held the wreck of the household gods. A mattress, a clock, kitchen pots and pans, a birdcage, an old dilapidated trunk, a basket of vegetables, some trussed hens, and always an image of the Madonna and Child Christ.

As far as I could see along the winding road stretched this river of refugees—women, children, men, cattle, carts—all flying from the danger that threatened. So might a crowd have fled before the rumble of an earthquake, or the boiling lava of a volcano. Fire and shell were sweeping athwart the country that only a week before smiled in fruitful harvest.

All this was but the beginning of the horrors that accompany war. More dreadful trials were to follow. Those villages that stood between the lines were the scenes of constant skirmishing. A patrol of Uhlans would ride down some village street. Their lances, painted slate-grey, they carried ready for attack. Every blind of the houses they passed was drawn, every door barred. The villagers huddled in the cellars. If the faint echo of clattering hoof-beats came to their ears, they trembled. Sometimes a patrol of Belgians would gallop down on the Uhlans. There would be a fight in the village street. Carbine bullets would tear through the plaster of the walls of the houses. The shouts of the battling men, the scream of wounded horses, the clash of sabre on lance, broke the deathlike quiet of the street.

Soon the clangour of the conflict would pass. Silence reigned again in the streets. Here and there a fearful face appeared, ready to withdraw at any further sound of danger. A few of the terrified inhabitants would steal into the streets. Tremblingly they would approach the scene of the conflict. Their own dead they would carry off for reverent burial. But they dared not touch any grey-coated corpse that lay in the village street.

After the Uhlans had passed the infantry of the Germans would come. Whenever they found the body of one of their own men in or near a village, they claimed that he had been done to death by *franc-tireurs*. For this crime they demanded the lives of ten of the men of the village. Try and picture the agony of those who took part in this gamble with death. With brutal rapidity the victims were singled out. Torn from their families, they would be marched to the wall of the village graveyard. The crying women and children of the town would hear the echo of the volley. After that they might drop their tears on the bodies of their loved ones.

Is it to be wondered that thousands fled panic- stricken to Liége? But they were not safer there. On came the ever-pursuing Germans, hurling iron-cased death before them. To the terror of each was now added the terror of the many. All who could clambered aboard the last trains to leave the city. The rest swept like an ever-increasing tide westward towards Brussels. In this flight mothers lost their children and wives their husbands. As they toiled onward they sought frantically for the missing ones. But dread was stronger than their love, and the fear of what followed kept them from turning back.

Whenever they might stop and rest, they told and retold the stories of their harrowing experiences. In this way the alarm that filled each breast grew tenfold. It was, indeed, a pitiful crowd that surged into the nation's capital. But again the invaders were on their heels. They could not rest here. As they once more took up their weary pilgrimage, the red flames of burning villages lit the night behind them. Within a week the world shuddered as it read of the wanton destruction of beautiful Louvain. Nothing is so typical of the brutal savagery of the German method of warfare as the destruction of this ancient city.

At last the flying throng were halted by the sea. They crowded into Ostend, a weary band of homeless wanderers. The already crowded town had no place for them. The bathing machines were drawn back from the beach and lined along the streets, and in these cabins the homeless found shelter. It is beyond the power of pen to picture the tragedy that now filled the spot once known only for gaiety and lightness. The gambling casino was changed into a hospital: surely the wheel of Fate had turned.

Those who still remain in Belgium are in a pitiful plight. Through no fault of theirs their livelihood has been suddenly wiped out; and it must be remembered that these are people of industry and thrift. Through their own efforts they had built up one of the most prosperous nations of Europe. Now they are a broken nation, crushed under the heel of the invader. The kingdom that has been brought to this pitiful estate through fighting for the cause of humanity has a right to our help. You who are sheltered from the grim actualities of war, remember the people of Belgium.

CHAPTER 14

# Conclusions and Impressions

The initial German campaign, so splendidly planned, failed because of two circumstances: the delay at Liége, and the moving of certain corps from the western to the eastern war zone during the last week of August. The unexpected strength of the Belgian army was of the highest military importance. In the first place it gave France time to complete her mobilisation and to hurry an army forward for the defence of Paris; in the second place it gave the English army time to mobilize and land on the Continent. In accomplishing these results the Belgians rendered signal strategic service. Also the defence of Liége inflicted heavy losses on von Kluck's right wing. This must have had an effect which showed itself at the time this body was so close to Paris.

Again, the check at Liége had a wonderful moral effect. In Belgium this effect was astounding. Untried troops considered themselves the superiors of the most vaunted soldiers of the Continent. It was the fact that the Belgians fought so splendidly at Liége which gave them the spirit for making so many sacrifices in subsequent encounters. I think also the moral effect of the holding back of the Germans by this army of King Albert led the soldier of England and France to say to himself, "If the Belgians can take it out of the enemy in this manner, why, we can do the same."

At the time of the attacks on the Liége forts, I wondered why one retaining force was not left at this point and the main army of Germany pushed on along their path of invasion. This would have been easily practicable and was obviously the better plan, when we know how important was the factor of time. I have since heard that it was by command of the emperor himself that the German forces remained at Liége until every fort had fallen. His theory was that the war should begin with a striking victory. It is said that he persisted in his theory despite the strong suggestions of the Great General Staff.

The second circumstance, the sudden reduction of the fighting strength of the armies advancing on Paris, certainly saved that city to the French. In the ordinary course of events, taking the military situation as it had developed, there is no reason to believe that von Kluck and von Bülow's armies could not have overrun Paris almost as easily as they had the north-east section of France.

I do not say that this would have meant the end of the war, for I know that the French people were ready to make supreme sacrifices, and that the French Army had learned from the bitter lessons of 1870 that they must not be caught within city walls. Grant that Paris would have been taken, General Joffre's army as it had been deployed would still have kept the field. To have ended the war in France, it was necessary for the Germans to meet and decisively defeat this army. But the enthusiasm which would have been aroused in Germany if Paris had been taken, and the depression that would have ensued throughout France, are factors that might have had a strong bearing upon the subsequent course of the war. These speculations, however, are of little value.

Information on this whole subject is so scanty that it is very difficult to discuss the strategic side of the early campaign intelligently. Of the several other circumstances of the war, the one which created the strongest impression at the time was the fact that the German troops advanced in line of battle in close order; in other words, shoulder to shoulder. As this was contrary to all accepted ideas on tactics, I questioned one of the officers on the German Staff for an explanation.

> We consider that close order develops intensity of fire at a given point. If, for instance, we wish to break through an enemy's line, and our troops are massed and he is in open order, we smother opposition under superiority of fire. It is a simple mathematical problem, and victory should rest with the greater number of guns concentrated in a specified area. Then we also think that the moral of troops fighting shoulder to shoulder is vastly heightened. Courage is contagious. Also at the critical stages of a conflict it is much easier for an officer to direct troops massed than those deployed with considerable intervals. In a charge this is most advantageous. I know that you will contend that the casualties are higher in our formation; but granting that

the ratio is higher, it is not in such percentage as to offset the advantages which I have mentioned. Besides, with the modern bullet so many of the wounds are of such slight consequence as often not immediately to incapacitate men for duty. Those who are knocked out generally get back in the fighting line within five weeks, if they ever get back at all.

The official lists of wounded published in Germany show that 8 *per cent*, of soldiers hit are unable ever to fight again; 36 *per cent*, after a short stay in the hospital return to service with their regiments; 56 *per cent.*, although not immediately available for duty, are used as instructors at recruiting depots. Eventually these men also return to the front. This calculation does not account for men killed in action.

From a military point of view the question is extremely interesting. In the first place, as Germany is the most advanced nation in the field of theoretic tactics, it can be taken for granted that this formation has not been adopted without study. The case for close order, as outlined by the German officer, has its merits. But I think, from what I have seen and from what I have learned from men long in the firing line, the Germans have overlooked one important factor— the machine gun. Wherever this weapon could be effectively brought into play, the havoc it wrought in closed ranks far exceeded German calculations. At the Battle of Mons one machine gun handled by a sergeant, who kept his piece in action even when wounded, held back a German column and contributed signally to the successful retreat of the division it covered. At Dinant machine guns were also used with great effect; and the wave of German invasion in north Belgium was surely smashed through the agency of the machine guns handled by the Belgians on the Yser. Mounted on armoured motor-cars, these weapons are the ideal support for reconnoitring troops.

When I was in Berlin the German General Staff laid before me their side of the evidence of the case of dum-dum bullets. They showed me original packages, unopened, which proved to contain the regulation French bullet with the nose bored out. This was certainly a very effective method of dum-dumming. At the time I told the officers of the general staff that as I myself had not seen these packages of cartridges in the possession of the French soldiers, I could not testify that the bullets had been used by those troops. I will give here, however, the *ex parte* evidence, as it was presented to me, upon which Emperor William based his letter of remonstrance to President Wilson.

The so-called dum-dum bullets were supposed to have been found on the persons of prisoners captured at Longwy.

They were of four types. The first, to which I have already referred, was an ordinary infantry rifle bullet which carried a projectile made of soft lead with a covering of white metal. The point of the projectile had been drilled through the white metal covering to the soft lead. Thus the nose, instead of being convex, was concave. Treating a bullet like this of course destroys its range and its accuracy beyond two or three hundred yards. Up to that distance, however, it has high "stopping" power. According to the German reports, the French troops had ten of this type of bullet in every hundred rounds of ammunition. It was supposed that they were to be used against charging troops.

The three other dum-dum bullets were simple mutilations of the regulation French copper-jacketed projectile. Two of these had the fine pointed nose of the bullet drawn out as one might pull out putty. The other had a nick just below the point. The Germans claim to have captured tens of thousands of this type of bullet. I, however, never saw more than the two samples which were brought for exposition in Berlin. As additional evidence that the practice of using dum-dum bullets was common with the French Army, the German staff claim to have captured the drill used in mutilating the projectile. I asked that I might be allowed to see this drill, but it was not shown me. My request that I might be allowed to visit that part of the fighting line where the dum-dum bullets had been found on French prisoners, the wounded and the dead, was refused.

The German complaint against the British revolver bullet cannot stand. I have been informed that all British officers and non-commissioned officers captured with this revolver ammunition on their persons were summarily shot. If this is so, the Germans have committed a gross breach of military law. The British bullet is nothing more than the ordinary pistol cartridge that has been in use for years. In size, material and shape it closely resembles the American service revolver ammunition. The projectile is lead. It is very nearly the weight of the Colt "44" bullet. Wicked-looking though it is, it conforms in every way to the requirements concerning ammunition as laid down by the Hague Conference. To take exception to this bullet and classify it as "dum-dum" is mere quibbling.

The range of the revolver is limited, and in the British Army its use is limited to the officers and non-commissioned officers of mounted troops. That the service rifle ammunition used by the British is anything but regular cannot be questioned.

There was a claim made by the French that the character of the wounds received by their troops at Dinant proved that the Germans were using an expanding bullet. I do not believe that this is correct. Many of the wounded I saw here had the typical lead pencil hole which the modern bullet makes, and if there were any tearing wounds, I think they were due to ricocheting shots. As the French were fighting from a limestone ridge, many of the German bullets were deflected.

On this point—the use of dum-dum bullets—I feel sure there has been much misunderstanding. From my own experience I have found that under certain circumstances it is almost impossible to prevent individual soldiers from mutilating their cartridges. This may have happened on both sides in the present war. If it is so, one can only charge it against the perversity of human nature.

The question of censorship in time of war and the treatment of correspondents is one I approach with considerable hesitation. Unquestionably the moves of armies in the field should be inviolable secrets. Censorship which suppresses news that may be of value to the enemy is necessary. It should be of the most rigid character. But the suppression of all news from the front is a hardship both on the men in the fighting line, and on those who are dear to them at home. There are so many details of life at the front of no military importance, yet of enormous interest to the friends and families of the soldiers, that ruthlessly to cut off news of this character is simple officiousness. My complaint of the censorship is that it is unintelligently conducted. I will illustrate what I mean by "unintelligent." The news of the transportation of the Expeditionary Force to Belgium was a splendidly kept secret.

There were, of course, rumours, and certain details were perhaps known before the English force arrived on French soil. Once in the war zone, however, the English censor seemed to think it was no longer necessary to suppress the fact that this force had landed in Boulogne. Columns appeared in all the English papers boasting of the success of this movement, and giving innumerable details which would be of great value to the intelligence officers of an enemy. I have the word of two officers of the German General Staff, one of whom had spent much time in England, that they were not certain in Germany that a British force was opposed to them until they read this news in English newspapers. Knowing the main facts, it was not difficult for them to piece all the information together and locate exactly the position and composition of General French's army.

The fact that correspondents were forbidden to witness any of the engagements of the British Army has worked great injustice to the troops of the Expeditionary Force. General French's reports are all splendid, but a commanding general has not the time to spend on elaborating his reports so that they may include the exploits of different regiments; neither has he the inclination for this work, as it savours somewhat of boasting. The acts of heroism shown by the different regiments at Mons and Le Cateau which have gone unrecorded are a loss to English history never to be remedied. No country is more proud of the splendid sacrifices made by her sons than England. And no country has greater right to such pride.

Yet who are to be the examples for the coming generation, if there is no one to tell of the gallantry of the officers and men who held back the Prussian tide at Mons? Another unfair effect of this censorship has been recently shown in the tremendous advertisement given to the London Scottish Regiment. I do not begrudge these Territorials one line of praise that has been bestowed upon them, but why should no word of the splendid work done by the Second Dragoon Guards or the Lincolnshire Regiment, or any other of the units that have been fighting since the war began, ever be published?

As a specific instance of how inconsistently the censorship works, I give another personal experience. I arrived from France in London on Saturday, October 3. I had at that time a dispatch of about five hundred words, which dealt in general terms with the movement on the French left flank. I handed in to the office of the *Daily Telegraph* the original of this dispatch on Saturday night, at the same time giving a carbon copy to the correspondent of the *New York American*, in order to make it available for the Sunday edition of that paper. The dispatch as originally written, with some very minor excisions, went through that night to New York, and was published broadcast Sunday, the 4th. The *Daily Telegraph* does not publish on Sunday.

When I opened my Monday morning paper and saw no line of my dispatch, I surmised that the censor had been busy. Arriving at the office about eleven o'clock, Mr. Le Sage showed me my original message entirely blue pencilled, and returned with the note: "Nothing of this can be published." Seeing that the news was already published in sixteen of Mr. Hearst's newspapers in America the previous day, why should the censor have forbidden its publication in London?

I will summarize the French attitude towards the correspondents in a sentence. They look on all journalists as pariahs.

Again and again I have been questioned about the atrocities in Belgium. Although I made assiduous search, I must say that I nowhere met evidence, which I considered sufficient, of any of the cruelties said to have been committed by the German troops. I did not have the opportunities afforded the Belgian committee of investigation, and I cannot add testimony of individual cases of savagery to the long indictment they present. What I can testify to is that entire towns near the German frontier have been wiped out of existence. On the main road from Aix-la-Chapelle to Liége in every village the houses are gutted. I never would have believed such devastation possible, had I not seen it myself.

Of the little town of Battice, with a population of about ten thousand, not more than six houses remain untouched. In street after street, nothing remained save the *débris* of what had once been the homes of thrifty, peaceful people. Hervé has passed out of existence. The same conditions are found in every one of the small towns which bordered the roads which the German Army used. They have left behind a trail more terrible than the plague.

I attach as an appendix the description of the massacre of Dinant, which is typical of the German treatment of the population in the frontier towns.

Another feature of this great war which must be regularized is bomb-dropping. The plan pursued by German aviators of dropping bombs indiscriminately on non-combatant populations is to my mind the acme of cowardice. The aviator need take no more risks in war than he does in peace. In fact, I think that the men of this corps are in the safest positions in modern warfare. When they operate over large cities, dropping death-dealing missiles on women and children, their work is so dastardly as to merit the severest condemnation. I was in Paris during one of these air raids.

Three or four bombs were dropped in different parts of the city. One of these killed an old man and blew off the leg of a small girl. I think the aviator who accomplished this may well be proud of his morning's work, but how he can pretend to call himself a soldier I do not know. Assassin is his title. To drop death on the innocent from an impregnable position is surely no soldier's work. That the German emperor sanctions this character of warfare, I know from Lieutenant Wierner. Bomb-dropping should be considered a greater crime than piracy.

The poxmarks on the walls show where a German air assassin dropped a bomb successfully, killing an old man and wounding a little child.

The actual damage done by the projectiles dropped from aeroplanes is inconsiderable. Unless one is unfortunate enough to be directly under the falling missile, one is safe. In Ostend a Taube dropped three shells within a hundred yards of where I was standing. No one was harmed. The bombs fell in the fish market, which fortunately was empty at the time.

There is a question that I have been asked a great many times: "How long do you think the war will last?" Before stating what I think on this subject, it must be distinctly understood that I cannot pretend to be a prophet. What I put down here may be modified by what happens tomorrow. All that I say is simply what I think at the moment. When there are so many factors to be considered, opinions change constantly.

In the first place, I want to warn all those who are in sympathy with the Allies not to underrate the strength of Germany, who possesses today the most marvellous military organisation the world has ever seen. This organisation is the result of years of study and preparation. The best brains of Germany have been devoted to this work. An organisation built on such a foundation does not topple easily. Next it must be remembered that Germany is heart and soul and undivided for victory in the war. I have nowhere seen the enthusiasm and outward expression of patriotism as it exists in Germany duplicated in any other of the fighting countries. Russia alone approaches the same spirit. With a nation so determined on victory, and one that has carried the war into the territory of its foes across all its boundaries, it is difficult to fix a date of defeat.

My original idea was that the war would last only six months. I considered that financial conditions would make it impossible to carry on such a tremendous conflict for a longer period. But the success of the recent war loans has caused me to modify my first guess.

Again it seemed to me that the violent efforts made by Germany to occupy the territory of the Allies was an indication that the emperor was placing himself in the most favourable position from which to negotiate peace terms. This is mere surmise. It cannot be said that Germany is the loser in the actual field of operations. Our maps tell us a different tale. Where Germany has suffered is in her commerce. The Berlin business man is in the gloomiest possible frame of mind. Even should his country emerge victorious, he cannot see how he is going to stave off ruin much longer. Despite this, he is heartily in favour of the war. Deluded they may be, but the German people believe that this war was forced upon them.

Under the circumstances they are willing to go to any lengths to achieve victory. That the country is suffering from lack of food, men or money, I do not believe. That they have some splendid strategists has already been proved. There is no want of ammunition. How, then, are they to be defeated?

The first thing necessary for the Allies is to achieve numerical superiority. Under the conditions developed by modern warfare, no decisive victory can be expected where the forces engaged are equal or nearly equal. When the French, British and Belgian armies are sufficiently strong to take up the offensive with success, then we may say the beginning of the end of the war is in sight. I do not take into consideration the Russian frontier, and the forces engaged there, as I have not sufficient data on which to base judgments of conditions on that side.

But even with a greater force, the defeat of the Germans will not be a matter of weeks. Granting that they are driven back to the line of the Rhine, they only lose what they have already taken. Carrying the war into Germany would be a task calculated to daunt any general. The thought of the sacrifices demanded will make the attacking nations pause. As far as I can see, there is only one factor that will defeat Germany, and that is exhaustion.

# Appendix

A report drawn up by a member of the Commission of Inquiry on the Violation of the Rights of Nations and the Laws and Customs of War, has been communicated by the Belgian Legation in London.

### Sack of Dinant

The town of Dinant was sacked and destroyed by the German army, and its population was decimated, on August 22, 23, 24 and 25. On Friday, the 21st, about nine o'clock in the evening, German troops coming down the road from Ciney, entered the town by the Rue St. Jacques. On entering, they began firing into the windows of the houses, and killed a workman, wounded another inhabitant, and forced him to cry, "Long live the *Kaiser*." They bayoneted a third person in the stomach. They entered the cafes, seized the liquor, got drunk, and retired after having set fire to several houses and broken the doors and windows of others. The population was terrorized and stupefied, and shut itself up in its dwellings.

Saturday, August 22, was a day of relative calm. On Sunday morning next, the 23rd, at 6.30 in the morning, soldiers of the 108th Regiment of Infantry invaded the Church of the Premonastrensian Fathers, drove out the congregation, separated the women from the men, and shot fifty of the latter. Between seven and nine the same morning the soldiers gave themselves up to pillage and arson, going from house to house and driving the inhabitants into the street. Those who tried to escape were shot. About nine in the morning the soldiery, driving before them by blows from the butt ends of their rifles men, women and children, pushed them all into the Parade Square, where they were kept prisoners till six o'clock in the evening.

The guard took pleasure in repeating to them that they would soon be shot. About six o'clock a captain separated the men from the women and children. The women were placed in front of a rank of infantry soldiers, the men were ranged along a wall. The front rank of them were then told to kneel, the others remaining standing behind them. A platoon of soldiers drew up in face of these unhappy men. It was in vain that the women cried out for mercy for their husbands, sons and brothers. The officer ordered his men to fire. There had been no inquiry nor any pretence of a trial. About twenty of the inhabitants were only wounded, but fell among the dead.

The soldiers, to make sure, fired a new volley into the heap of them. Several citizens escaped this double discharge. They shammed dead for more than two hours, remaining motionless among the corpses, and when night fell succeeded in saving themselves in the hills. Eighty-four corpses were left on the square and buried in a neighbouring garden.

The day of August 23 was made bloody by several more massacres. Soldiers discovered some inhabitants of the Faubourg St. Pierre in the cellars of a brewery there, and shot them.

Since the previous evening a crowd of workmen belonging to the factory of M. Himmer had hidden themselves, along with their wives and children, in the cellars of the building. They had been joined there by many neighbours and several members of the family of their employer. About six o'clock in the evening these unhappy people made up their minds to come out of their refuge, and defiled, all trembling, from the cellars with the white flag in front. They were immediately seized and violently attacked by the soldiers. Every man was shot on the spot. Almost all the men of the Faubourg de Neffe were executed *en masse*. In another part of the town twelve civilians were killed in a cellar. In the Rue de l'Ile a paralytic was shot in his armchair. In the Rue Enfer the soldiers killed a young boy of fourteen.

In the Faubourg de Neffe the viaduct of the railway was the scene of a bloody massacre. An old woman and all her children were killed in their cellar. A man of sixty-five years, his wife, his son and his daughter were shot against a wall. Other inhabitants of Neffe were taken in a barge as far as the rock of Bavard and shot there, among them a woman of eighty-three and her husband.

A certain number of men and women had been locked up in the court of the prison. At six in the evening a German machine gun, placed on the hill above, opened fire on them, and an old woman and three other persons were brought down.

While a certain number of soldiers were perpetrating this massacre, others pillaged and sacked the houses of the town, and broke open all safes, sometimes blasting them with dynamite. Their work of destruction and theft accomplished, the soldiers set fire to the houses, and the town was soon no more than an immense furnace.

The women and children had all been shut up in a convent, where they were kept prisoners for four days. These unhappy women remained in ignorance of the lot of their male relations. They were expecting themselves to be shot also. All around the town continued to blaze. The first day the monks of the convent had given them a certain supply of food. For the remaining days they had nothing to eat but raw carrots and green fruit.

To sum up, the town of Dinant is destroyed. It counted 1,400 houses. Only 200 remain. The manufactories where the artisan population worked have been systematically destroyed. Rather more than 700 of the inhabitants have been killed; others have been taken off to Germany, and are still, (as at time of first publication), retained there as prisoners. The majority are refugees scattered all through Belgium. A few who remained in the town are dying of hunger. It has been proved by our inquiry that German soldiers, while exposed to the fire of the French entrenched on the opposite bank of the Meuse, in certain cases sheltered themselves behind a line of civilians, women and children.

France Bears the Burden

THE TRENCH SENTINEL EVER-WATCHFUL GUARDIANS UPON WHOM THE SAFETY OF FRANCE DEPENDS.

# Contents

| | |
|---|---|
| Foreword | 169 |
| The Glory of France | 173 |
| Monsieur Poilu of Paris | 182 |
| Verdun; The Battle Epic | 192 |
| In the Argonne | 203 |
| In the Stream of the Somme Fighting | 213 |
| The Business of War | 222 |
| The Flying Fighters | 233 |
| Thoughts on Shrapnel and Tanks | 243 |
| Who Pays for the War? | 252 |
| The Burden France Has Borne | 265 |

TO
MY MOTHER
WHO LOVED FRANCE

# Foreword

Letter From His Excellency, The High Commissioner of France, M. André Tardieu

My dear Major Fortescue:

That which, in my opinion, gives special value to your book on France in war time, is that you have not been content only to gather therein the excellent articles sent by you from Paris and the front to the *Washington Post*, but you also, from your observations and experiences, develop a picture of the whole subject. Yours is the work of the historian.

To your vivid and accurate articles, to your accounts of the fighting on the Somme, at Verdun, in the Argonne, you have added a methodical delineation, exact and instructive, of the organisation and practice of war as developed in France during three years.

Systems of transport, artillery with its new method of firing, *liaison*, aviation, new tactics, new arms, as well as the co-operation of the different branches in defence and attack, are actually described by you in their functioning as "the business of war"—the gigantic war enterprise of today—and you recognize in this new war machine and these new tactics, a new work of the spirit of the French people. Another proof, the most eloquent perhaps, of the creative genius and adaptability of our democracy and our race.

With sympathetic understanding and friendliness, on the other hand, you have known how to show the inner side of this organisation for war, to express those moral and spiritual forces which explain the efficacy of this technical work.

If, to use your own words, the French Army has "saved the world from the domination of Germany and despotism," it is, to again quote you, because our army "has been the soul of the nation;" because it has been without peer, the army of democracy and liberty, the army of citizen-soldiers. For this reason, if I may avail myself once more of your strong words "the French who hate war, are the finest soldiers in the world."

Do not say, however, that "the soul of France today was born at the Battle of the Marne." The Battle of the Marne was for nation, only the occasion of a new awakening under trial. If the Battle of the Marne has been won, if the invasion of the German hordes has been stopped, it is because that soul pre-existed, because it was present, entire, in the breast of every French soldier, and, because in defending our soil and our existence, every soldier knew that he defended at the same time, the cause of democracy and liberty throughout the world. Here again, is the reason why, through three years of struggle, behind the armies and the front, the steadfastness and spirit of sacrifice of the whole nation has never wavered.

You have happily explained how this identity of our national spirit and democracy is reflected in the special discipline of the French army, an army of a free people under a discipline of intelligence, a discipline, fair, humane, and fraternal.

This you have seen in France. All those Americans who have seen what you have seen with us, are thus convinced of the absolute agreement of minds and aims which the participation by the American democracy in the war reveals and will reveal between your nation and our nation, between your army and our army.

From the close co-operation of the French and American armies on our soil, we can further expect, out of the war, other results of great importance. Between America and France only one thing is lacking: to know each other better. In the past, distance has hindered the establishment between us, people to people, of the personal contact; I mean to say a contact between the mass of Americans and French.

The Americans who visited France before the war were but few, and these only tourists, people of leisure, financiers, representatives of great commercial houses, students or professors. Now, for the first time, with the presence of the American Army in France, we see and will see among us those who heretofore have never crossed the Atlantic; farmers, workmen, clerks, representatives by the thousands of the great mass of the American democracy.

In the battle lines, in our villages or cities, as companions of our soldiers and guests of our civil population, they will live a long time in daily intimate contact with our peasants, workmen, *employés*, and small merchants, with all that constitutes the body and substance of the French democracy. On one side and the other, they will get to know each other at first hand. From this will result an understanding, an esteem, a confidence that will be mutual. It will be difficult to exaggerate the good of this. Nothing is more necessary than to develop and strengthen, actually and firmly, between the American and French people, this good feeling, this mutual understanding, this close union, this material and spiritual co-operation which is dear to us, and which is of such great value, first for the common good of our two nations, and second for the progress of democracy and the future peace of the world.

Please accept, my dear Major Fortescue, the expression of my high esteem, and believe me cordially yours

André Tardieu.

Washington, September 22nd, 1917.

NOTE

Some of the material used in this book appeared originally in the columns of the *Washington Post*. The author begs to thank the editor for the permission again to use this material.

Granville Fortescue.

Camp Lee, Va.
September 27th, 1917.

Chapter 1

# The Glory of France

France fights for her firesides. In that sentence we touch the chord that stirs the soul of the Nation. The legions that line the trenches from the Somme to the Vosges hold back with their rifles, their machine guns, and their cannon, the enemy who would overrun French fields and put the flame to French homes. All the rhetoric of the politicians, who juggle the blame of the war, cannot hide this fact. Who started the war is a question almost lost in the lurid haze of the past. But, with her sons bleeding and dying on her very soil, France today is roused to a condition of heroism that matches the glory of Sparta.

It has been my fortune to see France in three periods of her trial. In the first weeks of the war I was swept back from the Belgian boundary to Paris with French armies that struggled hopelessly against the savage onrush of the enemy. France of that period was a dazed, panic-pursued nation. The bogy tales of 1870 haunted all, from the President and his advisers down to the clerks, the artisans, the shopkeepers, and all saw, for a brief paralysing moment, a vision of their beloved country once more beaten down by the brutal Uhlans. Paris in those days held something of the terror of the graveyard.

But, with the turn of the war tide on the Marne, the spirit of France was born anew. The ghost of Fear faded. Out of the ordeal by blood and fire the nation came to its strength. I saw this agony of the rebirth of the soul of the people. It reached its climax with the bombardment of the Cathedral of Rheims. That outrage crystallised the sentiment of the whole nation, and stiffened it for the sufferings and sorrows of war.

Now I see France enduring these sorrows. It is the dolour magnificent. It finds its reflection in the resignation pictured in the faces of the black-garbed women. It sparks in the scornful eyes of the blue-uniformed men. It even seems to speak in the calm of the children. Yet it shows its strongest in the manner these people go about their daily work—yes, and play—for they have not forgotten how to play in France. Outwardly you see a normal nation engaged in the business of life.

Yet the scars of battle appear on every side. Hardly a woman passes whose black bonnet and dress does not tell of a husband, a son, a brother, dead in defending France. And the strange mixture of uniforms, pale blue, khaki, with a few of the ancient red breeches and blue coats, still worn. Here is the backwash of the misery of the trenches; for many a trouser-leg is pinned up and many a sleeve hangs limp.

I met a bit of this wreckage when my ship first touched at Bordeaux. To me, he typified the courage of France in this time of affliction. He was the guard, posted at the gangplank, to see that no passenger landed without a proper passport. He wore the new pale-blue uniform of the army of France, it was soiled and rubbed. I noticed the strap marks of the pack crossing the shoulders. Then I caught sight of this soldier's face. The first view was a shock. The forehead from above the right eye to the cheek bone was broken in. He had been hit by a bit of iron and the skull had cracked as an eggshell struck with a spoon. A star-shaped cicatrix closed the skin around a glass eye. The healed wound was a triumph of modern surgery. But the greater triumph was the cheerful spirit of the man who had suffered this wound. His rifle slung over his shoulder, he scrutinised carefully the papers of each disembarking passenger, meeting all with a smile. Here was the courage of France personified.

If I had to choose a symbol best to picture all the evil and energy of this war, it would be the Octopus. The battlefields form the body of the devil fish, while its tentacles stretch out interminably drawing up all that goes to feed the trench- turmoil; men, munitions, food. These great tentacles are sucking out the life of Europe. One of them reaches down to Bordeaux. Already it has drawn into the devouring maw all the men that city can give. Still it sucks up great quantities of wine and food, and carries them on to renew the waste of the struggling millions in the trenches. Yet the women work with stronger arms in the vineyards, because they know the fruit of their labour helps in the defence of France. The old men and boys gather a rapid harvest, happy in the thought that the flour ground from the wheat they thrash, is baked into the bread to feed the men fighting for their hearths.

All this labour throbs through Bordeaux. The city bustles with business. The riverside teems with unloading ships. All day winches rattle, donkey engines snort, in the work of dragging out great cases from the steamers' holds. The quays are crowded with mountains of bales and boxes. Here are the worked-up sinews of war. A thousand carts form a double line that runs like an endless chain from the quays to the freight station of the railroad.

Thence all this sustenance of war is whirled out to the depots of distribution, till at last it finds its way to the very outermost listening post. The enormous hogsheads of wine that I see loaded today on the freight cars, within a week mean drink for some lonely sentinel who dare not take his eyes from his narrow loop-hole while a comrade fills his tin cup. Those sharp-pointed wooden stakes stacked so closely in that box car, will be built into a forest of wire entanglements beyond a bit of dearly bought enemy trench before a dozen nights have passed. All those hundreds of cars of straw with the black tarpaulins stretched over them soon will be welcomed with joyful neighs by the thousands of artillery and cavalry horses picketed behind the battle lines.

When the train has carefully steamed out from the shadow of the neat houses of Bordeaux, the beauty of France unfolds in broad fields and deep forests that spread away in varying shades of green from the line of the railroad tracks. Yet as you watch the busy harvest scenes your eye catches a false colour in the landscape.

A new spur runs out from the railway, a cut of raw earth in the green, and above it sits a soldier, nursing his musket. He does not raise his eyes as the train passes, but keeps them fixed on the workers toiling along the spur. These men wear queer, little round, grey caps, banded with red, the remnants of green-grey uniforms and battered army boots. They turn their stolid Teuton faces up as the train passes, staring with puckered eyes. Here is another vision of the front. What thoughts are behind those staring eyes? What a story is each of these German prisoners living?

Throughout the journey from Bordeaux to Paris, Peace and War mix incongruously. The peasants labour in the vineyards, paying little heed to the young soldiers of the newest class who crowd into the railroad stations. Here trench-stained uniform rubs against sober dress of the civilian. All this mingling of the activities of war and peace gives the clue to the attitude of the French people in face of the invasion. The army is the soul of the nation, and every man, woman and child of France glories in it, honours it, loves it.

These feelings find expression when a group of *permissionners*, men on leave, debark from a returning train. At the station in Tours I saw the welcome of a veteran by his family. He came straight from the *abris*, as the trench shelters are called. Under his dishpan helmet his beard blossomed like that of a Spanish pirate. Two brown haversacks sagged from his shoulders. His sky-blue coat had faded to dusty grey.

As he stepped from the compartment he was engulfed by his family. His mother, fat and red-faced, pushed his helmet far back on his head and planted a resounding kiss fair on his lips. Both her hands were clapped tight around his back in a strangle-hold. Together they rocked, hugging and kissing and emitting all the terms of endearment included in the French dictionary, while father, thin with a grey beard, and three buxom sisters bumped in on the hugging couple and snatched a kiss here and there whenever the gyrations of the mother permitted.

Such a reception is typical. It gives you a queer lump in your throat to watch the joy of the mothers, fathers, sisters and younger brothers, over the return of the soldier; so many sombre thoughts flash into mind. Beside the joyous group stands an older woman—in black. She holds a little tray on which are spread knives, scissors, corkscrews and other bits of cutlery. Passing from window to window of the train she offers her wares for sale. It is a sweet, low voice that importunes you, a voice that must be wont to talk to children.

It was when the train swept past the banks of the Vienne that I saw the spirit of the French truly symbolised. Under the shade of the poplar trees, following the winding course of the narrow river as far as one could see, stretched a line of men, fishing. All were in uniform. One of the nearest fixed my attention. He was a *Chasseur Alpine*. He wore his Tam o' Shanter hat perched jauntily over one eye. A "bull dog" pipe dropped from the corner of his mouth. His uniform made a spot of blue in the grass. There he sat, puffing contentedly, watching his line, for the moment the last thought in his head was concerned with war. Back of that line of fishermen I seemed to catch a vision in the skies of other uniformed figures, along other rivers—the Meuse and the Somme.

As we draw nearer and nearer to Paris the sidings are more and more crowded with war material. But despite this, life seems in many aspects normal.

Even Paris, superficially, is the same ancient, gay capital. The streets show a lively contrast to my first war visit. *Cafés* and restaurants then closed at nine, and a taxi-cab was a rare and fleeting bird. Tonight you dine in comfort and light until ten-thirty, and the taxis are ranked at every customary corner. In fact Paris has all that old charm of movement radiating from the stream of life that flows without stop, up and down the *boulevards*.

It was in the Rue de la Paix, a street in name and aspect the antithesis of all that war connotes, that I made close study for signs of the struggle the French uphold so valiantly. When I saw this path of luxury in the first onset of war, it was the Street of the Pestilence. From the *Place de l'Opera* to the Place Vendome, iron shutters had snapped down on the jewels, fine linen and purple that were wont to lie in tantalizing array behind the plate glass of the great shops. A hot August sun beat down on the blind doors and windows. Here and there a furtive figure passed, waking Sunday echoes in the canon of quiet. Even the sparrows had flown. Now all is changed. The jewellers whose names stand for wealth, workmanship and art, throughout the world, push their baubles once more under your nose. The poseurs of fashion, whose names on a frock add a thousand *francs* to the bill, have returned like homing pigeons. The warning horn of the taxi sings an all-day chorus in your ears. Hurrying shoppers fill the street from curb to curb.

So for the moment you think the city once more the Paris of old. Has France of the Rue de la Paix forgotten the war before it is over? But in some jeweller's window your eye catches the glint of a golden *soixante quinze* minutely fashioned. Beside it are pendants and brooches, diamonds surrounding a red cross. Here is a miniature silver projectile made to hold a tiny bottle of smelling salts. There hangs a tiny gold aeroplane with silver wings. You have the story of the war in these trifles. The cannon, the shell, and the red cross. And if from these you cannot fill your mind with enough associations of the misery of the world slaughter, close to the curb there passes a soldier wheeling a chair, such a chair as travels the boardwalk at Atlantic City or the shaded paths of Palm Beach. But here no grinning darky pushes it; no picture of parasol and lace lounges in the seat. A sky-blue coated soldier trundles the chair; on it another soldier, a boy, sits tailor fashion, both trouser legs neatly sewn above the knee. Yet he smokes his cigarette with an air and takes lively interest in all that passes.

If it were not for the wounded, one could almost forget the war in Paris. Soldiers have always been part of the picturesque setting of the city. But when they come hobbling along balanced on crutches, or wearing an empty sleeve pinned across the breast, you feel the pity of it all.

Cheek by jowl with the shop of the master worker in gold, silver and jewels, where the skill of trained fingers and the sharpest eyes have created a marvellous watch or some delicate diamond and platinum hair ornament, you find a window filled with brushes. Hat brushes, clothes brushes, toothbrushes, nail brushes, sink brushes, scrubbing brushes, shoe brushes, all forming a homely contrast to the luxury beside them. Here is the output of the wounded blind. Their hands have been slowly and painfully trained to this work. There are other articles the blinded soldiers make, baskets, network table covers and lamp shades. In such trifles the French ingrained spirit of art finds expression.

In other shops where the work of crippled soldiers is on sale, one finds a bewildering conglomeration of toys, knick-knacks and what-nots, from a life-sized pasteboard poster of a *zouave* to a full-rigged ship. Rings and bracelets made from the metal of an exploded shrapnel fuse are the most popular gimcracks sold in these shops. Such a ring or bracelet will be the soldier's first present to his *marraine*.

The *marraine*, I must explain, is the soldier's fairy godmother. Some girl or woman, who, having no calls upon herself from any relative, adopts a soldier in the trenches as her special charge. There is no paragraph of the French army regulations which says that a soldier should not have a young and chic *marraine*. However, one chooses this fairy godmother sight unseen, so it is with fluttering heart perhaps, that the young *permissionnaire* (furloughed soldier) awaits his first interview with the one who has been writing him, to whom he has poured out his confidences, to whom he has appealed for sympathy. But be she fair of face or not, the French soldier hardly cares. In his *marraine* he sees the beauty of the spirit that tries in all ways to share the burdens of the trenches.

Do not think there is any lightness in the relation between the godmother and her godson of the trenches. Thousands of men fighting the battles of France have no family ties. Thousands of women have lost sons, brothers, husbands, in the battling, and they write the letters and send the little comfits and kickshaws to their adopted children in pious memory of those dead sons, husbands and brothers.

If her *fillieu* should be wounded, the *marraine* devotes her best efforts to lightening the cares of his convalescence. And if he should come out of the hospital crippled, or blinded or carrying the broken wreck of a once hale body, she it is who searches night and day to ease the broken soldier's path in life. Such an institution as our American pension list is inconceivable in France. Here is a burden the women shoulder. They know the short-lived glory of war. Yes, the wounded are heroes—for months—but they are young men. The surgeons have saved life, but with mutilated body the sons of France must struggle down the vale of life through the years when their heroism lies cold.

This problem of the wounded is one that will take the best brains of our economists of the future to solve. For the present it is a question of charity, but let the war continue, with each day adding new thousands to the ranks of the maimed and blinded, and a condition must arise which will demand prompt solution. These sacrifices to war must be made as self-supporting as their physical state will permit.

I have made it a rule in writing of war to touch lightly on the story of the hospital. Wounds, to those who see them for the first time, are horrifying, hideous revelations. The pity you feel as you stare at the ghastly rent of flesh is often smothered in revulsion. The cry that is sometimes wrung from the stoutest heart wrenches your soul in sympathy, but the festering gangrenous sore fills you with disgust. I leave this curious cross-purpose of feeling to be explained by the psychologists.

To study this side of war I visited the American Ambulance. As an American I felt the pride in my countrymen and countrywomen increase as I passed from ward to ward. As a nation we have not paid our debt to France, but as individuals thousands of good Americans help to repay in some measure our obligation to the people of the Marquis de Lafayette and Rochambeau.

It is one of the disheartening reflections on civilisation that the science of healing has not kept pace with the science of destruction. Still, let the ingenuity of man devise a mighty engine of war, and the ingenuity of some other man will endeavour to supply a means for modifying the effect of this engine. It is a struggle in many ways approximating the competition between the naval gun and armour plate. Except that the surgeons who repair the ruin wrought among humankind have nature always fighting on their side.

The high explosive shell is the most puissant destructive agent achieved by man. It blasts its way through wood, iron and earth, tearing and rending everything within the radius of its explosion. The French "75" shell breaks into four thousand fragments, the German "77" shell flies out into twenty seven hundred bits of iron. These fragments will vary in size from a long jagged splinter to bits no larger than birdseed. Let a shell blast strike down a man, and granting he is not killed, his wound would baffle the highest skill of the surgeon thirty years ago. The high explosive shell is a new development in the art of killing. To offset this instrument of death and maiming, surgery has invented the Roentgen Ray.

My visit to the American Ambulance—I use the word ambulance in its French meaning, hospital—took place when the fighting on the Somme reached its climax. Wounded soldiers arrived that morning after a night in a dressing station, straight from the battlefield. Already X-ray photographs had been made and printed showing the nature of each wound and the result of the *eclat* or burst.

These photographs are Cubist pictures. A fractured bone will stand revealed, its jagged edges splashes, the bits of iron buried in the wound. From the radiograph the surgeon gets a clear understanding of the problem before him. Then he pits his skill against the havoc of the shell. While it may be that wounds of the arm or the leg or the body have certain general characteristics, yet each special wound varies in its progress. The surgeon does not stop at the first photograph, but has X-ray pictures taken whenever he wants to check up the results of his operations. And the men as they recover become as interested in these pictures as debutantes in the snapshots of their doings that fill the illustrated society papers.

The surgeon's greatest enemy is infection. He knows that no matter how badly damaged the human body he works on may be, if he can keep the wound clean, he can save life and limb.

One soldier who had been brought in with both legs broken and a great gash across his abdomen, had these hurts almost miraculously cured. But a bit of the shell had clipped off the tip of his finger. Here infection set in. First the hand, and then the arm was poisoned, and from an insignificant beginning the surgeon found himself battling for the very life of his patient.

The X-ray makes possible the marvel of modern surgery—bone grafting. In this curious process the victim furnishes his own graft. The vision of substituting bits of the bony structure of dogs, sheep, monkeys for similar injured sections of man have not materialised. The experiments forced on the surgeons by the wounds of this war have shown that man best absorbs his own material.

Throw your mind back to the days when you studied the structure of your body, and you will remember that in the lower leg you have an extra bone running from the knee to the ankle. In the anatomical diagram it is called a *tibia*, but in plain English we call it a shin bone. It is to this shin bone that the surgeon goes for supplies when he wants to build out any of the lost bony substance that has been blasted by bullet or shell. With a wonderful little saw he cuts out a splinter of it the exact size he needs. This is clamped in place in the wounded limb, and nature does the rest. Sometimes nature, just to show that she is the most wonderful of all surgeons, will perform this operation herself. Dr. "Jim" Hutchinson showed me an X-ray photograph where nature had anticipated him in such an operation, and under his attractive smile I thought I detected just the faintest hint of jealousy when he said "Fine piece of work, wish I could say it was my own."

But Dr. "Jim" has one remarkable operation to his credit. It was a matter of bone grafting, but here the patient could not furnish his shin bone as a substitute, for both were already shattered. Almost at the moment the surgeon was patiently repairing the hurt as best he could, at the next operating table a soldier's life ran out. He had given his soul for his country, why should he not give a bit of the bone that was no more use to him to make whole a broken comrade?

In making the rounds of this house of misery, watching the silent deft-fingered nurses move from cot to cot; listening to the clean-cut surgeon tell in short, simple words of his fight for a limb, a life; gazing down on the simple trusting faces on the pillows, you are oppressed with the horrible futility of war. You conjure up the story of any one of the men on the cots. A peasant, he takes his place in the ranks and follows his training much as one of his own horses works. Then, he is swept out to the battlefield. He knows nothing of the strategy, the purpose of the powers that move him, a pawn in the game, over the face of France. He meets the trials, the privations, the cold, the heat, the hunger, the weariness of his duties with a smile. "It is war," he says philosophically, hardly knowing his philosophy is an inheritance from forebears who fought under Napoleon

"It is war" that he should dig trenches, stand guard all night, march miles in rain or dust. "It is war" that he must charge in the face of the merciless machine-guns, the devastating shells. "It is war" he will say with a smile when his flesh and bones are torn to fragments by the *eclat*. And though he may not know the strategy or the purpose of the chiefs, he knows that he is fighting to win back the homes of thousands of his brothers, he knows that he is fighting for the right to be a Frenchman, for his thatched house, his little field, his wife, his children. More, he fights for an ideal pictured in his heart by the words "*La France!*"

Chapter 2

# Monsieur Poilu of Paris

Starting from the Latin "*pilosus*," and following a long linguistic road, we arrive at *poilu*, defined in the French dictionary as "hairy, shaggy, bristling." *Poilu* is an adjective in its original use, but by custom becomes a descriptive noun applied to any member of the French army who has served his tour in the trenches.

I fail to recall at the moment whether it was Cicero or some other war correspondent who, when describing a triumph in honour of a certain line regiment of the legion, wrote of the Roman veterans as the *pilosii* who smote the Germanii. And to indicate the impossibility of striking a new vein in war writing, all the French war correspondents are today singing a similar chorus in honour of their regiments. We witness, therefore, the long association between whiskers and war.

Those of us who were in Paris during the first months of the war recall the various emotions through which the Parisians were supposed to pass under the trials of that time. Some of the vivid paragraphs, I may say, having written my share of them, are still in mind. But nowhere have I read of the shock, the shiver, the surprise, the cross feeling of apprehension and approbation that smote Paris when, after three months of trench life, the first French soldiers on leave strutted along the boulevards.

While these veterans sought a well-earned respite from the toils of war, Paris stared, rubbed its eyes, stared again and stammered *tiens! tiens! tiens!* Whenever a Frenchman meets a problem having no apparent explanation he exclaims *tiens!* And what Paris saw had no explanation short of the one that General Joffre's army had turned pirate and was wearing its beard to suit the part. The soldiers from the Marne came into Paris entirely surrounded by whiskers—black whiskers that would have made Blackbeard the Pirate commit suicide, walking his own plank, out of sheer envy; blonde whiskers that might have adorned the cheeks of a Viking; brown whiskers that recalled thick-bearded evangelist portraits; red whiskers! like the sunset behind the Arc de Triumph. When a Parisian greeted a friend from the trenches he felt that the soldier's eyes peeped out of an ambush of hair. The nose was concealed in the bearded face like a cannon hidden from aircraft. Only the tips of the ears emerged from the hairy jungle.

When squads of the bearded ones burst upon Montmartre, the district where Paris patois rises like bubbles in champagne, the Montmartrians with one accord exclaimed:

"*Oh, les Poilus!*"

The phrase might be freely translated into American slang as "Get onto his whiskers."

*Poilu*, the soldier of France, has since remained. In its original sense the word defined a quality in no way complimentary. A shaggy moth-eaten cinnamon bear was *poilu*; scientists used the word impartially in describing the fur of the orang-utan or the beard of corn; until the happy inspiration of the Montmartre gamin, it was an adjective with reverse English. Today *poilu* is a term of endearment, admiration, honour and respect.

After the beard, which almost conceals it, the most characteristic attribute of M. Poilu is his smile. Rather disconcerting and quite definite is this smile. You see, when a man has stopped a section of German shell with his arm or leg and unhappily has lost the arm or leg in the encounter, you do not expect him, back at work, to view the incidents of his day with any large amount of humour. So the smile of M. Poilu is surprising. There's Charlie, the *chasseur* of the *Café de la Paix*. A *chasseur* is a runner who stands outside a *café* ready to run errands, help guests out of motors or buy a newspaper for any of the diners. Charlie has only one arm now. In case some unobservant person might think he lost his arm in a railroad accident Charlie wears four war medals across his breast.

One of the duties of the *chasseur* is to doff his cap and open the doors of cabs or motors for arriving or departing guests. Charlie, with his one arm, has developed the skill of a juggler in this feat. And it is all done with a smile that seems to say, "Now we are going to have a good time," or "We did have a good time, didn't we?" It is a respectful smile, ready for whatever wind, weather or fortune the day brings.

Charlie when he left the hospital "cured," asked for and got this job of *chasseur*, which he had before the war. Edouard, the doorman at the

Hotel Maurice, who now wears a glove over what was his left hand, had the same good fortune. You would never know, unless someone called your attention to his slight limp, that Adolph, headwaiter at the Restaurant Mazarin, got through his work on a mechanical foot. Out in the trenches, M. Poilu is certain that if enough of him ever gets back to Paris he will find his old job waiting for him.

Not quite in the same class is the artist Ferbel, who, referring to the fact that he now buys his shoes by the half pair, said:

"It is an economy, is it not, *Monsieur*, now that the price of shoes is so high? And,"—he was shading in one of his vivid war sketches as I talked with him—"what luck that the bosche shell missed my right hand."

If for any reason his old job is not open to him, M. Poilu is soon assured of a new one. His physical condition determines which of many he may choose, from tinsmith to chartered accountant.

The Grand Palace, where in better days the auto mobile shows were held, is a manual labour school for the retraining of wounded. Besides the manual arts, the *poilu* may be instructed in stenography, typewriting, practical bookkeeping and accounts.

You can be a very good tailor, even with two wooden legs; you can make soap with one hand—I have seen it done—and regular feet are no better than artificial ones to the stenographer or the accountant, as far as the work is concerned. Carpenters, cabinet makers, ironworkers, frame makers, shoemakers, soapmakers, tailors, saddlers, barbers were taking their first lesson in their new trades in different corners of the exposition building. It was a thriving trade laboratory solving a dozen human economy problems.

The master workmen who instruct the *poilus* in new trades pass from soldier to soldier teaching the secrets of the work. Here is one soldier learning to handle a saw and steady the plank against his peg leg. Over there another one-legged worker is cutting out a pattern of a coat. Beyond him another moves his fingers hesitatingly above the keys of a typewriter. And so on throughout the hall in the booths that marked the floor space of some former automobile exhibitor these maimed men are preparing themselves to go out again and fight the world.

They are preparing in a double sense. Not only do they learn a craft, but they turn that craft, if possible, to their own particular needs. An artificial hand costs more money than many of our *poilus* can afford, yet they are not content with the simple hook, so these amateur carpenters, tinsmiths and iron workers have contrived an improvement in artificial hands almost as cheap as the hook, and much more useful. It ends in a snap something like a patent spring clothespin, and with this the *poilu* can pick up a pin, handle a fork or hold a pencil. Sergeant Bertrand, who has used his new hand for six months, will gladly write you his autograph.

Or if the bit of shell or bullet has carried off only a part of your forearm, say the radius, the iron-workers have invented another mechanical aid to fit your particular need. Nowadays all surgery is conserving. If any part of a man's leg, foot or hand can be saved, the surgeons concentrate all their skill on the problem. They make every effort to turn out all patients as nearly whole as possible when they leave the hospitals.

Even when large sections of bones are shattered the surgeons will mend the flesh as best they can and rely on some artificial device to take their place. In the *poilu's* manual labour school I saw some ingenious substitutes for radii. The radius is the bone in your forearm to which the muscles are fixed. If it is destroyed, the muscles have no leverage to work on and you cannot move your fingers.

A shoemaker who was using one of these mechanical bones slipped it off and dropped his hand into mine. The fingers were as limp as pulp. Then he explained to me the working of his "outside" bone. It was a combination of steel splints and springs, a sort of mailed fist. First, a long steel splint was strapped from below the elbow to the wrist, forming an exterior bone; at the wrist, joined to the long splint yet movable, were five small jointed splints that backed the thumb and fingers, these small splints were held in place by coil springs. When the shoemaker slipped his fingers into the rings of these jointed splints they, with the exterior steel radius strapped to his forearm, gave him the leverage upon which he worked his still intact muscles. When I left, the shoemaker had his mailed fist clamped around the toe of a boot as he pegged away at the sole. When he goes home I'll wager he will get most of the shoemaking business of his home town.

Whenever a new man joins this labour school it is always a matter of ceremony to measure him for a new peg leg or mechanical arm. The head carpenter, ironworker and tinsmith, gather around the newcomer and discuss his particular difficulty in all its aspects. Each maimed limb presents features that call for special care.

A tape is run here and there around what is left of the member, and each measurement checked. Then the workmen separate, each setting to work out his part of the artificial leg or arm. From time to time they consult on the fit of the different parts. Finally, when the leg or arm is finished, comes the problem of fitting it to the patient. This is a moment of triumph for the workers. You see it in their eyes as they watch the delighted soldier manoeuvring his stump or practising picking up tools with his clothes-pin hand. "*Ca va, ca va*" ("It's all right"), say the workers, with satisfaction. It must be satisfying to the spirit to think that you have cheated war out of some misery.

This work at the Grand Palace is but a sketch of what is going on all over France. Everywhere the maimed *poilu* goes back to his old work in a new way or learns a new work, so he may make his living. That is the strongest impression you carry away with you from one of the workshops for the wounded, the will to work. Just because a man has lost his leg, his arm, or his fingers, he does not think he is entitled to be supported by the nation for the rest of his life.

Old "Papa" Gaston, whom I sometimes meet in a certain cafe across the Avenue D'Antin from the Grand Palace, where, unless you wear a soiled uniform and are short an arm or a leg, you are distinctly an outsider, put the French idea of pensions before me very succinctly. I had tried to give him some notion of the American pension system.

He listened till I had finished, then exclaimed: "But where is the glory of fighting for your country if you do it for a life of ease and doing nothing ever after? If a man gives his life for his country, well, let his country look out for the wife and the children. That is fair. But the man who gives a leg, an arm, a hand—bah! what is that but an honour? He loves his country all the better since he has proved his love—it is like that with people. And where is the honour if every week you get so many cents to pay for the leg, arm or hand that has long since ceased even to be fertiliser?"

Gaston, who was so old-fashioned that he wore the primitive hook, waved it to emphasize his words.

"All the money in the treasury could not have bought that hand from me in time of peace," he said, bringing the hook under my nose; "but in war I am honoured to give, give it to my country."

"But the blind?" I interposed.

Papa Gaston dropped his hook to his knee. Tears shone in his eyes.

"The poor blind, the poor blind," he murmured tenderly. "Yes, France must take care of them."

And there are others who must receive all care. Love of life is the strongest instinct in man. The most miserable, misshapen thing will cling to it, living on through long black days that hold no hope. Often the brutal shells make frightful havoc of the body without destroying the soul. Hidden away in a forest outside Paris in a hospital for the hopelessly hurt; it is the House of Sorrow Unending. I shall not tell of those who dwell there. France in pity draws a veil over their terrible afflictions. Let us respect the sanctity of their sufferings.

But Paris does all she can to brighten the long days of Monsieur Poilu's convalescence. Sightseeing automobiles festooned with laurel, and filled tier upon tier with sky-blue uniforms speed around the boulevards, so that the wounded may enjoy the sunshine and the beauty of Paris. Monsieur Poilu is still gay and as a rare treat he is taken to the theatre. His choice of play is always a comedy. I followed a hobbling crowd into the Olympia Theatre one day. The Olympia is a sort of Parisian Keith's, although in the strictest sense the vaudeville is not over refined. Monsieur Poilu, however, having been close to the clay, is no stickler. Major, Captain and Lieutenant Poilu filled the reserved seats of the music hall. He came, spick and span as is always the French officer.

Behind him shuffled the Privates Poilu, chatting and laughing as schoolboys on a holiday. First came a tall grenadier, whose clean, white head bandage pointed the way to the derelicts who followed him. Furbished and freshened, his uniform fell a bit loose about his figure. The comrade of the grenadier was an undersised infantry man, his tunic spruced, brushed and carefully mended over the left arm hole. He had dropped his right hand into the palm of the tall grenadier, and followed him as a child its nurse. Next followed a *zouave* on crutches, his *fez* cocked at a defiant angle and his one boot shining as bright as an advertisement for shoe polish. Two artillerymen came next, one of whom made the distance from the door to the seats balanced on two canes.

"*Dis donc*, Paul," his comrade insisted, readjusting his sling, "you will have to clap for the two of us if we see a good turn."

"Certainly," answered Paul, making a two-yard hop.

So M. Poilu went to the music hall, limping and laughing, favouring a foot or an arm in the push for seats, but wholly centred on the show.

I trailed in after. I found myself brushing elbows with a girl wearing a streaming crepe veil. She gripped the arm of the last wounded soldier. He did not laugh. The side of his face toward me, from temple to chin, was smooth and waxlike. The lights reflected from it, as from a highly polished surface. He turned. Then I saw the line where the painted copper mask met the true flesh.

What first surprises you is the boisterous health of these derelicts. A leg gone, an arm crippled, a head trepanned, has made no hurt on the uninjured section of their bodies. They bubble with animal spirits. Then you remember that they have led the lives of farmhands with plenty of air, exercise and food, when the enemy did not interfere, as they will themselves tell you, they have taken on a robustness that defies the worst, short of death, that the shell can do. After the first shock of amputation, if there are no complications, Monsieur Poilu comes back to the vigour and strength he has been storing up in the trenches. I have seen a lad who had lost both arms who could still smile.

But let us get back to the music hall. What I wanted to know was, could those remnants of humanity still enjoy the delights of unrestricted laughter. On this point my curiosity was soon satisfied.

The first turn, a gymnastic trio, was generously applauded. A tramp turn, redolent of all the "business" seen on every vaudeville stage from Maine to California, followed. The bewhiskered, crimson-nosed ragamuffin had hardly rolled out from the wings when the *poilus* were snickering. When he took off his moth-eaten fur coat and plucked from its lining, in pantomime, a phantom flea, tossed this vermin on the floor, when it supposedly hopped off the stage to a base drum accompaniment, our tramp touched a responsive chord that set the *poilus* rocking with laughter. Not one among them but had met these vermin of the trenches on terms of easy intimacy. As the tramp developed his foolery, I studied the faces of his battered audience. Every face was stretched in a broad smile. Each new bit of nonsense brought out a surprised chuckle or a base guffaw.

The tall grenadier with the bandaged head barked out a laugh at every point made by the tramp comedian. The one-armed, undersised infantryman doubled in his seat and slapped his knee, shaking with hilarity. Paul, the artilleryman, pounded his two canes on the floor to express a double joy. When the tramp finished with a face fall a wave of laughter wafted him back to his feet. He bowed himself off in a burst of shouted gaiety.

After the tramp, a song turn—one of the pre-war soldier comedians who have been a feature of the French variety stage for a generation. A moment of curious quiet followed his appearance. He wore the red *kepi*, dark blue tunic, and baggy red breeches, the old uniform, not the khaki or the horizon blue of today. He belonged to the dark days of the war. In the hushed moment of his first appearance it seemed as if this heavy comedian called up a picture out of the past, a picture that must have many associations for these cripples wearing the new uniform. But when he launched into a French barrack-room ballad, interlarded with the soldier slang that serves in the trenches today, the *poilus* were with him to a man.

So it went throughout the performance. Turn after turn, trick bicycle riders, Australian skaters, an Irish slackwire walker, the inevitable *comedienne*, all met a joyous reception. As shout after shout of pure unfettered laughter rose to the cluster-lights in waves, I knew that Monsieur Poilu had lost none of his gaiety. Even that poor, disfigured one, he of the painted copper mask, he forgot a sorrow that must weight him deeply. His eyes twinkled, his lips spread, as the rough humour of the stage and the infectious chuckles of his comrades echoed in his soul.

The *boulevards* were still light when I left the Olympia, so I turned my steps to the little cafe opposite the Grand Palace where I hoped to meet "Papa" Gaston for his appetiser.

In the walk under the beautiful trees of the Champs Elysees, I caught another phase of the life of Monsieur Poilu. On the long summer evenings all Paris that does not drive up and down the Avenue des Champs Elysées sits under the trees to stare, to chat, to gossip. It is the custom for friends to meet in groups at the same time and place each day to exchange rumours. So the whole Champs Elysées becomes a collection of open-air clubs, strictly limited in membership and confined in location. Of course you expect to find the Messieurs Poilu here.

As I made a turn under the trees, I came suddenly on a group of chairs, not of the kind that you rent for a few cents from the local chair woman, but roller chairs, with wheels. On each chair sat a wounded soldier. All except one could manage to move about by manipulating the wheels, for though all had lost both feet or legs, they still had both arms. They sat smoking, talking, disputing, gesticulating—such a group as you might find ensconced in the corner of a club. Surely this was a unique club, and an exclusive one. War medals glittered on their breasts. They would have scorned your pity. The world still held plenty of interest for them. That you could see by the way they watched the throng on the Champs Elysées, by the animation of their talk, by their indifference to the stares of some rude watchers.

Each seemed to say, "Well, suppose I have lost my legs, crying about them won't bring them back. And one gets along well enough on these wheel chairs. Here we are, pleasant companions, plenty to smoke, the crowd to watch. What more could I do here on my two legs?"

They draw on an inexhaustible fund of native philosophy for their contentment. I passed on with a silent wish of "good luck" for the wheeled chair club.

At the Café du Grand Palace I found "Papa" Gaston with a half-dozen cronies, sipping drinks. Seated with them was a boy, not over twenty, dressed in a new sky-blue uniform. From cap to *puttees* he was a sky-blue symphony. His haversack swung from his shoulder; a neatly wrapped bundle rested on a chair behind him. Evidently he was the newest of recruits. As he sat among the veterans they chaffed him. "Had he a whisk broom in his pack? No! Oh, that was bad. It was often dusty in the trenches and without a whisk broom it would be impossible to keep such a nice uniform clean. Yes, it was dusty in the trenches." For some undisclosed reason the idea of dusty trenches set all the veterans laughing. The boy blushed under their banter, but it was plain he was proud to rub elbows with their soiled and ragged uniforms.

Now "Papa" Gaston put the boy through his catechism.

"Have you warm, soft socks?"

"Yes, papa." Everybody called Gaston "papa."

"Two warm shirts?"

"Yes, papa."

"Do your shoes fit?"

"Yes, papa."

"Have you some chocolate?"

"Yes, papa."

Gaston paused, searching for further practical interrogations. The boy glanced at the watch strapped to his wrist.

"I fear I must go," he said anxiously.

"What, is it already time?" There was a strong shade of disappointment in "Papa" Gaston's voice.

The newest recruit gathered his pack, shifted his haversack and stood.

"Wait!" Papa Gaston commanded. He motioned the waiter to fill the veteran's glasses. Gaston stood and lifted his glass. The other veterans struggled up, leaning on cane or crutch, and followed his example.

"My friends." All listened. "Good luck to the newest recruit." Papa Gaston drank.

"Good luck! Good luck! Good luck!" the others chanted, and drank. When the newest recruit stammered his thanks, Papa Gaston hugged him to his chest and kissed him once, twice, thrice. The wounded veterans crowded round until the boy broke away and hurried off in the gloom toward the Quai d'Orsay railroad station.

Tears stood in Papa Gaston's eyes as he stared after the sky-blue uniform.

"A nice boy," I ventured fatuously.

"A nice boy, a nice boy," repeated Papa Gaston. "Thank you, *monsieur*, he is my only son."

## Chapter 3

# Verdun; The Battle Epic

Verdun, the greatest battle of the greatest war of all time. As a rock this citadel stood in the path of the armies of Germany that battered and broke themselves in the last desperate effort to raze its walls. But it was not the swart and grim walls of the fortress that baulked the Germans, but walls of flesh and bone, walls wherein each stone was a son of the soil of France.

These human walls saved France. The men of France poured out their blood and laid down their lives until their very graves were mounds to hold back the foe. They not only dammed the lava-like flow of fire and iron, with their bodies, but turned it back upon itself. Day after day the ring of Krupp cannon that half encircled the city widened and weakened. Day after day the sullen cohorts of the foe were driven back from shell-pit to trench, from trench to dugout. Day after day, the lines of hang-dog prisoners lengthened.

"Each day we eat a few more bosches."

In English the words lose some of the idiomatic significance they held when spoken to me by Captain Le Blanc of General Nivelles' staff. But they aptly personified Verdun as a great sluggish monster that dined on human fodder.

Come with me into the brain of this monster. If you took a sixty foot section of the New York Subway, buried it beneath seventy feet of dingy stone wall, fitted it with plain board tables, rough kitchen chairs, telephones, typewriters, filing cases, dropped from the ceiling a dozen Mazda bulbs, shelled in yellow copy paper, and wall the room with maps, you would have the stage setting of this brain. For actors, fill up with a dozen French soldiers in faded grey uniforms working at the typewriters, the telephones and the filing cases; stand three smart French officers, booted and beribboned, with compasses in hand before the maps, and in the spotlight place a white haired, white moustached, brown faced general. That is the brain of Verdun.

The telephone booth is the motor centre from which the nerves stretch out to the farthermost listening post of the most recently captured shell pit. Every move of the foe is instantly flashed back from the listening posts. Along the wires speed messages, commands, the reactions of the brain. Quick as the sense of sight, this brain of Verdun registers impressions of the battle. The check of counter-attack, the success of a charge, a great gun silenced, the roll of the wounded, the prisoners, the dead, are here recorded. Here victory and its cost is counted. Here is collated all the material that afterwards appears, severely edited in the *communiqués*.

It is curious to reflect that the hundred deeds of gallantry in charge, counter-charge, attack and repulse, all the drama, all the tragedy of a battle lasting throughout twelve hours of the night, goes down to history in a "stick" of type.

The days of my visit to Verdun the French fought two battles that in other times would have won at least a chapter of history. All day and night the cannon blazed. In the earliest dawn the infantry swept over the ground, now broken into a thousand craters—for it was no longer a war of trenches in front of Verdun, but a war of shell-pits—and after desperate hand-to-hand fighting that went on in the shell-pits and later in the dugouts, the French mastered their foe.

In the number of men and guns employed these two "operations" of this French Army could be compared with the Battle of San Juan Hill. Yet here is all the official report stated about the fighting.

> *Thursday, 3 p. m.* On the right bank of the Meuse about nightfall yesterday our troops carried out two operations with brilliant success. Southeast of the Thiaumont work we carried several trench positions, capturing more than 100 prisoners, two being officers, and two machine guns.

Could a battle story be more emasculated? Not the name of general or regiment. Not a word recording the furious fighting that raged from lip to lip of the shell pits. Not a syllable of the stirring story of the struggle around the machine guns. Nothing but the bald facts relieved solely by the injection of the adjective brilliant.

But summarised in those few lines of type we have the history of this great battle. They bring to mind that day when the soldiers of the crown prince came out of the east "like leaves of the forest when summer is green." They remind us of the first days of the fight when the armies of France staggered and reeled under the tremendous onslaught of the Germans. We can picture again the sudden snowstorms—that storm that fought for France—the fields white, the roads impassable, all of which meant a respite for the French, giving them time to turn in here the unending supply of men, munitions and guns that has since been watered over the hills that surround Verdun. We recall the smash and counter smash of the might of German flesh and blood matched against French flesh and blood. We remember when the world waited, tense and expectant for the news that Verdun had fallen. But that news never flashed along the cables.

Instead we heard the story of the genius of General Petain, of the superb valour and steadiness of the French under the pounding of the greatest guns that Krupp could forge. We remember how the Germans lost the impetuousness of their first dash; how they slipped back foot by foot from the ground they had captured at the cost of uncounted lives. The few lines I have quoted tell the end of the story of Verdun. What is more significant than that phrase, "capturing more than a hundred prisoners." Let us follow the fortunes of one of those captives.

He is Carl Swartz, second company of the Brandenburg Regiment. He marches first behind the two officers in the line of haggard, leg-weary prisoners in smirched uniforms, that winds down the Etain road toward Verdun.

It was not thus that the Brandenburger Swartz pictured his entry into Verdun. His mind harks back now to that day when his regiment bit its way into the heart of Fort Douaumont, and hung on in spite of the tidal wave counter-attacks of the French.

The morning broke clear after a week of hail and snow. Below his post in the newly won position, across the wrack of battle, lay the village of Fiery. Beyond that village, hardly four miles away he saw Verdun. Verdun was his goal. When the German armies would sweep over that scant distance, then Brandenburger Swartz knew his work would be done. There was the end of the war in sight.

Had he not been so assured by *hauptmann*, *oberst*, yes even the august crown prince himself. He remembered now the thrill that had gone through his soul as he looked down upon the city that was the symbol of victory. How they laughed and joked, his comrades of the Second Regiment. They had lost some fifty men of the company that night, the wounded were being carried out of the fort, but they thought nothing of their mangled bodies or limbs, they gave back wan smiles to the jokes of their comrades. "We can see Verdun. One more rush and it is ours."

This picture passed through Swartz's mind as if he had turned back the pages of some well-known story. How the shells rocketed into Verdun that March day. The whole city sparkled with red fire that flared against the buildings and died in clouds of black smoke. What was it little Heindrick Myer had said as he watched the ceaseless succession of explosions that burst off the roofs of the houses of the city; "If the artillery keeps that up another day, there'll be no work for us Brandenburgers. We'll walk into the town without firing a shot."

"Walk into the town without firing a shot. Yes"—thought Swartz—"that's what I'm doing. But how different, how different!" He and his companions were all that were left of the original two hundred and fifty men of the Second Company. The end had come after a bloody fight around the lip of a mine crater. The French had driven them into the pit of the crater. Caught in a ring of bayonets, the remnants of the Company surrendered.

Swartz marvelled at what he saw as the guards hurried him past the battle line. Trench after trench, field work after field work, battery flanking battery, all so jumbled together that they seemed splashed in by a giant's brush across a canvas stretched through four miles of earth. He and his comrades had been driven on the run through the first line positions. It was hardly daylight then, so he could see little. But the *crescendo* crackle of rifle and machine gun fire told the story of the strength of those positions.

As they passed the reserve trenches, a group of French soldiers rushed out to see them. "*Voila les Bosches!*" they had shouted. They had studied him critically, thought Swartz. He had straightened his shoulders and thrown up his chin as he walked past them. But out of the corner of his eye he had seen that they nudged one another and joked. They were cheerful. Long months had passed since any one had joked among the Second Brandenburgers.

It was clear light when the little band of prisoners were marched past the battery positions. Swartz measured them with his soldier's eye and marvelled. For months on end he had suffered under the smothering shell fire of those batteries, but till he got this glimpse of them he had not conceived their number nor yet the tide-stream of shells that poured across the country behind them.

For Swartz noticed the network of Decauville railways spread out in rear of the batteries, and the hundreds of cars, loaded with projectiles, their painted points upward, shunted along the narrow rails. The line of prisoners moved not so fast but the mind of Swartz gradually assimilated the marvellous preparations of the French. It seemed to him that though the French batteries fired so constantly that never could he say—"Now no gun speaks," yet the mounds of shells that were dammed up back of the gun shelters did not melt. They grew.

As the significance of this shell supply worked into the Brandenburger soldier's mind, for the first time he began to feel resentment against his officers. "Did they not know the French had these mountains of ammunition? Why, they have as many shells for their great and small guns as we Germans have cartridges for our rifles."

With this reflection came other thoughts into the mind of Private Swartz, thoughts that he would not have dared to have whispered to himself in the night, thoughts that drowned his soul in an acid sea of depression. During the last two months the beginnings of these thoughts had dawned, but he had thrust them from him as treason. Dare he doubt the assurance of his Master? But then, when he was fighting, things had not been so clear to him, he made himself believe he was winning.

As he tramped along, a prisoner, inside the circle he had been fighting so long and so fruitlessly to pierce, he saw things that turned his doubts to demoralizing convictions. Even an army of devils—could never take Verdun, he thought bitterly. An army of devils the French themselves deserved that title. Could these confident quiet men in their uniforms of light blue be the same breed as those fiends who shot, bayoneted and surrounded him and his comrades last night? The picture of the bloody struggle on the lip of the mine crater flashed on the curtain of the German soldier's brain. It was a ghastly terrible picture of ghost men who slaughtered, with only gun and grenade flash to lighten the night.

But Swartz did not want to think of last night. He turned his eyes above the steeples of the cathedral, and caught the sight of the black bulbous shapes of the captive balloons, swaying slowly upward in the sky. Six he counted. The same six he had counted day after day for more than two months now. It seemed to him they were a monstrous mockery, those bloated "sausages."

They swung between Heaven and Earth, a target for every gun, a temptation for every airman on the German side. But no shell ever reached them, no aviator dared venture thus far from home. For as the balloons rose, Swartz caught the drone of an aeroplane engine. A Nieuport biplane swooped out of a cloud, graceful as a swallow, swift as a bullet. No silvered Albatros from Germany could race these French machines; and to the fighting airman, speed is life. The Nieuports hovered about the captive balloons, alert and constant guardians.

When Swartz had arrived at the station where he was searched and questioned, he was completely bewildered. The searching was rapid, thorough, and finished in a few moments. But he could make nothing of the questioning. Why had they asked him if Charlemagne was a Frenchman or a German? Then, when he stood confused, they quickly questioned "When had he heard from his family? Were they well? What was the date of their last letter? Before they had harvested the potatoes?" Potatoes! Did they not know the potatoes had rotted in the ground, Swartz had answered. What foolish questions these French asked, he thought, as he took his place once more in the line that marched under guard to Verdun.

Swartz smiled as he swaggered down the Rue Etain. It was a sullen smile born of the havoc he saw. It was nearly true what little Myer had said, the German guns had battered the roofs, breached the walls of the houses, until nothing stood upright except jagged silhouettes of rock and plaster. Here stood one house with the roof blown off, leaving the debris as hideous as a smashed skull.

There stood another, a section of a house, with parlour, kitchen, bedroom exposed immodestly to the gaze of all who passed. Bed and table and chair were tossed as if some drunken giant had raged the home. The still white face of the clock marked five minutes past seven, the hour of the tragedy. For here great rambling brown stains marked where warm blood once spread across the floor.

Through roof to cellar a shell had pierced the next house, and the explosion had sprayed the building into the street. A once peaceful home was thus transmuted to an indistinguishable heap of lath, plaster and brick. Beyond stood a house with its walls split from top to bottom, another pierced through from side to side by a shell. But one building in that city where once stood the peaceful homes of twenty thousand souls, escaped the scathe of the shells. Swartz saw all this scarification—his heart filled with secret joy.

But the fury of the German fire has concentrated on the top of the street of the Beautiful Virgin. The old museum building standing there was an improvised hospital. A great Red Cross is painted athwart its roof. "Some German gunner scored a bull's eye," thought Swartz,

German captives taken at Verdun

This parade of prisoners was not in accordance with the programme of the crown prince

noting the shell hole through the very centre of the cross.

As the line of prisoners neared the citadel, a sound so long familiar that Swartz was slow in perceiving it, came over his head from the German lines. Only when the shell burst did he realize that he was under the fire of his own guns. He was glad to hurry on.

The captives turned into the keep of the citadel to wait the train that would take them back to the prison camps of France. When the ancient dungeon door closed, Swartz was conscious of the sudden quiet of the place. He no longer heard the guns. This relief almost reconciled him to being a prisoner. Swartz could not know that all the underground passages of the citadel had been turned into barracks for the French soldiers. Here they came for rest and repose after the tempest of the trenches. Side by side their beds were lined along the tunnels. Here where no echo of battle reached them, they slept. Here they ate. Here they chatted, wrote post cards, did their laundry work—the steam pipes were excellent dryers—and forgot the strain of fighting. In a branch tunnel a moving picture screen was hung. Songs were sung and little farces which the soldiers acted, were given between reels. During the days of their rest, the French battalions became an underground people, never coming out of the tunnels except for exercise. One had a sense of peace, lying there seventy feet underground, that almost let one forget the horror of the fighting.

But Swartz and his fellow prisoners of war were allowed little time to enjoy such peace. Soon they found themselves huddled into freight cars, and they heard the puffing of the engine that dragged the prison train. For them the war was over.

It is a new railroad which leads from the fighting zone over which they passed. Three months ago not a yard of it had been surveyed, not a cross-tie cut. Today it runs forty-eight kilometres (thirty miles) back from Verdun to the heart of the greatest advance base on the French front. No better symbol of what France has done in the strengthening of Verdun can be found.

We know a superhuman succession of motor trucks supplied General Petain's army during the tense days and nights of the first month's fighting. With the wonderful organisation of transportation which took place at the time of the early desperate battles, the fate of Verdun was decided. The genius who planned this transportation stands on a pedestal but little lower than that accorded General Petain.

But this motor transportation belongs to the first chapter of the story of Verdun. The new railroad is an achievement of the last chapter.

And it gives us a scale by which we can measure the magnitude of the world's greatest battle. It is a giant scale. But this is a giant war. In former times a battle was fought in not more than three, four, at the longest seven days. Now a battle rages for as many months.

As the time scale has lengthened, so also has the scale of munitions and supplies used, and men killed and wounded. We must adjust our minds anew to the stupendous proportions of this war, in order to understand how the building of a railroad thirty miles long was possible while a battle was in progress.

The Verdun Short line, as we might christen it, grew out of conditions that would bring a railroad into being in any other part of the world—an imperative demand for the most efficient transportation. The motor trucks were beginning to be less and less reliable, and the need for refitting and repair became each day a more harassing problem. The first onslaught of the Germans had been checked, through the aid of these trucks. But there was every sign that the Germans would hammer and hammer at the walls of Verdun. They would try to repeat the victory of Warsaw. So when the French saw the problem before them, they solved it on masterly lines. The result today is that the siding at the advanced base reminds one of the freight station in Kansas City.

Food and war material in crates of every size and shape are crowded in the stations. Special shell trains, loaded with nothing but the heaviest ammunition, are sent on daily time schedules, out to the fields behind the batteries of Verdun. Acre after acre is covered with steel cones. Here are the fabulous Dragon's teeth springing out of the ground.

Seeing field after field of these shells you get the impression of some extraordinary crop about to be harvested. While most of the fields are planted in yellow tulip-beds of shell cones, yet on occasion you see an acreage of trench bombs, sprouting like pre-historic mushrooms.

In other fields great canvas curtains painted green and brown are stretched over a hidden shapeless bulk. If the wind lifts a corner of the canvas, you catch sight of mysterious boxes, thousands of the same size and shape, with broad red bands painted around their middles. Red is the colour of danger. Each of these thousands of boxes in itself is concentrated danger. The most reckless motor dispatch-rider, the most supercilious and daring chauffeur who drives staff officers' automobiles behind the lines, gives the wagon with the little red disc stuck out from its tail board, the right of way. All roads are cleared for the powder boxes.

Close to the shell and powder fields are the aeroplane hives. These are arched corridors of canvas, painted green or yellow. As the honey bees leave their hives in the morning, so do the aeroplanes drone out from these canvas corridors at daylight. And as the bees, when their work is done, at sundown the flyers come homing back to the hive.

The strongest impression you carry away with you from Verdun is one of movement. The snorting, smoking engines, pulling endless trains of munition cars is movement. The interminable line of motor lorries that run like a chain up and down the Metz-Paris road spells movement. The loading and unloading of the thousands of Decauville cars with shells is movement. The swift flying aeroplanes are the quintessence of movement. Even the clouds swirling past the bulbous balloons give the illusion of movement.

Gradually it breaks in upon you that this movement, this unceasing activity of every department of the organisation behind the fire trenches, symbolises victory. Day and night the arteries that feed the fire-spitting dragon at the front function without losing a pulse beat. Day and night the wastage of battle is renewed. More, this dragon finds, as is the law of nature, that with exercise his powers grow. Since that short period when indecision hampered results, Verdun has gained daily in strength.

I have tried to give you some impression of the vastness of the preparation carried out during the months of fighting at Verdun. But one's mind grapples ineffectively with an estimate of the millions of shells, the tons of ammunition, the train-loads of supplies that were banked up behind the fighting line. Perhaps we would get some idea of this estimate if we tried to imagine the Verdun army as the wall of a dam, the Elephant Butte dam of New Mexico, then picture the war material of France flooding into it.

The Battle of Verdun ended the first phase of the war. Now, when the mighty events that marked its beginning, its continuation and its final chapter, have faded a little into the past, so we get a clearer perspective of the Greatest Battle of all wars, it stands in the balance of history as a French victory.

Remember a victory can be effectively measured in terms of resistance. If you thwart your enemy of his most wished-for and worked-for objective, you inflict a defeat on him that may count to your credit as important in result as an offensive success. When the Germans realised the enormity of their failure at Verdun, they tried to minimize defeat by measuring the ground they had gained there against the ground gained by the Allies on the Somme. But the balance sheet of battle is not computed on such a simple basis. The Germans lost more than men and guns and ground on the Somme. They lost morale. While the defence of Verdun gave the French a quality of *morale* that made each simple soldier a giant in the fight.

I have said little of the soldiers of Verdun. What is there to say? Their deeds are beyond praise. Their heroism beyond comparison. One day perhaps some new born Homer will arise to chant of this battle in glorious verse. For Verdun is an epic. An epic chorused to the peal of cannon, the rush of the raging charge, the blast of shell, grenade and rifle, the hoarse grunting of men meeting men with sharp edged bayonets.

CHAPTER 4

# In the Argonne

War burnt a path through this forest primeval as consuming as a prairie fire. Picture a forest so dense that the branches of the young trees twine and intertwine so closely you think the soldiers could cut out sections of them for trench wattling. Only the straightest rays of the sun pierce the crowning foliage of these trees to brighten the heavy undergrowth that flourishes about the trunk roots. Yet where the trench lines run, the trees, giant pine and stripling beech, have disappeared.

Here and there a gibbet trunk still rises, a sort of skeleton tree standing as a stark symbol of the results of war. Scattered over the soil are rotting branches that bleach in the sunshine and the rain. The armies of France and Germany, where they pushed through this beautiful woodland, were as the plague of locusts that sweep through the green grain fields of Argentina. And as is the path of destruction of the locust, so is the path of destruction of the armies, sharp and defined. The primeval forest grows dense up to the edge of the fortified positions. But where man battles, nature dies. Here is a "No Man's Land" by contrast made doubly desolate.

It was a day of clear sunshine when I went to the front through the Argonne forest. The first tang of autumn filled the air. Walking up the broad road leading through the trees towards the dugouts, I was strongly reminded of the Adirondacks. The soldiers had cleared away much of the underbrush behind the lines, and in the clearings had built collections of log cabins. The thin blue smoke curling out from their chimneys, the odour of a cooking breakfast, aroused such a series of association in my mind that I longed for rod and gun.

Compared with the other sectors of the front, these rest camps behind the Argonne trenches seem like pleasant picnic grounds. But if you study the faces of the soldiers who are spending their four days of relief from the firing line in these shaded glades, you lose the thought that their lot is easy. Now, after these years of war, experience has cut its mark with grim, hard lines on the faces of the soldiers. Their eyes hold a glint of defiance. Yet, if you catch these eyes off guard, they brood. They seem to be the eyes of men seeing visions. These eyes speak of absorbing, unfathomable thought filling the soul behind them.

The chief occupation of the trench soldier in rest camp is washing. He comes from his tour in the front line caked and covered with several layers of soil. He has walked in mud, he has eaten in mud, he has slept in mud. Of other dirt he has collected all varieties with unconscious ease. Trench work brings out the sweat of the brow. Oft-times the daily wash is perforce postponed because of the activities of the enemy. So, on duty, the soldier puts aside all pretence of cleanliness.

But when he returns to the comparative comfort of the reserve lines, he revels in cleanliness. He begins with a complete bathing of his person. Incidentally, a soldier had as lief lose his water bottle as his bath towel. After his bath he indulges the long postponed joy of shaving. When he has satisfied himself of the cleanliness of his person, he turns his attention with a sense of pleasure to his week's wash.

There is a sensation, soothing and satisfactory, in washing clothes. It is an occupation that makes for a philosophic outlook on life. So our soldier dawdles over it, scrubbing and smoking, examining results with a critical eye that frowns on the faintest stain. He enjoys sinking his hands deep in the suds and swashing his clothes about, then rinsing them in cold clean water. In the Argonne he spreads them over the branches of the trees to dry. So as you pass the camps, your eye is filled with a strange assortment of men's outer and under clothes swaying in the morning breeze.

A fortified position does not consist only of the first and second line trenches. The whole scheme of defence is carried back to the rest trenches, so that point after point is turned into a strong supporting position. In the Argonne the strength of these positions is founded on barbwire entanglements. I had seen much of the wire entanglements in many fields of this war, but nowhere had I seen a network of wire ribbon and steel thongs so impenetrable as that spread under the trees that still stand in the Argonne forest. The situation was ideal for the use of entanglements. The underbrush concealed the field of wire, and the standing trees made natural supports for the strands. During the summer creeping plants wound themselves along the strands, as if

Nature strove to hide the unseemly work of man.

In the centre of the webwork of wire entanglements stood a ridge; coming on it from the rear, one discerned at intervals of about fifty yards, six door-like openings to tunnels bored into its core. I passed down one of the tunnels to a square underground chamber, the moist earth sweating through the boarded walls, where a machine gun poked its hollow muzzle out on the forest. I had come under the backbone of the ridge to the far slope, which, still bedded in barb wire, fell away below the lengthwise slit through which the gun barrel peeped. The machine gun squatted on its tripod, staring into the wood like an iron watchdog. Measured in a direct line, the foe was but six hundred yards distant.

From the machine gun positions the way to the front led through a deep winding ditch. The soil had a curious semi-petrified quality that made the ordinary expedients of revetting unnecessary. I am no geologist, but the soil seemed to me to be in the first stage of the formation of granite. This quality made it possible to construct defensive positions of great strength, and it turned the fighting in the Argonne into a war of mines. The ditch I was traversing led to the entrance of the famous Argonne tunnel.

But before I could be shown the mysteries of the tunnel, I must don the helmet of the French soldier. In the shelter of the ravine, the commander of this sector had his burrow. After I had paid my call of ceremony on him, I was led to the helmet store. The latest styles of trench headgear were stacked on the shelves. I deposited my Stetson and was offered my choice of the grey helmets in exchange. They are simply made, something like a derby hat with the brim off, light and not uncomfortable. The value of the helmet lies in the protection it gives you from shell splinters, shrapnel, or bits of a hand-grenade that may burst on the ground above a trench should your head show over the parapet.

It has a value beyond this, for putting on the helmet, you feel your *morale* rise at least fifty *percentum*. If you were to ask a group of soldiers which part of their anatomy they considered the most vulnerable, nine out of ten of them would answer, the head. Men who come under shell fire for the first time invariably duck, and wind their arms around their heads. It is an instinctive movement.

When you pause in cold reason to consider the slight protection it gives against the hurtling shell splinter, you may not repeat the movement. But you will long have the inclination to duck your head when you hear the whine of the coming shell. So like the ostrich, when you put on one of the steel helmets, you have a feeling of security that makes a visit to the firing line almost comfortable.

While I fitted my helmet, a French battery hidden in the trees started a leisurely shelling of the enemy. At about the sixth shot, a distant machine gun chimed in, playing treble to the battery's bass. It promised to be a busy day in the trenches.

At the time of my visit to the Argonne front, the Battle of Verdun still continued, and the fighting on the Somme was at its height. With these two powerful efforts in progress there was little chance of heavy fighting in another sector. The western front is divided into live and dead sectors of fighting. Under the restrictions of the war of position, it is physically impossible to provide enough guns and men to maintain battle operations throughout the total stretch of the siege line. There are sectors where the belligerents seem almost to draw apart, like boxers sparring for wind, making only enough demonstration of force to convince the opponent that the sectors are strongly held.

In the vicinity of Compiegne, the apex of the Laon angle, the two armies sat glaring at each other since the Battle of the Marne, yet for over two years neither dared attempt a forward movement. The condition was much the same in the Soissons sector. And in the Argonne, while there had been a continued state of mine warfare, yet neither side dared launch an assault.

There were two chief reasons for such conditions. First, the natural and artificial strength of the position. Second, its unimportance from a military point of view. While the Germans drove an attack at Verdun, a naturally strong position, yet from the military point of view a success there, would have been worth all the losses involved. That the Germans failed is but added proof of the futility of attacking a position of such strength. On the Somme there were a number of reasons for carrying through an offensive. The position was not so strong as other sections of the line, and the potential compensations justified the effort.

In the dead sectors, one felt all the tense strain of war with none of the relief of action. Men were on the watch day and night. Surprise, one of the potent factors of military success, is an eventuality that must be guarded against at all costs. Therefore, even in those in-active divisions of the battle front, the role of the sentinel was paramount. The sentinel must be alert not only for any indication of important activity of the foe, but he must be eternally vigilant for signs of minor activities, such as raids, bombing parties, or sapping work. In daylight, this task is comparatively easy. The time for "putting something over" on your foe is night. So, in the darkness the trenches take on an atmosphere of energy in leash that approximates the thrill of the wait before battle.

For every night brings its minor engagement. Unimportant as this engagement may be in the general plan of war, yet to the individual soldier who may be wounded or killed in the encounter, the engagement is of supreme concern. The night before my arrival in the Argonne, the Germans had exploded a mine, killing eight and wounding ten of the defenders.

Captain Delmas of the staff, explained the character of Argonne fighting to me on the way to the tunnel. His explanation was interrupted by a voice calling to me in English—

"Say, are you an American?"

I turned to see a St. John's ambulance driver coming out of the brush. The red cross on his cap and the insignia on his coat lapels were the only touch of colour on his khaki uniform.

"Yes," I replied.

"Well, I lived in your country for eighteen years. Down in the Panhandle, Texas. I worked on the J. A. ranch. My name's Jenkins."

When he said Texas, we shook hands. I know the Panhandle and had ranched with the X. I. T. outfit in the old days when their range joined the J. A.'s. The long arm of coincidence must have been pulled out of its socket to bring two old hands from the cow country together in the Argonne. We swapped a few reminiscences, then I followed my guide once more towards the tunnel.

Down a sharp incline I entered under the crust of the earth. By the light of a flickering candle I noted the shoring of wall and ceiling, and when I reached the bottom of this entrance shaft, I found myself in what might be the gallery of a silver mine. Briefly, the soldier adapted the craft of the miner to serve fighting ends. This adaptation inaugurated subway warfare. At long intervals incandescent bulbs lightened the gloom of the damp tunnels. Their rays shone on the strong boxes of small arms ammunition ranged against the walls. Cross tunnels lead from the main gallery to shafts that climb up to the fire trenches and the cartridges are stacked safe, yet convenient for emergency. Beyond the boxes of cartridges, a wooden door opens into a subterranean sleeping chamber. Two cots, a table and two chairs furnish it. For ornament a cartoon from *Life* is pinned against the wall. The cartoon

THE SERRIED RANKS OF SHELLS
PART OF AN INEXHAUSTIBLE SUPPLY. THE SHELLS HERE PICTURED WERE SHOT AWAY IN AN HOUR'S TIME ON THE SOMME.

represented Uncle Sam in a state of petulant annoyance, and the caption beneath it read,

"What, is there a war going on in Europe?" A little beyond the sleeping room I passed another cavern wherein a dynamo—made in America—was installed. This furnished a power for the lighting of all the underground passageways. Further along the tunnel I became aware of a sound that for a moment I confused with the clatter of a machine gun. Following my guide, we went a short way down a branch gallery, and there stood a soldier cutting his way through the soft slag with a compressed air drill. But for his stained and faded uniform, he might have been a miner drilling down a vein of quartz. I reflected on the labour expenditure of this mine warfare.

Here was this man cutting a tunnel that would take weeks to complete; and when finished, several hundred pounds of explosive would be touched off underneath the German trench. Probably the explosion would result in the killing and wounding of some twenty men. Surely this was an exceedingly small result for the cost in labour and material of the military land mine. Then, there was always the risk of a counter mine, destroying this work of weeks. It is not difficult to detect mine workers, for the soil is a good conductor of sound; also to aid in the detecting of mine work, an instrument contrived on the principle of a Dictaphone is carefully deposited near the edge of the enemy's trench. And on occasions it is possible to overhear not only the tapping of the mine workers but even conversations.

Leaving our soldier miner, we ascended to the second line trenches. For a moment I was blinded by the bright sunshine. The battery that I had heard before my underground walk was still firing methodically. Now and then the machine guns sputtered. Except for these sounds all was as quiet as a Sunday morning.

This calm had a dramatic quality. Behind the breastwork of sandbags, we crouched, as the hunter watching his prey. Captain Delmas and I spoke in low tones as if we feared the enemy might overhear us. Over the parapet, I looked into the rear of the fire line trenches, hardly a hundred yards distant, and beyond them a scant ten yards ran the enemy's line.

A rough, irregular furrow of stubble, running along the crest of a hill called *La Fille Morte* (the dead girl), bounded the enemy position.

But the picture I got of the French line gave graphic evidence of lurking danger. The loophole through which I peered framed a view of a group moulded rigid as stone. There was no movement in the fire trenches. At a lookout post, a sentinel posed still as a statue. His coat fell from his back in those ample folds that are the delight of sculptors. Further carrying out the illusion of statuary, were the figures of two other soldiers, one on either side of the sentinel, stretched out on the soil sleeping. Remember, the time when the sentinels must be most alert is night, so these sleepers were taking their rest as only soldiers can.

Up and down the line of the fire trenches I glanced. Wherever I looked on the back of a soldier he was tensed against the side of the earth wall that stood between him and death. Sometimes I caught only the glint of a grey helmet showing above the ground. Yet it was so still it might have been fitted on a tree stump. This concentration of watchfulness characterised the whole line.

It seemed irrational that these men should be staring so intently at nothing. Strain my eyes as I did, through a pair of the best binoculars Mr. Zeiss ever made, I could see no indication of a foe. But he was there. These sentinels knew every tree trunk, every hummock in the stubble, every picket of the enemy's barb wire, better than they knew the details of their own farmyards. If the morning light shows a tree trunk cut, a boulder displaced, or the barbed wire changed, the activity of the enemy stands revealed. Immediately it became the purpose of the defenders to divine and check his object.

The sentinels did not even turn their heads to watch a silvered Albatross aeroplane that swam out of the sky above the German lines. That was the duty of the anti-aircraft gunners. Four puffs of feathery smoke burst against the blue of the sky about the aeroplane, surrounding it like the pips on a playing card. Then the flying machine passed from view into the bosom of a friendly cloud.

Leaving the lookout, I walked behind a strongly built parapet to one of the forward machine-gun positions. It was but little larger than a comfortable grave. A horizontal slit gave through the wall of the grave towards the Germans. This opening was concealed with a curtain of burlap, through which the light of the outer world filtered, revealing the blue-barrelled gun.

The machine gun in the Great War is the master weapon. I always look on these sprinklers of death with awe. From the beginning of the world fighting, I have been witness of their frightfulness. Turn that spout of lead free into a charging line, and men will drop as clay pipes in a shooting gallery.

On our way back from these trenches, the Marquis d'Andingné, who had been my companion from Paris, told how, on his last visit to this front, an ill-natured German had thrown a hand-grenade at him. Evidently the Germans were in better humour the morning of my visit.

After retracing our steps through the gloom of the tunnel, and then passing along the zigzagging communication trench, we came again to the helmet shop, where I turned in my iron hat, and received in return my Stetson. Then, with an hour's stiff walking, I arrived at the chief artillery observation post in this sector.

The walk through the forest was interesting, for what I saw and more than interesting for what I did not see. It is obvious that the officer at the front has not too much confidence in the correspondent. He is jealous of the secrets of his position. He is quite indifferent whether the world knows of his wonderful achievements, or whether they continue a hidden mystery. If anything, he prefers that his work remain a mystery. Yet he is all courtesy. So when you are his guest at the front, he shows you all that he feels justified in revealing, often at inconvenience to himself. But such is the perverseness of human nature, it is the things that remain hidden that we want most to see.

I soon became aware that there was a mystery in those woods. Perhaps this mystery concerned one of the giant French guns that are hidden in the dense thickets of the Argonne. Immediately I was fired with curiosity.

When I met the commanding officer of this new division of the front, I noted that he wore the dark uniform of the artillery. He was a handsome elderly gentleman. His burrow was hollowed out of the side of a hill. From what I could see through the open door, it was furnished with characteristic simplicity. Yet it boasted one improvement. It had a window. The window was ingeniously made of empty claret bottles, the necks broken off, and the remainder of the bottles fitted six or eight in a row in a wooden frame. Such a window admitted a soft church-light into the commander's chamber.

His men also were very comfortably dug in. And they too, had the claret bottle windows let into their cabins. There is no favouritism in the French Army. The men were at breakfast when I saw them. A long table was built out under the trees around which they sat, while a luscious aroma steamed up from a half dozen deep mysterious pots. They were in the easy undress allowed the French soldier off duty, but I noted they wore artillery soldiers' breeches.

Finally I was escorted to an observation station. I might have been in the conning tower of a battle ship. A long slit, that made a half circle of the conning tower, gave a view of the whole country in front of the French positions. A powerful telescope, and an equally powerful periscope, through which I looked, brought the German trenches so close I felt I might reach out with my cane and strike them. At one end of the line stood a lone hill with its side gashed out. My guide told me the Germans had exploded seventy-five tons of dynamite under this hill. Yet, between the observation station and the distant ridge that marked the German positions, the tree tops made a green carpet.

The first purpose of an observation station is to observe artillery fire. From the character of this station and the powerful glasses there installed, it was to observe artillery fire at a great distance. My deductions more and more convinced me that this was the post of one of the mighty cannon, guns that are a hundred millimetres greater in calibre than the 420's of Germany. Perhaps this was the home of the famous "Rosalie," the largest cannon in the world.

When I left the observation tower I caught sight of a range chart hung against the wall. Here was the final link in the chain of evidence. Beyond doubt within the radius of a few hundred yards was the hiding place of a mighty gun. Etiquette forbade my asking to see it, but I devoutly hoped I should be shown the gun. I was disappointed in my hope. *La Lourde* (the heavy one), was not to be revealed to my profane eyes. I passed close to it. Yes, I saw the powder magazine that fed the gun, but the gun itself remained unseen in the densest thicket of the Argonne forest.

Yet I had seen enough to understand the strength of the French position. The wall of the impenetrable forest was made doubly secure by every device known to the military engineer. If the whole weight of German military strength had been thrown against the French lines in the Argonne, it would have shattered like the sea on a rock-bound coast.

CHAPTER 5

# In the Stream of the Somme Fighting

As a stream swollen with the rains cuts under its banks till the earth falls into its waters and is carried away, so did the French battle current on the Somme cut under the German bank of defence. Tramping over the battlefield between Peronne, and Chaulnes, the simile of the stream in springtime came to mind as I watched the rivulets of rain water draining into the myriad shell pits. These pits cover the ground as if it had been scourged with smallpox. They are filled with pasty mud of the consistency of newly mixed mortar. From them the rain water seeks the level of the roads, now turned into ribbands of yellow paste spotted with pools of yellow water. Along the roads working parties of French sappers are busy with pick and spade, cutting drains to lead the water to the shell holes.

They work gingerly, these mud covered sappers, because the battlefield is sown with shells and hand grenades waiting only the slightest touch to bring a long delayed explosion. Danger is hidden in every shell pit. Other hidden things are now revealed by the rains—gruesome, repulsive bundles of rotting grey uniforms, which send out sickening odours like marsh gas. The sappers spade the mud decently over these bundled forms.

Distant German batteries fire their sullen rounds at the groups of sappers. The shells pitch into the mud to burst with a roaring eruption of wet earth and black smoke. French batteries, guardians of the workers, give answer, their shells quitting the guns with poignant detonations.

The battlefield is a section of the world in decay. Rot, disintegration and disruption go on, rapidly turning the fields, fences, the trees, the crumbling rubble of the ruined homes into a weltering mass of raw wood, twisted iron, broken stone, imbedded in dank earth. Above this desolate scene, a saffron sun struggles through the mist that covers Picardie.

In this dreary waste, leading lives little less horrible than the vermin that plague them, the soldiers of France exist. I do not say live, for to pass days and nights amid scenes terrible with the blood and blight of war, is not living. The death strife, the wounds, all the frightful incidents of fighting, are no more soul trying than eating and sleeping in a grave-like ditch, deep in slime with the grey rats fighting for your food, and no fire to dry the coarse clothes, dank with rain and sweat that chill your body.

By day these soldiers build up the trench where German shells have torn it, or clear out the mud that has land-slipped into their shallow ditch. By night they lie deep in the dugouts listening to the gun-thunder and feeling the tremble of the earth as it quivers like a living thing under the pounding of the shells. Thus they wait for the new order of battle.

For the fighting goes on in spasms. New guns, new shells, new men must be hurried forward after each battle before a new effort of attack begins. Winter war is a mind-numbing, soul-scarifying, body-breaking trial.

Chaperoned by an officer of the French General Staff, the correspondent could leave the Gare du Nord in Paris at noon, and arrive at the front in time for the five o'clock bombardment.

What a contrast the martial crowd at the railroad station make with the travel crowd of peace days! The harried American and the misunderstood English voyagers have vanished. A swarming assortment of soldiery fill the places of the peace time traveller. Every army of the Entente contribute a sample to this martial mass. On the Amiens special stolid, self-contained English officers pre-empt the choice seats in the waiting trains. Dour Scotch soldiers, their faces brick-red under their "glengarries," and bare knees peeping beneath their swishing kilts, climb in with some khaki-clad chums of the Army Transport Service. A whole train is reserved for a regiment of Belgians bound for Dunkerque. Soldiers from India, Algiers, Morocco, show their swarthy faces in the throng. But by far the greater part of this assemblage wear the horizon blue of France.

The French soldiers give a blue tinge to the mosaic of uniforms. Watching them depart and arrive you realize in the concrete the "before and after" of the trenches. The men of the new class are spick and spotless in azure great-coat and vibrant blue helmet. Their eyes sparkle out of smooth, unwrinkled faces. You almost smell the newness of their boots and accoutrements. The furloughed men make a shabby contrast to their brothers. Sore and stiff, they step from the trains. Mud in thick layers cakes their faded uniforms. Helmets are dull and dented. Sombre eyes stare out from under the visors, above cheeks that are rough and sunken. But recruit or veteran, they all carry an atmosphere of what the French call *fierte*, bold dignity that marks them as men ready for the final sacrifice.

The soldiers are engulfed in the crowd that greets or Godspeed's them. The poignant humanity of that crowd! Held back by wooden-faced *sergeants de ville*, they stand outside the barrier breasting the platform, a sea of white faces and straining eyes.

Those eyes sparkle with tears, tears that break into a joyful shout when father, husband, son is recognised plodding down the platform, soil-stained and grimed, but safe from the trenches. The loved one is smothered in embraces. Hugged, kissed and patted by mother, sister and child, all laughing and crying by turn, he is led off grinning to such a dinner as only a French woman of the country can cook. They are good to their men, these French women.

Beyond the crowd waiting for the men on leave, the pendulum of emotion swings to the other extreme. Here the last sad goodbyes are said by the loved ones. Brave they are, and voluble, filling the departing soldier's haversack with patties, meat pies, cigarettes, and stuffing his great-coat pockets with bottles of wine. The tears are held back, but they burn the fiercer in the swelling hearts that restrain them. There is a boy, his blue eyes a shade deeper than his helmet, being kissed in turn by brother, sister, father, mother. And when they kiss in France, it is no self-conscious salutation to be ended as quickly as possible, but a sacred ceremony of affection, full of lingering emotion. How that mother kissed her boy!

Standing near is another group. A woman, a girl rather, wearing deep black and carrying a child. She is looking with proud yet wistful eyes up into the face of the soldier beside her. He prods his tiny offspring with his forefinger, smiling broadly at its gleeful cries. The whistle blows, the bell rings. Husband and wife crush each other in a long last embrace, the child between them. As the blue-coated soldier hurries away, the girl waves her handkerchief, now damp with tears, and holds the baby aloft while the long train shunts out of the station.

Amiens, before the war, was celebrated for its splendid Gothic cathedral, and as the home of Jules Verne. The cathedral is still undamaged by German shells. As for Jules Verne, if he were alive today, he would sit around reading the submarine reports, saying, "I told you so."

But Amiens hereafter will enjoy a greater claim to fame than it ever did in prewar time days. It was the main base of the British and French Armies in Picardie.

It is difficult to convey the exact meaning of that sentence. Imagine Jersey City crowded with a polyglot military population, its trafficking trucks turned into military motor transports, for a first impression of Amiens. Grey automobiles of all sizes and shapes, from the elephant-like lorry to the mouse-like runabout, scuttle through the streets, engines panting, and horns braying. The horns must be kept pleading incessantly for room from the crowd that fills the street from sidewalk to sidewalk. The motors and the yellow overhead trolley cars plough through the crowd like destroyers through a tossing sea.

The crowd links Amiens to the farthest corners of the earth. No small part of its bustling activity is expended in the purchase, the writing and the mailing of postcards. It is a safe statement that post-card pictures of the Amiens cathedral hold the travel record. They have found their way to Aukland, Sydney, Calcutta, scribbled with a greeting from the front.

Australians in flopping felt hats, New Zealanders hatted in the American army style, and turbaned Pathans are the outstanding elements of the crowd. For at first you only distinguish heads above the multitude. Here the colonials and the Indians seem to tower above their European brothers. Gradually groups of Coldstream Guards, of Fusiliers, of Royal Engineers stand out in the picture, giving it a drab tone. Brushing elbows with these are the azure blue coats of the French. While the dominant colour of the streets is a kaleidoscope of drab and blue, yet there remain in Amiens nearly the whole of the resident citizens, whose dark *habiliments* tone down the colours of war.

The bustle of Amiens rivals that of a bonanza town. And the local shopkeepers have raised all prices to the bonanza town scale. The guide book will tell you that a room in the *Hôtel d'Univers* costs four *francs*, but when you get your bill you are charged twelve. If a battle-weary soldier of epicurean taste comes back from the front with a longing for lobster, he can satisfy that longing for twenty five *francs*, nearly five dollars in American money. It is not only the American who grows rich through the war.

The remarkable feature of the city is that all the business of war is carried on with but little interruption of the routine of civil life. School children, their books packed on their backs, follow the burdened soldiers along the Street of the Three Pebbles. Business men in sombre black hurry to and fro under the press of urgent affairs. Business was never better in Amiens. Clothing stores, drug stores, shoe stores, hat stores, haberdashers, silversmiths, jewellers' shops, and a hundred other varieties of buying and bartering present a picture of a Christmas shopping season.

The war stream passes through the centre of the city. It sweeps through the main arteries of traffic, a rushing symbol of fighting strength. It is a febrile stream. Its waters are never still. The bread, the meat, the drink, the cannon, the powder, the shot, the shells rush through the town like a winter torrent down a mountain. Here is the flood of war.

When you reflect on what this flood of war stuff means, you get some dim understanding of the cost of the world struggle, and its inevitable end. The lands held by the Central powers can be likened to an island, the war strength of the Allies to the sea. And the tide is rising.

If you turn out of the war arteries into some quieter street, you meet one of the grim ironies of war. The magnificent building of the law courts, the *Palais de Justice*, no longer serves as a stage for forensic combat. From its tall, forbidding windows, figures in white dressing gowns are staring. A bandaged head, an arm in a splint, mark these figures as the mildly wounded, wreckage thrown out of the rushing war current.

Beyond this improvised hospital stands the cathedral. With the rumble of distant guns in my ears, I thought of that other beautiful cathedral, and how it had suffered in the war. I had seen Rheims Cathedral under the fire of German guns. I had seen the carvings of the Saviour, the saints, the holy ones smashed into scattered slag. I had seen that other glorious Gothic church blackened and scarified by the scourge of gun fire. Would the vandals repeat their infamy?

To protect against another such outrage the *façade* of the cathedral is covered with a fortress wall of sand bags. All the magnificent carvings, the work of centuries, that decorate the exterior of the church are hidden. Even in the interior, under the high, vaulted, nave, the choir, with its exquisitely carved pews, lies safe from aircraft bombs under a thousand bags of sand.

Before a side altar women kneel. Some are old, with deep wrinkles spreading out from their trembling lips; others are young, yet sorrow speaks from their supplicating eyes. All are gowned in black. They bow before an image of the Christ crucified. The agony shadowed on the carved face of the Christ finds reflection in the faces of the kneeling women. Above them the vaulted roof echoes the booming of far-off cannon-fire. In the streets the war vortex surges and rumbles unceasingly. Can the Saviour hear the whispered prayers of these women?

Amiens lies at the apex of the triangle made by two of the longest and straightest roads in France. Today, (as at time of first publication), these roads carry more traffic than the busiest *boulevards* of Paris. The northern leg of the triangle leads to the British Front; the southern leg runs straight east without twist or turn to the heart of the French army.

All day and all night an unending chain of war traffic shuttles back and forth over these two roads. Trains of grey motor lorries, vaguely resembling the prairie schooner of the pioneer West, clumber one after the other over the rough macadam. The links of the lorry train will be joined by an automobile battery, banging and bumping along the route. Skirting these a speeding staff motor will pass like the wind. All are hurrying under the exigent call of war.

A low winter mist covered the stubble fields of Picardie as I journeyed out to the front. Our motor passed beyond the outskirts of the city the microphone signal station, with its curious instruments like enormous gramophone horns, pointed towards the eastern sky. These were tuned to catch the hum of the aeroplanes, or the menacing whirr of the Zeppelin. Flanking the microphones, two anti-aircraft guns were hidden under a cover of rusty corrugated iron. Passing these, we turned to the main road, and met the greatest handicap of modern war—mud.

The rainwaters had covered the face of the earth, turning it into a thick yellow paste, soft, oozing and slimy. Here the problem confronting the French army was the maintenance of roads. The mud is an enemy more tenacious than the Germans. It is the ally of the enemy. It holds up the trains loaded with shells; it halts the cannon; it delays the plodding regiments of reinforcements. A muddy road may spell defeat to the best planned push. So the French as they have set about methodically conquering the Germans, now set about conquering nature.

It has come to pass that the steamroller is a war weapon second only to the eleven inch gun. I did not count them, but I hazard the guess that one of these steam rollers is busy every mile of the road behind the French front. Beside both gutters of the road, a mountain range of cracked stone is piled. As much care is given to seeing that this supply is never diminished, as is taken in keeping the caissons of shells filled. No matter how rapidly the prisoners, for it is the duty of the German prisoners to be road menders, shovel the rut or puddle full of stone and the roller crushes it into place, the stone piles grow no smaller. A constant stream of carts pass from the quarry, along the whole length of the road, dumping their contents at the call of a road mender. It is an army in itself, the corps of road menders, and their work is second only in importance to that of the fighters in the trenches.

The prisoners, young and stout enough, take to their enforced work sulkily. Perhaps it is the insult of the Moroccan sentry that chafes their spirit. Indeed it must be good for the soul of the proud Prussian Guardsman to find himself herded to his work by a turbaned negro.

The prisoners wear their regular uniforms, which are stamped with a big P. G. (*Prisonnier de Guerre*) and all I saw had overcoats. There is nothing in the appearance of these prisoners to bear out the oft repeated statement that the quality of the German soldier had deteriorated. They were all of good fighting age. They were ruddy cheeked, and bore the appearance of good feeding—though this perhaps is the effect of plentiful French rations.

Coming to a stretch of road where the menders had railed off half of the fairway, our motor was held up just as if it were caught in a jam at Fifth Avenue and Forty-Second Street. A soldier with a whistle and red flag acted as "traffic cop." The up-and-down stream of war stuff followed his signals implicitly. One halted while the other passed, and the whole moved without confusion.

I soon began to see and admire the system that is behind the French army. The whole machinery moved with the speed and swiftness and surety of a high-power dynamo. But what I saw at this time was as nothing to what I was soon to see.

I stopped with my courteous escort, Captain Block-Leroque, at the great shell depot of the Somme front. There are other shell depots, but few equal this in size and the number of shells stored. In this little village over half a million shells of all sizes are hidden.

I doubt if the prewar field artillery of the United States had as many shells, yet this is but the supply depot of an army corps. If the supply were not constantly renewed, every one of those half million shells would be gone at the end of a week. Roughly, the supply is divided into half for the "75" guns, and the other half for heavier batteries. It is not unusual to feed twenty-nine thousand of the "75" mm. missiles to the Germans in a day from this depot. When you have not seen an ammunition depot behind one of these European armies, it is almost impossible to imagine its vastness. If every man, woman and child in Baltimore were given a shell as a souvenir from this one depot, there would remain enough of the yellow projectiles to provide souvenirs for the populace of Alexandria.

In the beginning of this war I confess that I bowed before the fetish of German military organisation. In the American army we were taught that the world had never seen such perfection of system as that developed under the direction of the Great General Staff. One spoke of the supply, subsistence, transport, armament of the German Army, its mobilization plans, as if the development had been the work of geniuses. The mighty fighting machine was the achievement of the vaunted superman. No other nation could hope to approach it.

But under the stern demand of war, France has brought into being a system of transport and armament that surpasses that of Germany. This was borne in on me as I stood overlooking the five sidings leading into the munitions depot. Flat cars shunted in along two of these, each packed with shells as neatly as beer-bottles in their cases. A horde of Madagascar natives, singing as they worked, rattled the shells into the waiting munition trucks so fast that the yellow missiles seemed iron filings flying to a magnet. The first siding handled the heavy shells, the largest, equal in size and something of the shape of a spotlight gas tank. From these giant cases of high explosive, the shells gradually descended in size to the "85" mm. projectile which is somewhat greater in bulk than a Magnum measure. The next spur was jammed with "75" mm. shells, and it seemed that even the most wasteful battery commander would not be able to shoot away ammunition faster than it could be supplied him by the combat trains circling past the siding.

Beyond were other tracks crowded with clothing and subsistence stores, engineering material, hospital supplies, all passing rapidly and in order to their ultimate destination at the front. Cases of hats, coats, shoes, a new trench boot patterned after an Esquimo muck-a-luck, innumerable boxes of rations, a mountain built of barbwire spools and planking, and another of crated first-aid bandages. Of such is the store-house of war.

And the marvel of it all was the smoothness with which it was handled. No yard-master of a dozen years' experience can show a better freight system than the one devised by the French colonel in command of this supply station. Here was a sample of French organisation, and it compared with the best that Germany has perfected. If any added proof was needed to show how the Allies have wrested the superiority in this war from the enemy, it was found behind the lines that sweep the Somme. I found as much method in the labour of war there as I saw in that gigantic labour of peace, the Panama Canal.

As our motor sped away from the basin where the shells lie, I looked back half-wondering what might happen should an enemy aviator drop a bomb into this reservoir of compressed destruction. I could not imagine the hell picture that then would be painted against the western sky.

But up in that western sky swung a score of captive balloons, black sentinels watching over the war base. They were anchored in a great circle around the rim of the basin wherein lay the ammunition depot. Above and among these spheroids some twenty aeroplanes swarmed like a cloud of gnats.

No enemy aviator could hope to cut through this cordon of flying sentinels. At least, not while the, sun shines. In the night there is danger, for then it is difficult for the airmen to distinguish friend from foe. Yet were it all destroyed, it would only mean that the supply departments and the shell factories would have to make up the loss of a week's material. Gauge from this the coefficient of destructiveness of a week's warfare.

With these thoughts running through my mind I sped faster and faster towards the battle front. The rumble of the guns became more and more distinct as the speedometer ticked off the miles our motor covered. The war traffic thickened. We met a mud-stained regiment just from the trenches. The motor slowed and stopped. We were on the edge of the battle ground.

Chapter 6

# The Business of War

Battle is a business problem. The questions of supply and transportation fall naturally into like grooves behind a battle line, or behind the plant of the Steel Corporation. The battle problems of production and distribution baffle the generals as similar difficulties perplex the heads of great commercial organisations. In the United States we have come to know something of this condition through our commercial relations with the fighting nations. But not only is the feeding, the clothing, the moving, the munitioning of an army, business in the strictest sense, but the plan and action of a battle itself is business of the most intensive character.

This conviction was borne in upon me in the office of General Maistre, while that officer explained the work of the French Army in the attacks along the line of the Somme. With the courtesy characteristic of all French officers, the general was making plain to me how his corps, week after week, cut out sections of the area that the Germans occupy in France.

These sections were marked on a map in yellow, red and blue, the different colours representing the work of three succeeding weeks. General Maistre was discussing the assault on Ablaincourt.

> We have, in our attacks, a definite and a contingent objective. These are fixed upon in our general plan, and depend upon the character of the country, the resisting powers of the enemy, and the particular purpose of the attack. The definite objective is limited by what effect our success may have on the enemy, and is an area beyond which we decide it would be dangerous to push, even against a demoralised foe.
>
> It was not necessary for the general to explain why troops could

not charge on indefinitely, driving the enemy before them. Several English battalions had tried this with the result that the German line closed in like water behind them, cutting off all communication with their friends, and thus, what had begun as a brilliant charge ended as an ignominious surrender.

"But," General Maistre continued, "we have found that we have often underestimated our area of contingent advance. Sometimes our front line commanders halt in accordance with orders and watch the German battalions leave a large section unoccupied on our front. Lately we have been increasing the extent of the ground we hope to take in each assault"—the general paused while a smile played around his mouth—"and our hopes have not been disappointed."

"Outside of tactical considerations, general," I asked, "how do you determine how far it is safe to push your attack?"

The officer picked up a photographic print from his table and handed it to me, saying:

"By taking a picture of the country."

I studied the print. At first glance it seemed an illustration for a book on insect life. It looked like a bird's-eye view of a city of ants.

"That is a picture of the country between the French and German trenches. It was taken by one of our aviators two hours ago. There," he said, pointing to what I had mistaken for a column of ants, "are the Germans in their trenches. Here the French. The photograph is taken on the oblique, so as to throw the main features into high relief. If you look closely you can see what the Germans are doing, evacuating some of their wounded. Here," pointing to what looked like an imperfection in the plate or print, a small white splash on the brown ground, "is where one of our heavy calibre shells has just exploded over a German battery."

The eye of the camera had caught the shell just as flame and smoke were clearing. Beneath it I could discern vague outlines of the ant-like figures.

"The aviator who took the photograph flew about fifteen hundred feet above the enemy's guns, and was himself in much danger."

The more I studied the photograph the more plain the different landmarks became. The rectangular outlines of the houses of a village, Ablaincourt, a long straggling building with a tall broken chimney, the Sugar Mill, where a desperate skirmish raged later; long, meandering fretwork lines, where the trenches ran; pits that spotted the print like pock-marks, some with Lilliputian figures hiding in them—the shell holes. The lens had omitted no detail of the ground. Under a magnifying glass the whole country came out as clearly as a plaster relief map.

> After the staff have studied the photographs, and the plan of attack is arranged, these pictures of the landscape are given to the officers commanding the assaulting battalions so that they can familiarize themselves with the ground over which they advance; and know where to expect the chief resistance of the enemy and judge what measures will best overcome this resistance. They take the photographs into battle with them, so that even in the heat of action, they can tell from them exactly where they are, and what positions friends or foe should occupy in their immediate vicinity.

In conclusion the general stated his opinion "that these aerial photographs mark the most valuable development of technical warfare."

The aerial photographer is not only the aid of the infantry, but also of the artillery. When posing the enemy for the purpose of the guns, the air photographer "shoots the piece" as the moving picture operators say, not from the oblique, but from the vertical position. He flies directly over the battery or section of the front that the artillery commander wants to pulverize, points his camera straight below him, and presses the bulb.

The result tells a better story to the artilleryman than the slanting picture. Of course it is the object of the enemy to conceal his battery positions, headquarters, and all other points of crucial military importance. He takes elaborate precautions to accomplish this object. But the lens will often lay bare the site of the most carefully hidden battery.

For instance, should the photograph show four white, semi-regular patches, spreading out in front of a suspiciously dark patch, that would be a sure guide to the station of four enemy guns. The four white patches would indicate the effect on the ground in front of four gun muzzles of repeated firings—the black patch would represent the protective covering of the battery.

For the artilleryman, the prints from the groundwork of maps are drawn carefully to scale, from which he reckons the exact range to any of the enemy fortifications.

This application of photography to the needs of war is only in the first stages of development. It promises to become one of the most fascinating branches of that already fascinating occupation, war-flying.

Nevertheless, the photographic work is but a small incident of the business of battle. It is out of the ordinary and thus interesting. But the results obtained by the photographer would have no value if the routine of war business did not go on in the dull, monotonous way of all routine work. It takes some imagination to think of battles becoming routine, but so they have become, in the trench-grilled fighting zone. Day after day, week after week, month after month, the long trains of bread, beef, shells and powder, limber and load, travel and unload, return and reprovision with time-telling regularity. The old woman living in the little cabin on the Chaulnes road, ten miles east of Amiens, when she sees the first of the crawling *camions*—as the French call the big war motor trucks—reach her gate, knows that it is six o'clock.

The supply of men moves almost as regularly. Battalions march in and out of the trenches, through tour after tour of duty, with only the incident of actual battle to break the monotony. And now at last the recurring orders to advance have been so often repeated they have become a stale story.

Even the appearance of the new Cyclopian cannon, the 20-inch howitzers, hardly disturbed the even dullness of the war business. At least it was so in the war zone. Back of the lines, where the people have more time to talk and speculate on the incidents of war, the debut of these monster pieces was a gala occasion that surpassed the singing of a new opera.

In the clubs and *cafés* of Paris stories went the rounds of how long it took to cast the gun, of the tons of iron required for one barrel, of the marvels of its mounting. Then there were speculations on its power, its graceful construction, and more astounding than all, its comparative lightness. The breach, the bolt, the elevating mechanism, the loading slides all fitted and worked so smoothly that an "infant could operate it."

Much of this gossip was the exaggeration of the untechnical, and was discounted by the serious-minded French officers. Yet when the first of these great howitzers was tested before President Poincaré, it surpassed the claims of its designers.

A group of artillery experts accompanied the President to a certain military camp, where a target had been erected. The target was built as a fortress of reinforced concrete, strengthened with steel rails and plated with battleship armour. The whole was surrounded with a sand-bag barricade. Beneath the fort deep chambers were dug, and these were protected with concrete and steel. Thus a modern fort of the strongest type was built in preparation for the latest trial of strength between the offensive and the defensive, the most powerful shell against the strongest armour.

The new gun, mounted on its broad-bellied flat car, with its long barrel pointing to the North Star, recalled in outline the ancient ichthyosaurus. It was run along a spur leading from the main track and onto an ingenious portable structural iron platform, and groomed for the tryout. The inhabitants within a radius of ten miles were warned to leave doors and windows open during the hours of firing; otherwise they would have heavy glass bills to pay.

The loading crew went through their drill for the last time. The gun pointers checked up his figures on the range and elevation to the ten-mile distant fort, and verified them to the fraction of a degree. When President Poincaré arrived with his staff the captain of the gun gave the command to fire. The shell left the muzzle with a roar like an ice-crack in the Arctic. A distant, dull explosion followed. The officers, with their glasses focused on the fort, saw it burst like a bubble of sand.

President Poincaré and the professional members of the party motored under the arc of the shell trail to the place where the fort had been; for when they reached the site they found little more than a gigantic sand pit. Cement, steel, sand bags were jumbled together in a jagged hole. The subterranean chambers were covered with a sand and cement mulch, made from the walls of the fort. Armoured plates were hurled fifty yards from their original positions. The best protected fortification that modern military engineering could devise had disintegrated under the power of the mightiest shell that modern military genius could produce.

Nothing human can survive the blast of these weapons. Even the troops out of range of the flying missiles are so unstrung by the terrific explosions they cannot be held to their work. These are the weapons that won the Battle of Vaux. Theirs are the mighty voices that opened the battles on the Somme.

The tactics the French staff have devised for the employment of heavy and light artillery in attack, are extremely simple and highly effective. The area of the German line which is to be smothered under the heavy gun fire is blocked out, giving each battery commander a short section on his immediate front to smash. The strongest salients are assigned to the mercies of the 20-inch guns. Other sections of the front are divided among the 15-inch, 13-inch, 11-inch, 9-inch and 6-inch cannon. The first blast of the great howitzers is the signal for the general bombardment. Then every battery opens fire. Shells drop from the sky in a deluge.

It would take a skilful mathematician to calculate the total weight of iron sprayed over a five-mile front. A 13-inch battery of four guns fires sixty tons of metal in one day. (It begins to look as if there would be profit in gathering old iron from the battlefields after the war.) As a rule the heavy bombardments are continued for two days which is time enough, under the incessant rain of shells, to reduce the strongest fortress wall to the status of Swiss cheese.

The enemy usually pursues two courses. First, he brings all his heavy guns to bear on the opposing batteries, and makes the best effort possible to keep down the bombardment. Owing to the present superiority of the French artillery, most of his struggles in this direction are abortive. Then he will withdraw all but the machine gunners and observation pickets from the front line trenches.

It was thought at first that the men who had dug themselves in some thirty feet beneath the soil would be safe, even from the explosions of the 20-inch shells. But if you measure the shell-pit of one of these projectiles you find that it often has a greater depth than the thirty feet formerly considered the limit of penetrability. Often such a giant shell will land fair on the superstructure of a dugout, sealing the men in a living tomb.

But it is not only the killing power of these enormous shells that make them of high military importance, but also the extraordinary demoralizing effect they have on the unfortunate men who come under their fire.

I am of the opinion noise is one of the most trying factors of fighting. This has been my own experience, and I have had it confirmed by many men who have lived day after day under artillery fire.

Even though soldiers are in a safe position, a fortification that lies in a dead angle, for instance, where the formation of the ground makes it impossible for the shells to strike their shelter, yet they find their nerves "turning to water," as one man expressed it to me, after a few hours blasting from the heavy guns.

Thousands of shells go wide of their mark. I have heard it estimated that it takes one hundred shells, regardless of calibre to kill one man. Some of the observers put the figure much higher, and declare that not more than one shell in five hundred makes a kill. For the present there is no method of getting at the facts; so we must be satisfied with the generalisation—thousands miss their mark. Yet while this is true, the paralysing effect of the before-battle bombardment is so great on the whole organisation of the enemy that he can make little or no effort to go to the aid of the battalions in the menaced sectors. When the staff judge that the enemy has been sufficiently pulverised they send an order to slacken the heavy gun fire.

Before the last of the heavy gun detonations have ceased to echo, the light artillery sends a new shell stream through the air. These are not aimed at the points smashed by the big guns, but at the roads and level country four or five hundred yards beyond such points.

Technically, a barrage fire is developed. Which in simple language means that the rain of bursting iron is so constant on all the approaches to the first line positions that no ammunition or reinforcements can be sent forward. This is the moment selected for the infantry to attack. The foot soldiers climb out of their trenches, clamber through the barbed wire and stagger on through the sea of mud and shell-pits till they meet what remains of the enemy.

Then comes the climatic period of the attack, and the ubiquitous flying fighter is once more called into the fray. He takes no photographs now, but gives comfort to his friends and information to his general.

No simile can picture the confusion of troops in contact. Hell has no horrors comparable with the flame and frenzy of the modern battle. In such a scene, friend and foe become inextricably entangled. The wave of fighting tosses, falls, and flounders, strewing soldiers, like storm-whipped wreckage, over the battle ground.

Field telephones are smashed as soon as erected. Messengers are killed as fast as they mount their motorcycles. The commander has no word from his troops. The troops can send no message to the commander. Here and there a handful of reinforcements would turn defeat to victory.

Then it is that the battalion officers leading their men against stubbornly served machine guns are cheered by the sight of friendly aeroplanes. They know that an observer sits at a wireless key in those machines, sending word to the general of their plight. Then it is that the gallant remnants of a brigade that has captured a town from the enemy and lie in it, the target of their own and the enemy's shells, know that word will be flashed to the artillery commanders to elevate the muzzles of their guns. When the troops that have pushed so far forward that they are in danger of capture look to see one of their own aeroplanes circling above them, they greet it with a cheer. They know that reinforcements will soon be marching to their aid.

This manoeuvre of keeping up communication with headquarters during the battle by aeroplane, was invented by the French. It is one of the most dangerous duties yet assigned to the airman. The difficulty of distinguishing friend from foe in the turmoil of battle makes it necessary for the reconnoitring aviator to fly close to the earth. He cannot see distinctly enough to send an intelligent report unless he sails less than a thousand feet above the struggling lines. He is, of course, a target for every available gun, and what is more discouraging, finds himself peppered with a steady stream of enemy machine gun shots. This is a most exasperating experience. It is on record that one aviator so far forgot himself under such a trial that he swooped down within a hundred and fifty feet of a machine gun that had been pestering him, and gave it a belt full from his own *mitrailleuse*.

But these reconnoitring aviators are not supposed to fight. They are watching for the rocket signals of the infantry and must interpret those signals to the chief as rapidly as possible.

Time is one of the vital elements in battle. Owing to this new system of communicating from firing line to headquarters, the general commanding often knows more of what is going on in the battlefield than the brigade and division commanders who are close up to the scene of fighting. The saving of time usually lost in transmitting reports from commander to commander has often meant a mile more front or a thousand more prisoners captured.

The signal aviator not only sends news of the conditions of his own troops, but he also sends reports on the movements of the enemy. Should he sight a column of the foe moving to attack any section of his line, the position and probable strength of that column is immediately clicked off to his chief. When new enemy batteries come into action, he sends word of their number and situation.

In fact, he is a super-scout. He must have all the technical and perceptive training of the cavalry man, be a wireless operator of the highest speed, and, in addition, be an expert airman. Only the elite of the most elite service are selected for the role of reconnoitring flyers.

What is the business of war after a battle has been won and certain sections of the enemy's lines taken? In the words of the military expert, it is consolidation. But a great many different tasks are included in that term. In the first place, the wounded must be evacuated. Both from a humane and a practical point of view this work must be carried out promptly. From the humane side, if a man is sent within eight hours to one of the great hospitals his chances of recovery are much greater than if his transportation is delayed. Men can be taken from a Somme battlefield to Dr. Carrel's hospital, in Compiegne, in that time, and Dr. Carrel will guarantee to cure all except the most hopeless cases.

Delay will mean the difference between life and death sometimes, and often the difference of saving a limb. From the practical point of view, under the enormous wastage of human units in this war, the side which can save the most from their war wreckage will gain on their enemies. The saving of a limb may mean the saving of a fighter for France. Hence the importance of getting the wounded out of the trenches. The sight of the wounded has a demoralizing effect on the other troops. Here is a minor reason for quickly clearing them out of the way.

Be it understood that all this war-work goes on while the foe is attempting to stop it with a smashing fire from rifle, machine gun and cannon. That side of the picture I am leaving to the imagination of my reader. What I am analysing is simply the grind of war.

The assaulting battalions have captured all the points of the pre-determined objective. The foe has been "cleaned" out of his hiding places. The trenches must be held.

Now comes the dire drudgery of war. The man digging a sewer ditch in the city streets works leisurely compared with the soldier throwing up an earth protection in a newly won trench. Picks and shovels are plied with feverish energy. Sand bags are filled and fitted with automatic speed. Men who had thought they were completely exhausted by the shock and struggle of battle call up a new reserve of strength. They spade up the earth as levee builders erecting a dam against the flooding Mississippi.

To this new position the system of supply must thrust out a new feeler. Food, drink, munitions and medicaments must be sent immediately to the part of France the French troops have reconquered. So we complete the circle of the war routine.

This business of war, unlike the business of peace, has for its end—destruction. How thoroughly that object is achieved you see within the radius of the battle.

I have tramped over one of the recently won battlefields between Ablaincourt and Chaulnes. The Germans continue a sullen bombardment of the sector they have lost. The French reply with smashing cending any height from the ground, such as looking out the tenth-story window of a skyscraper. But he never felt the slightest giddiness no matter how high he flew free from the ground. He made no attempt to explain this apparent contradiction in sensations. Such explanation he put up to the psychologists.

They are all the same wild type, Cowdin, Prince, Biglow, McConnell, Rockwell and the rest of the American fliers, and when they are not heroically risking their lives, they amuse themselves to the limit of physical endurance. And their training makes their endurance high standard. Also, youth has its privileges.

Those of us who have passed the period of late adolescence need not be reminded that our nervous centres react more sensitively than when we were in the twenties. It is the hard fact of history that young men are more daring than their elders and this fact rings the whole subject of aerial warfare.

After youth the two predominating characteristics of flying fighters are recklessness and resourcefulness. I search in vain for comparisons that will picture to you the recklessness of the aviator who spins the propeller of his aeroplane at daybreak and sails up into the void of heaven against the slowly rising sun, knowing that his fate may turn on the whim of a wind current, on the jamming of his machine gun mechanism, on a broken rudder wire. For sheer nerve, I used to consider the youth, who, at the country fairs, parachuted from a balloon, to be the ultimate limit. My wonder and admiration for such exhibitions of nerve were mightily swayed by the knowledge that the performer who came down from the heavens swinging from a trapeze supported by an overgrown umbrella received as wage exactly five dollars.

But such temerity, with its reward, sinks beneath notice when gauged against the rashness of the fighting aviator. His risk runs a thousand degrees higher than that of the parachute artist, and his pay as a private in the French Army is five cents per day. Even if he makes but two flights a week, the aviator can claim the minimum wage for the maximum danger.

Strongly allied to his recklessness, if he is to survive, is the flying fighter's quality of resourcefulness. Perhaps it were better to define resourcefulness in this instance as instinct.

No action in an air duel is calm or reasoned. To arrive at a conception of how men's minds act in such a struggle, imagine if you can the mental processes of two fighting hawks. When the birdmen battle,

THE FLYING FIGHTERS
FIVE OF THE FAMOUS ESCADRILLE LAFAYETTE. FROM LEFT TO RIGHT:
LIEUTENANT LUFBERRY, SERGEANT HINKLE, CAPTAIN LELARGE,
SERGEANT BIGLOW, LIEUTENANT THAW.

they swoop, circle, strike, struggle, with the swiftness demanded of all flying things. More is asked of them than that rare virtue of quick thinking. The flying fighter must act on instant, impulsive thinking and his act must always be the right one. In an air duel the prize is life, the penalty death. The Darwinian *dictum*, the fittest shall survive, finds no more conclusive illustration than the air battle.

Having these three qualities, youth, recklessness and resourcefulness, any one may aspire to become a war air-pilot. But even if he have these qualities he cannot hope to command a battleplane until he has completed a gruelling novitiate.

You may have read that one of the tests for flying aspirants is a sudden, unexpected explosion near the victim, such as a revolver shot behind his back, after which his pulse is tested. If the unexpected explosion develops an abnormal blood pressure, the aspirant is passed on to the recruits for the hand grenade squad, where he is slated for such safe work as preceding infantry charges. Here, in his case, the French Government only risks losing a man and a gun, not a perfectly good and valuable aeroplane.

When the candidate has passed the physical tests, he is ordered to the beginners' training ground at Buc, a short distance from Paris. He dons the grey uniform of France, a jaunty aviator's cap and a brassard with a silver wing.

He is ready for his first instruction.

The aviators' training ground at Buc resembles in general outline a race track, but instead of thoroughbreds filling the stalls that surround it, we find aeroplanes. This substitution does not strike you as incongruous, as there is some association between flying machines and race horses. The field is the old testing ground used by M. Bleriot in tuning up aeroplanes of his manufacture. He still uses it for this purpose, though it is under government control, and on one of my visits I witnessed the tryout of a new giant flying machine Bleriot had constructed.

It was built on the general lines of all aircraft, except that it was approximately thrice the size of any machine heretofore constructed. The nacelle could accommodate a crew of seven men and had the appearance of a yacht cabin. The wing spread had been proportionately expanded and four motor engines, each one hundred horsepower, were supposed to lift the giant bird. I write "supposed," for, though I saw the machine thrice tested with motors whirling and crackling at racing speed, the great aeroplane budged not an inch from the ground.

Meanwhile, other aeroplanes quickly leave the ground. Above the flying field all types of aeroplanes are manoeuvring. They hover in the lower sky, sailing and circling in a fashion that reminds one of gulls following a ship. In walking about the field the lowly ground man is under constant apprehension lest there be a collision in the air and the wreckage descend upon him.

The men who guide them are the sixth form aerial scholars. The beginner starts in no such spectacular manner. In order better to conserve the lives of the prospective fliers and the government property—aeroplanes being more valuable than men—the first lessons in flying are given in machines so constructed that their engines cannot lift them more than six feet above the ground. They have all the appearance of a standard aeroplane, an old-fashioned one, but the engine power is limited. The beginner seated in one of these goes buzzing about the field for all the world like a primordial grasshopper.

In this stage he is called a "penguin." Learning the levers and control of his machine is his task. He is kept at this preliminary work until he shows proficiency in handling his hopper and can successfully pass tests contrived to determine his ability to keep his machine straight, to turn, to balance and manipulate the control with dexterity.

Most of the fliers will tell you that this "penguin" state of their education is the most trying. The machines are clumsy, the engines unreliable and accidents are considered a necessary part of the day's work. Yet this first training is the most important in the whole schooling of the aspirant aviator. It is at this time he acquires the instinctive reactions that make for his future success as an aerial pilot. In mastering the awkward gyrations of the "hopper" the novice aviator gets his first inklings of how the "loop the loop" is accomplished.

There are several advancements in the "penguin" stage of flying. The first machine can do nothing but foolishly slip about the field. From this the candidate graduates to a higher power engine, which lifts the machine in jumps of fifty or sixty feet. Finally the fledgling is given an aeroplane capable of circling the whole field at a height of twenty feet. Generally he ends this thrilling experience with an inglorious nose-dive.

That nose-dive impressed upon him the one real difficulty of flying, which, paradoxically, is landing. And it is training in this line that occupies most of the time and attention of the young flier. Judgment, under conditions where his ordinary impressions are of little use to him, must be developed in the aviator. He must learn when to cut off his engine, to estimate the distance from the ground, his speed, when to tip, and all the delicacies of movement which must be combined to make a successful landing.

When the recruit has shown he can handle his machine without sending it to the hospital each trip, he is seated in an aeroplane with a full power engine. As a rule, this is a tried and stable Farnam biplane, guaranteed to be more or less foolproof.

Stepping into this aeroplane for his first flight in the upper regions, the flier experiences an unrecordable variety of sensations. He settles himself in the nacelle, the engine is started and with a clatter of racing propellers the machine hurtles a hundred yards across the field, then mounts in the air.

Instantly life becomes replete with quickening interests. With the first snort of the engine the pulse of the aviator rises as the bubble in a suddenly heated steam gauge. The first stage of the trip, while the wheels below the body bump over the rough surface of the field, recalls automobiling over bad roads, but as soon as the earth falls away below him, the tyro aviator suddenly realizes that never before did he give our good old globe sufficient credit for its steadfast and solid qualities.

Always in the back of his head is the knowledge that he is carrying his life in his own hands. His ear is attuned to the slightest miss in the time of the engines. His nerves feel every quiver of the ailerons. With the levers pulled hard against his breast, he mounts toward the sun.

On his first flight he perhaps touches a thousand feet altitude. In this air strata he circles right and left, cuts a figure eight and executes any other manoeuvre his instructor may have assigned him. He feels he is the brain of some mighty force that obeys the levers as readily as his muscles obey his nerves.

One aviator described his sensations in his first flights as "like a driver seated in a sulky, hitched behind a hundred and fifty galloping horses, pulling with all their might." Also your "sulky" is travelling a thousand feet up in the ether.

But confidence comes as the aviator sees the machine mount, turn, descend, all in answer to his will. One of the American *Escadrille* gives the following rule for all flying: "Never start any movement unless you are prepared to carry it through completely. Indecision in the air tempts death."

After the flier has shown ability to handle his machine around and about the flying ground and when he has successfully accomplished the tests in mounting, planing and landing he is sent off on a triangular cross-country flight, which includes a stop in some distant town. His only guide in this flight is an ordnance map of the region. This flight finished without mishap, the aviator receives his certificate or brevet as an air pilot. As an indication of this honour, he wears two silver wings on his collar points.

But the flying fighter's schooling is far from completed when he has learned to navigate the air. The course at Buc once finished, the aviator goes to Pau, where he is instructed in military flying. Here he learns all the tricks of air fighting. Also he is put through an advanced course of fancy flying, looping the loop, spiral planing and quick ascensions. The technical side of his work is learned at Pau, handling the machine gun, signalling, aerial photography, bomb dropping, until the aviator is sufficiently expert in his art to take his place at the front. As an average, the total course requires six months.

As is always the case, the aviator finds his best instruction in actual experience. When he once arrives at the front he soon becomes familiar with the many uses of the aeroplane in modern war. Here the character of the new birdman is analyzed by his superior officers and he is assigned to one of the four different branches of aerial service.

The daredevils of the air are assigned to the attacking aeroplane squadrons. Their work is to kill or be killed. The risks they take are well known, but they, in France and Germany, get all the glory of their work. Guynemer[3] in France and Boelcke in Germany are the arch types of fighting airmen. The English fliers fight anonymously. Yet they are not outdistanced in this dangerous work. There is a well authenticated rumour of an English schoolboy with forty-five of the enemy as his record. And this after he had been expelled from every school he attended.

Steadier and more level-headed men are picked as infantry aviators. Their work is to watch the infantry attacks and report its development, step by step. They fly low over the lines, often at less than five hundred feet altitude, for it is only when near that they can be sure of the details they report upon. Of course, this brings them into easy range of the enemy anti-aircraft guns. The work of these infantry air scouts is invaluable to the generals in the field, for often the informa-

---

3. *Guynemer: Chevalier of the Air* by Henry Bordeaux & Mary R. Parkman, *Georges Guynemer, Knight of the Air* by Henry Bordeaux & *The Chevalier of Flight: Captain Guynemer* by Mary R. Parkman also published by Leonaur.

tion they obtain can be gathered in no other fashion.

Artillery air scouts work in a similar manner, but the character of the information they send back deals strictly with the field of the artillery. They are "spotters" who sail over the enemy battery positions and cut figure eights in the air above them so as to indicate the range to their own gunners. To do this in a haze of bursting shrapnel requires great nerve.

The newest branch of aerial service is photographic scouting. The results obtained are nothing short of magic. I have seen one of these air photographers leave camp behind the lines on the Somme, fly out over the lines of battle and return with an accurate photograph of the enemy positions, and the time consumed was five minutes short of two hours.

Special cameras are used in this work. And when the prints are ready, maps with the enemy positions indicated are immediately printed and sent out to the various commanders while the battle continues. So far this is the maximum of information efficiency developed in war.

These are the chief duties of the flying fighters. The danger that surrounds them adds a lustre to the service and perhaps one of the most inspiring things in war is the activity of the aviators, whether in camp or in the air.

The chief concern of the airman is his aeroplane. In war this concern is raised to the nth power, for not only would a defect of structure mean certain death, but inferiority in engine power or armament will probably prove equally fatal.

This condition has led to deadly rivalry in the designing and constructing of aeroplanes for war needs. Naturally, machines are being developed in France, England and Germany far faster and more stable than any constructed in the United States.

In France the two types that have given almost complete satisfaction are the Nieuport and the "Spad." The Farman is the most reliable for slow and steady work and is much used in reconnoissance duty, but it cannot develop the speed necessary for attack work. France as the nation that always led in military aviation has many other types of aeroplanes in service, but the ones mentioned are becoming standards.

The two German machines that stand out in war are the Albatross and the Fokker. The latter, because it was fitted with a 160-horsepower engine, for a time dominated the air. The Germans were particularly successful against the English, but under the spur of competition, England has designed a new Sopworth aeroplane which promises, from the results of its first battles, to sweep the air free of the enemy machines.

The engine is the soul of the flying machine.

In the power of the gas engine lies the secret of the success of flying. Europe still leads United States in engine construction, and unless war gives this country the stimulus of competition, we shall fall further and further behind in this vital department of aeronautics. The demand now is for a 200- and a 250-horsepower engine and the French machinists are meeting this demand. The engine designed for American war-planes will also develop 250 horsepower.

Speed is essential, not only because of the advantage it gives in manoeuvring against a slower enemy, but also as a factor of safety against the anti-aircraft guns. An aeroplane travelling at a high rate of speed and varying its course as it flies through the air is a very difficult target. I have seen a French aeroplane circle above the German trenches for a half hour, with the feathery bursts of shrapnel spotting the sky all about it, yet none of the shells touched the machine.

Systems of range finding and aiming are being constantly improved, however, and the plan of mounting anti-aircraft guns on automobile trucks and operating these trucks over triangulated country where range bases are quickly found makes the work of the flying fighter more and more dangerous.

Air fighting is the newest branch of war. No one can foresee to what extent this service will be expanded in the future. It is not impossible that in time air fleets numbering thousands of aeroplanes will meet to decide the fate of nations. That is the dream of the coming age.

What is essentially important at this time is that the United States should achieve a position in this department of the art of war equal to that of any of the other great powers. General Pershing, out of his discouraging experience on the Mexican border, is reported to have said that he would rather have one aeroplane for reconnoissance duty than a squadron of cavalry.

Can there be any higher recommendation for the flying fighters?

CHAPTER 8

# Thoughts on Shrapnel and Tanks

When the philosophy of war is at last made clear to finite minds, and the killing passion is purged from the earth, some social economist will calculate and reveal the material value of the energy lost through battle industry. But no research philosophical will make known to the world the moral stamina which battle industry begets.

Should you inspect one of the munitions factories of France you would be convinced that the energy there engendered has a moral value. Something haunting in the eyes of the girls bending over the brass fuses, something defiant in the poise of a puddler grappling with a molten shell case, bespeaks in the breasts of the munition workers, souls burning at white heat.

Yet, you reflect with dismay, as you pause on the threshold of the munitions plant—breathing the smoke-laden air, blinking at suddenly opened furnace doors, deafened by the harsh, grinding song of high-speed machinery—all this energy spells death. And once again you ask why? . . .

The Renault automobile works at Billancourt, near Paris, has been reorganised into a munitions- making plant and when you approach the acres of red-brick buildings that house the industry, you realize the reason for the coal shortage in France. Coal carts follow one after the other for a mile along the road leading to the furnaces. And the sight of this unending line of coal carts is one of the most impressive and concrete examples of the wastage of war.

The effect of this wastage is more poignantly brought home to you if you cannot buy in the open market an ounce of coal for your own cooking and heating needs. At every step I took through this munitions factory I felt the heat of a blazing furnace, yet back in my apartment in the Rue de la Pompe, with the thermometer registering freezing weather, my children huddled around a feeble gas-log fire, while the cook complained loudly that gold could not purchase its equivalent weight in coal. Here it stood heaped in mountains.

As a complementary reflection on war wastage, in going through the Renault Works you remember that the manufacture of automobiles is constructive labour, the making of something for service, something built to endure, something that symbolised an advance in living; while the manufacture of shells, the work that has displaced automobile making, is destructive labour, creating something that disappeared into powder and fragments and symbolised an advance in dying.

With such thoughts I followed the process of shell making from the pig iron stage to the final painting and polishing of the finished projectile.

In a yard flanking the coal bins, the steel bars which form the raw material of the shells, are stacked. One by one these bars, a little greater in breadth, thickness and length than a section of ordinary railroad rail, disappear into a rough shack from which issues at regular intervals a mysterious bumping sound. The shack houses the cold-steel cutter and the sound proclaims it at work. It is a brutal machine made of a ton of cubed metal set atop of a marvellously tempered steel blade. The bar is carefully run beneath the suspended blade and its ton weight backing, a lever is touched, the metal drops, and from the end of the rail is guillotined an ingot of cold, raw-steel. These shell ingots are about the size and thickness of the silver ingots sometimes seen outside the Sub-Treasury Building in New York.

When you enter the plant to follow the careers of the shell sections, it is as if you suddenly opened a door into hell. A noise blast smites your ears as you enter, filling them with a harsh, discordant din, till your tympanic membrane seems a tight-drawn drum-cover upon which a hundred imps beat the devil's tattoo.

I tried to analyse the clangour. To me it seemed made up of the component noises of a boiler factory and a planing mill, supplemented by the chorus of fifty compressed air drills snapping like machine guns. The upper space of the domed factory building twanged with a resonance that beat back in waves from the roof. Below this was a middle *strata* of sound—a sort of giant pulse-beat that jarred the walls as if some mighty unseen power at regular intervals lifted the plant a little and dropped it with muffled thud. The lower *strata* of the factory was filled with a multisonous racket, the clank of steel on steel, the rumble of rolling iron, the sharp hissing of steam, the roar of the forced draught furnace, through which the unending whine of whirring lathes penetrated like a storm sound.

The human voice was lost. My guide shouted a warning in my ear as two red hot steel cones tumbled out from a furnace at my feet. The words came as a whisper. He tried to describe the process of shell making but his sentences were drowned in the din.

And gnome-like men slaved amid this noise. Smut-stained and grimed, they fed the furnaces, grappled with white-hot cylinders of steel, plunged the stamps into the burning iron, toiling amid the fire glare and spark shower, tireless fiends.

One of these toilers, because of the feverish energy of his efforts, I mentally christened the demon. Lithe and small in stature, his muscles coiled and uncoiled as he worked like those of a lightweight boxer. Soot and sweat covered his pale face shadowed under long black hair. But his eyes imprisoned sparks from the blazing coals he faced, while he plunged long pincers into the opening of the furnace, nipped their fangs into a cube of blue-white steel, dragged it forth, and with one careless motion, threw it twenty yards to the waiting press. He was the satanic spirit of war.

The cube of smoking steel rolled with vicious hissing over the stone floor, was caught up by another smutched worker who slipped it into the cup of the stamp. It snarled a protest at its impending fate; flaming sparks shot off at the men forcing it in place. Almost without warning, the three hundred and seventy ton stamp was loosed above the sizzling metal. Down came the plunger at express train speed crushing out the blazing heart of the shell.

When the great weight of the stamp shot up again, the lambent steel cube was hollowed like a flowerpot. It was pincered out of the stamp, then sent on its way to the cooling bath from whence it progressed to the lathes.

I turned off from the trail of the shell to watch the women making the death missiles destined to fill it. The casting of shrapnel seems a fascinating game; just the sort of pastime I should recommend for an up-to-date kindergarten.

The game begins with a pouring of molten lead into wooden moulds much like the moulds used in large hotels for stamping butter pats. The girls showed keen enjoyment in this process and scrutinised each bunch of balls as it loosened from the mould in satisfied appreciation of their own artistry. At this stage of manufacture, shrapnel looks like a cluster of silver grapes. The cluster is slipped through an automatic cutting machine that trims stem and branch from the grapes and shoots them out into receiving pails. The trimmings are sent back to be remoulded, while the round, leaden shots are now passed on to other women who sift and size them.

It so happened that I had spent the morning of my visit to the munitions factory with a wounded friend in the American Ambulance hospital, so the thought of the contrast of women's war work came sharply to mind. Could one ever find an example more naked of war's inconsistency? I watched the women running their lead-stained fingers over the shot destined to bring such cruel hurt to men, seeing in the eye of my mind the work of other women's fingers; the nurses tending the wound for which these lead-stained hands would in measure be guilty.

"We have four thousand women working here," said my guide as he led me into the lathe room. "In their lines of work, they are more skilful than men."

My only mental association for the lathe room was the loom room of a cotton spinning plant I once visited. Here were the same speeding belts, the same buzzing machinery, the same automatic clink and clank of metal and the same long ranks of women with eyes focussed on the whirring bars. But the grinding of the shells gave off a sinister note far different from the song of the shuttle. Already the shells shrilled the warning they would give when shot from the cannon's mouth.

After the polishing process, the shell journeyed on to the testing table where women dropped minute electric lamps within the case while the glistening steel was searched for flaws; others measured the shell within and without, and especial care was given to the weave of the thread where the fuse fitted.

Fuses were made in the upper storey of the munitions plant and here the women worked with the skill of trained clock makers. Cap, ignition needle, stirrup springs, all the delicate parts of the time fuse passed rapidly through the hands of these women, each charged with one part of the total work. At the table at the end of the line laboured the girl with the detonators.

She was dressed in deep mourning. Wrinkles came and went at the corners of her eyes as she worked. Yet she was not old, not more than twenty. A cheap, woman's watch hung on a peg before her eyes. She seemed to count the seconds as her fingers sped through the motions of fitting the exploding contrivance that would give the spark of life

THE REVENGE OF THE WIDOWS
FULLY EIGHTY PER CENT OF THE WOMEN EMPLOYED IN FRENCH MUNITION FACTORIES WEAR BLACK FOR HUSBANDS, FATHERS OR BROTHERS KILLED BY THE GERMANS.

to the shell. She gave off an atmosphere of feverish haste in her work, and watching her thin lips move as she counted the finished fuses, I wondered if it were brother or father she mourned and what tempered her thoughts as she toiled?

The eyes of this girl haunted me as my guide led me down to the ground floor of the factory again and into a carefully guarded wing of the plant.

"Now," he said, "you are to be initiated into the mysteries of the making of a tank!"

A distant and furtive view of a tank in action I was to have later, but that picture was not more interesting than the sight of a tank growing from raw steel and rivets to armoured completeness.

The tank was born in weirdly befitting surroundings. The clangour that filled the Renault factory was the correct accompaniment while the blast furnace flare and charcoal smoke gave the appropriate atmosphere. Vulcan himself would have approved the setting for the ceremony.

Two solid, squared rails of black steel formed the keel and keelson of the land battleship. Axles, to support the petalled wheels, branched from the keel forward and aft. Beneath the wheels stretched a jointed tractor chain. The ribs of the tank were formed of thick angles of pressed steel and the vertebrae were made up of sections of the same sort of metal, reinforced and riveted at the joints.

Slabs of armour plate stood ready to be moulded into the hull,—a curtain of these plates will hide the wheels which were exposed in the first tanks,—leaving no vulnerable joint in the armour of the land ship.

Here rose the miniature conning towers; the rudder wheels, leaned against the tail shaft; the engine, a tangled mass of pipes and pistons was already placed. You marvelled that such a small bit of mechanism could serve to move the mass, yet it was the heart of the machine, another triumph for gas engine.

It is the combination of the riveted beams, flower-shaped wheels, snake-like chain and curious tail appendage that prevents the ordinary mind from assimilating the fact of the tank.

But once let your fancy play around tank possibilities and your bran will spin out adventures that are the envy of the imaginative author. Why not a fleet of tanks? Why not land battleships cruising across country. This possibility is but a higher problem of weights, stains, stresses and engine power. Here is a new vision of warfare.

What makes such a vision seem but a glimpse of the future is the fact that the tank is designed on the same lines as a war vessel. There is the conning tower, the ports, the superstructure, where the captain of the tank takes command; the speaking tubes, gongs and the usual means of communication between a warship's bridge and engine room. And the engine chamber of the tank is a marine engine room in miniature.

Yet, when all is said, these land battleships are but the development of the armoured motor. During different periods of the war I saw the work of armoured motor cars, and though confined to the limits of good roads, they proved valuable war engines. They possessed two of the essential requisites of offence; mobility and killing power, but their mobility was greatly limited once trench lines were drawn across Europe.

The machine gun is directly responsible for the evolution of the tank in its present form. Some contrivance had to be discovered that would offset the effect of the death-streaming guns and as the value of the caterpillar wheel had been proved in moving heavy artillery, it was natural that this improvement should be applied to armoured motors.

But the problem of the cross-country fighting motor was complicated by the fact of balance. A battlefield is about as rough a bit of cross-country going as man and nature can produce. To the usual difficulties of the terrain, soldiers have added various ingenious barriers, grouped in the military books under the general title "obstacles," which includes anything from a simple barb wire fence to a ditch lined with sharp pointed stakes. Mine craters and shell pits are incidental obstructions. And the problem of balance meant providing a machine that would crawl up and down such holes in the earth.

The balance difficulty was solved by giving the tank its over-hanging bow and long double-wheeled tail shaft. With this design the tank can push its nose over and through all the ordinary and most of the extraordinary obstacles in its path. The weight of the machine, the driving power of the engine, combined with the caterpillar wheels, make short work of wire entanglements, stone walls and even the debris of destroyed villages.

The meanest obstruction in the path of the tank is the tree stump. Climbing one of these, the tank is literally and figuratively "up a stump." It is in the unhappy predicament of a turtle balanced on a pole. With wheel base lifted off the ground, "caterpillars" and clanking chains whirl through space in futile fashion. Lifted evenly, the wheels get no purchase or as is usually the case, if one set of wheels scrape the soil, the tank churns in a circle, a limping merry-go-round. While these gyrations are distinctly disturbing to the crew within the tank, they furnish the soldiers assembled without with much amusement.

Tank designers had to sacrifice speed to power, in order to overcome obstructions and this is the chief weakness of the contrivance. It is too slow. It cannot keep pace with a line of charging soldiers and if sent out alone, it draws the concentrated fire of the enemy's machine guns and trench artillery, running the risk of quickly being put out of action. The armour of the tank can turn small arms bullets but a well-aimed shell will smash it. Therefore the enemy must not be allowed to fire as he pleases at the tank, so the work of the supporting infantry is to spoil the enemy's aim with heavy counter fire. Thus the tank and the foot-soldier operate together so the pace of the machine must equal that of infantry advancing.

The tank marks an epoch in tactics. It is the symbol of the change from man war to mechanic war. It is no freak design but a development of permanent military value. We soon may look for a Dreadnaught tank, a land ship wherein the fighting crews will make their home. They will be perhaps better described as self-contained, movable forts, carrying ammunition, gasoline, food and water sufficient for week-long independent operations. This super-tank will break the deadlock of trench fighting.

The development of the tank is the logical outcome of the hardest problem of war, the protection of the soldier. To carry on war with the vigour shown on the British front beyond the Somme, or on the French front at Verdun, if continued indefinitely would mean the eventual extermination of the male population. What with the tremendous improvement in modern arms and the terrible destructiveness of the great guns used in every day battles, casualties in war have gone beyond all safe percentages. Too many men are lost for the result obtained. Warfare today is an interminable pitched battle. Men are thrown without stint into the whirlpool of death with little tangible result. To save mankind, this abnormal condition must be remedied, and the first remedy is to provide the soldier with some protection while he fights. Such is the purpose of the tank.[1]

I left the hive of war industry a prey to complicated feelings. It was bitter to reflect that all the thought, the work, the feeling concentrated in the murky atmosphere of the munitions plant centred around

---

1. *Tanks 1914-1918, The Development of Allied Tanks and Armoured Warfare During the Great War* by Albert G. Stern, and *With the Tanks* by Richard Haigh & J. C. MacIntosh, two first-hand accounts of British tanks & tank-men at war in Europe during the First World War, *Life in a Tank* by Richard Haigh & *Men and Tanks* by J. C. MacIntosh are also published by Leonaur.

death. And death in its most frightful guise. Think of the brain work alone represented in a single combination high explosive shell. Take its modern successive stages of evolution from the time Lieutenant Shrapnel, R.A., designed his original man-killing shell in 1784 down to the highly complicated bit of mechanism turned out by the millions today, and calculate the mental energy put into this production. Think of the research in physics, chemistry, ballistics, and the countless thousands of folios of mathematical computations all used up in the creating of a death missile. Then dispute if you can the dogma that man is but a higher order of ant.

CHAPTER 9

# Who Pays for the War?

Upon whose shoulders does the burden of the cost of war fall? This question today is of high importance to the people of the United States and perhaps from a study of the results of commercial re-adjustments, industrial revolutions and financial fevers in France, Americans may arrive at some understanding of what the future will bring in the way of changes to the household budget.

Plunging at once into the curious social and commercial changes effected in France let me quote the owner of one of the largest retail dry-goods stores in Paris, a store once blazoned as "cheap" throughout the business circles of the city. The "*Marchetaine*" numbers its customers among the working classes of Paris; families outfitted in the shop for three generations. The women who do the family buying conduct it on scientific bargaining principles, and are known personally to the heads of the departments of this great store. However, the idea of catering only to the cheap trade has made Monsieur Port one of the richest merchants of Paris. His boast has been that he has never displayed a dress beyond the purse of a working woman, nor an overcoat a working man could not buy.

One morning Paris awoke to find the windows of the "*Marchetaine*" dressed with fifty dollar cloaks, one hundred dollar furs, and festooned with laces and lingerie. Luxury was also expressed in men's fur-lined overcoats, in children's embroidered dresses, and all the other samples carried price tags on the same high scale. At the French business man's lunch which lasts from twelve to two, a friend demanded an explanation for this change of policy.

"I have not changed," replied Monsieur Port, "nor have I changed my customers—it is the customers who have changed. Many of them are artisans and mechanics, men who own little carpentering shops, who are wagon-makers, wheelwrights, iron-workers, tinsmiths, blacksmiths, tool-makers, coopers, brass-fitters. Their wives are the hard-fisted, hoarding kind that met poverty with arms *akimbo*. But that was before the war. Today my customers are war-wealthy. Some have lathes that never stop whirling shell cases, others are busy fifteen hours each day constructing fuses, still others are making more wheels, wagons, and uncatalogued quantities of ironmongery, from horseshoes to machine gun shields. This they have been doing with French industry, while their wives have been saving the profits, until now they find themselves rich beyond the similes of a fairy tale.

Like good citizens they have subscribed to the war loan, and find themselves *rentiers*, living on income, something they never dreamed of. Still the money comes flowing in. It comes so fast that even these thrifty souls find themselves yielding to the temptation of luxury. The women, who keep the bank book, verify fabulous balance sheets until the possibility of the velvet dress,—a life's ambition,—becomes a reality. Some aim higher, at furs, laces and silken under-things, beyond which the imagination cannot soar."

"But," interjected the friend, "all that you say may be true, yet why don't your customers go to the shops long known as *Magazins du Luxe*, the stores of quality and high prices? Why don't they leave you for the Rue de la Paix?"

"My friend," smiled Monsieur Port, "they do not go to such stores because of the French fear of being cheated. My people, excuse me, my customers, trust me. They know I give the best of its kind for the price. They are clever enough to understand that in articles of luxury, there is large latitude in price between the real thing and the not-so-real thing, yet these customers of mine know they cannot distinguish between the real and the not-so-real. They come to the heads of my departments confessing their sins of temptation, their fears of being cheated and demand the protection due old customers." Monsieur Port paused, lit a cigar that costs the equivalent of a dollar at the present rate of exchange, blew out a contemplative cloud of smoke.

"The rest," he concluded, "is business."

Here is a class that does not pay for the war. It includes in general terms artisans and skilled mechanics, men whose labour is in high demand in the manufacture and repair of war material.

Let me give another example. Just off one of the great thoroughfares is a small boot-and-shoemaker's shop. Monsieur Bottine in pre-war days managed to make both ends meet in the back of that shop, but he was seldom more than one pair of shoes ahead of the wolf. His capital consisted of a few pairs of show window boots, some leather and the lasts of twenty-seven customers. Among said customers was an English Guard's officer, formerly military *attaché* in Paris.

That is the plot of the piece. It is not necessary to tell how other British officers, finding how good and cheap were the boots of Monsieur Bottine, left their tracks in the little shop just off the great thoroughfare. When the gossip spread through the smart French regiments "the Guards get their boots at Bottines's" an invasion of the boot shop followed. Since in the nature of things boots wear rapidly in the trenches, the profits of Monsieur Bottine have mounted to the skies.

Alas, he finds himself in an uncomfortable quandary at the moment. The French Government exerts a watchful solicitude over the affairs of its citizens in time of warfare, and apportions extraordinary taxes among those who are making undue profits out of an abnormal market. Monsieur Bottine found in his morning's mail one day an official paper wherein he was requested to report the amount of "the exceptional and supplementary profits" from his business since the first of August, 1914, to date. Furthermore, he will then forward a check for fifty *per cent*, of this amount to the Treasury Department as his *contribution extraordinaire* in war taxes. What worries Monsieur Bottine is that the profits are to be calculated above six *per centum* allowed on original capital. As his original capital was nil, he finds that he has to split fifty-fifty with the Treasury. All is not gold that is war profit. Still, the wolf that used to hang around the back door of the little shoemaker's shop is dead, his hide tanned and made up into "pig skin" *puttees*.

We will leave the world of trade for a moment to discover if the *rentier*—the man of independent fortune, living on income and not actively engaged in business—pays for the war. Remember, I am discussing this subject from the coldblooded monetary point of view. Do not think that I fail to give my French friends credit for the heartbreaking sacrifices they are making every day on the battlefields. There are no tables that can sum up the misery, the sorrow and desolation this war has brought to French fathers, mothers, wives and daughters. The people of France have my deepest sympathy.

The Marquis de Belletone's property is situated in Paris and Brittany, and the bulk of his fortune is secure in gilt-edged French and American stocks and bonds. When he was in Paris on leave he is a lieutenant of heavy artillery—we lunched together, and at the propitious moment I put my question on how the war affected him personally.

"I never felt better in my life." He looked it. His eyes were clear and his cheeks russet red. In his light blue uniform with scarlet trimmings he was as slick as a decalcomania.

"I see that—but how about your finances?"

His fingers played around the stem of the four-*franc* glass of Port he was sipping. He waited a moment before answering.

"Well, to tell the truth, my income hasn't been damaged by the war. As a fact, I have more actual cash today than at any time before the fighting."

Here was a curious admission, for the name of the *marquise*, his wife, leads all the charity lists, and she has a battalion of "godsons"—men to whom she sends monthly "goodies boxes"—in the trenches. The explanation was not long in forthcoming.

"When war broke, I turned my five automobiles over to the general staff; my chauffeurs and washers were automatically absorbed into the army. At once my heaviest upkeep account dropped from my balance sheet. I did not think about this at the time, for as you know, we in France were too occupied to pay attention to such matters three years ago. But the first of January has been around three times since, so I have had three chances for taking stock. Each year I am surprised how the expense column has shrunk. Yet it is natural.

"First, nearly all our menservants were mobilised. That meant a cut. (Of course, *Madame*, my wife, carries them on her roster of *filliuls* but this liability is properly listed under charities.) Automatically the expenses of my *château* in Brittany fell. My wife only opens it for a short time in the summer when she and the children go for a holiday. No more house parties, no more dinners, dances, motor tours, and all the other amusements that make up French country life. In Paris it is the same. My wife is in half mourning, many of her friends, alas, are in deep mourning, so the social expenses dropped to nothing. Outside of my wife's room and the fourteen servants' rooms, the house on the Avenue du Bois is closed. She keeps the servants' quarters open as a sort of soldiers' boarding-house, where her 'godsons' lodge when they are in Paris on leave. Believe me those boys can eat—and drink."

A good natured smile spread to the corners of this French aristocrat's eyes.

"But it's coming to them, *les enfants*" he added.

"Let me see, the next heavy saving in upkeep appears in *Madame's* furrier's and dress-maker's account. The former is cut one hundred *per cent.*, and the latter fully eighty *per cent.*, which makes Monsieur Worth cry in his scented beard. All of this saving my wife puts into her war work. My own tailor's bill is the price of my uniforms. Yet my English tailor is not so downcast as one would expect. When I last saw him, he told me his London shop received ninety-two orders from the United States in one mail. Also he has made all the officers' breeches for my regiment as well as the Sixth Dragoons."

The *marquis* was not wasting much sympathy on his tailor.

"But to go on with my own budget, if you deduct the super-expenses of our winter trips to Italy, Switzerland or the Riviera, that about closes the retrenchment record."

"How about your income, has that been affected seriously?"

My friend hesitated.

"I am ashamed to admit that it grows. All our American stocks are booming. My own particular French industrial stocks pay regular dividends. I have bought blocks of our War Loan from the first, but I get good interest on my investment. So, as I have cut my fixed expenses over fifty *per cent.*, when I get my yearly statements from my bankers each January I find my credit balance growing. Which is surprising, as my wife spends a good sum, a rather generous sum, on her charities."

The case of the Marquis de Belletone is typical of the adjustments put into practice since the opening of the war by the wealthier French class. The result can be thus summarised: Expenses in all the large homes have been much reduced, economy is the fashion, incomes have suffered only slight, if any, reduction. This condition has produced a saving on the credit side of the yearly balance sheets, one half of which goes to charity, and the other half to subscriptions for War Loan stock. The last item is both patriotic and practical, it helps the government while it increases the individual capital account.

Certain exceptions fall outside of this summary of the average. Yet as far as chaotic conditions permit investigation, the exceptions counterbalance. Those whose fortunes were grounded in the industries of the invaded provinces have lost all. On the other hand, the wealthy families who hold stock of the Creusot-Schnieder Arms Company, Bleriot Aeroplane stock, Renault Automobile stock, shares which Wall Street labels "War Babies," have acquired the touch of Midas.

The fact that stands out as sharply defined as a red golf ball on the snow, is, despite the war, the rich grow richer.

Luckily the greater number of the wealthier citizens of France recognize the responsibility of their stewardship and share what has come to them through war with their less fortunate fellows. The generosity of the rich has been lavish. They give money freely, not at all in the spirit of charity, but as a matter of duty. France as a country has been attacked. All her citizens rally to her aid and such aid does not mean simply shouldering a musket and marching to the trenches. It means putting forth every effort to help less fortunate brothers of the same great family. This is the word that accurately describes the French people. They are one big, good natured, considerate family. Ties of kinship are strong in France and in a crisis the ties of blood tighten the ties of nationality. In the face of the calamity that threatens the nation, a closer relationship has sprung up in all ranks of society. As the French above all are a practical race, they translate their sympathetic impulses into good deeds. When the Countess du Valle gives an expensive artificial leg to a poor soldier who otherwise would hobble through life on an unsightly and unscientific peg-leg, she only does her duty to the family of France.

Human nature, in all countries has its unlovely sides, and it does not detract from what I have written when I add that among the rich there are a few insignificant exceptions to the general rule. The experience which I now recount simply shows the supreme selfishness of certain individuals.

Monsieur Tableaux has for forty years been a dealer in antiques. His shop at no great distance from the Place Vendome is filled with rare *objets de vertu* artistically arranged in glass cabinets. On the walls hang paintings; authentic old masters, and some fine modern canvases, Bouguereau, Corot and Whistler.

"Of course, the war has killed your business," was perhaps a blunt way of putting the question to a vendor of things aesthetic.

Monsieur Tableaux placed the tips of his long artistic fingers together and after a slight hesitation answered:

"The war has made little difference to me. Art always has its market. I have sold more this year than I have since the year of the Exposition."

"To war-rich Americans?" I suggested, knowing that Monsieur Tableaux had a large and rich clientele in the United States.

The hesitation of the dealer in antiques became positive diffidence. Finally he responded:

"No, to my own compatriots."

Here was food for thought. . . .

The problem of finding out who pays for the war was beginning to reduce itself to a process of elimination. Pursuing this process, let us turn to the bankers. The tactful concealment of facts is the rigid canon of banking. Yet under the law banks must draw up and publish periodic statements of their financial condition. But in time of war, it is a principle of political strategy to misinform your foe upon the status of your finances. So we need not take the banker's word for the business of the bank. We may, if we wish, be sceptical of published figures showing increased deposits. It is just possible these statements might be "fudged." But there are certain outward and visible signs which even to the layman of rudimentary powers of observation mean increased business.

Before the outbreak of the war, a certain banking company, which owns one of the largest quadrilateral office buildings in the money zone of New York, decided to wind up and close its Paris branch. War then postponed all proceedings. Suddenly after the days of chaos that ended with the Battle of the Marne, the business of this bank revived. As water loosened from the snow line by a spring thaw, the stream of depositors began to flow through its doors. The closing date is indefinitely postponed. More, the original office force has been doubled within the last year.

The smiling American manager will tell you "business is booming." Why? People are saving money. He speaks truly. Not that all the money saved goes into the banks, there are still a few primitive patriarchs in France who bed their coin down in the family mattress, but it is fair to infer that eighty *per cent*, of the cash put by because of war conditions, eventually finds it way into the hands of the bankers.

Turning to a Simon-pure Allied Bank, the outward and visible results can be simply stated and causes as simply deduced. This bank was born in England and baptised with one of the most famous Trade names in the world. Despite these happy auspices, the infant did not thrive in France. It was housed in small and shabby offices, and were it not for its famous name, would long ago have sunk in the financial sea. But with the coming of war, conditions changed. The small and shabby offices have been abandoned. The famous name is now gilded across the ground floor of the finest and most centrally situated building in Paris, and the bank can pay a yearly rent of 360,000 *francs*, and make money for its stockholders.

If the volume of business done by stranger and allied banking houses has increased in this remarkable degree, how can an estimate be made of the increased activities of the purely French banks? Keep in mind the fact that the government has impressed upon the people the vital importance of fighting the foe both in the field of battle and in the field of finance. "Pour out your gold for the defeat of the enemy." This phrase printed on a striking poster—a great golden "Louis,"—the French piece that corresponds to our American Eagle, crushing a German soldier to earth—greets your eye from the window of every bank in Paris.

To this appeal the people have answered by flooding the Treasury with rivers of gold. The symbolism of the poster crystallised the patriotic impulses of the non-fighting Frenchman and woman. They saw their gold coins overflowing the enemy. While their sons poured out blood to crush the invader, in the same cause the fathers poured out gold. Today, when no extraordinary effort is made to collect this gold, at the Bank of France over two million dollars in coin was exchanged for paper during one week. In a short time every *louis d'or* in France will be mobilised to fight the foe.

To get a general mental view of how this war helps the banks in France, let us analyse briefly national financial and trade operations in the bulk. The French Government has become an unlimited borrower and buyer. It borrows at home or abroad, from the individual or the institution, anywhere it can get the cash. Also, it buys wherever it can procure the wartime commodities. But in this matter of buying, when the government goes into the foreign market it pays with gold. When it buys at home, it pays with paper. Under these conditions the financial primer explains the advantage of buying in the home markets. Certain raw products must be purchased abroad. Let the gold be saved for such disbursements. But whenever an order can be placed at home, place it, and pay in paper. The tyro in finance sees the reason.

Governmental buying has reached the sizable figure of seventy-two billion *francs*, about twelve billion dollars, and a large proportion of this sum is distributed among the citizens of the country. Under this incentive hundreds of business organisations have accommodated themselves to war demands. Certain industries, essentially French, have expanded enormously under the impulse of supplying fighting material. Of these the more obvious are gun casting, shell making, and the construction of aeroplanes. The business done in these particular industries remain military secrets, but that the length of their pay rolls now compares with the height of their factory chimneys is no secret.

Labourers, skilled and unskilled, men and women, are earning more and saving more than was possible in pre-war days. The price of living varies in different parts of the country, but for an average we can say that it has gone up sixty *per cent*. To offset this, the wage earned in all the industrial institutions that have been accommodated to war-work, has increased, one hundred, and in some cases, two hundred *per cent*. At the lowest figure, here is a net gain of forty *per cent*. The thrift of the French is the subject of proverb.

To understand the origin of the habit of saving, which verges upon parsimony, you must remember that the well-educated and well-paid French working-man of today, (as at time of first publication), is only four generations removed from the pauper whom starvation drove to the Revolution and its consequences. Money is never "easy" in France. And in acquiring it no substitute for work of the hardest kind has yet been discovered.

That old saying that *some are so tight-fisted that they grip a dollar till the eagle screams,* would apply generally in France if you substituted dime for dollar. The war has accentuated this national characteristic. Figure the result of this ingrained thrift upon workers who earn more per hour, and are employed more hours than any previous industrial statistic tables can show. Your conclusion will be that the working-man is not paying for the war.

From the worker it is natural to continue the search among the butchers, bakers and grocers. A bare glance at any market place gives a picture of brisk business. French women with corpulent baskets and fish-net carry-alls besiege the stalls. From their clamour it is clear they bargain bitterly and denounce the climbing prices of food. But still they buy until the basket lids barely close and the fish nets seine a mess of cabbages, cauliflowers, chops and the incidental dinner catch. If the market-baskets overflow, one may be sure that the till of each butcher, baker and grocer qualifies under the same adjective.

Here in Paris I live around the corner from the Rue Bellefort, the chief marketing street for the quarter. Butcher Grasse, ruddy and robust despite his fifty years, does rush-hour business from six a. m. to six p. m., the five meat selling days of the week. There are two other *bucheries* farther down the long street, but Paul Theobald and Jean Dufour are in the trenches, so their shops are closed. Madame Dufour tried to carry on her husband's business, but she could not make it go. She missed Jean's good right arm.

Luckily women can carry on a grocery business, in a way. But some of the tricks of the trade are unknown to them so the "big business" victuallers find the lines of their customers lengthening every day. Felix Rotin, the Park and Tilford of Paris, with half a thousand grocery stores and wholesale purchases, has the inside track in the race with all his competitors. Your prunes, *patés* and potatoes cost four cents a kilo less at Rotin's, and you save on your coffee and tea.

At one time the word sugar was a synonym for gold in the south, and in wartime Paris one recognises the association. Sugar has become almost as rare as the precious metal. If in some mysterious manner, Monsieur Rotin is able to salvage from the diminishing supply more sugar than is apportioned to his rival purveyors, it follows that more customers will crowd the counters of the Rotin shops. Which is the exact situation. When this privileged grocer announces a sugar sale, his sugar line is twice as long as the queue that fights to buy seats at the circus.

But in order to keep unscrupulous and selfish persons from cornering the sugar market, something no honest grocer would think of doing, and in order to see that all get their fair share, Monsieur Rotin sells his sugar in small quantities, two pounds to each purchaser, and said purchaser is only allotted his two pounds of sugar after he has bought half-a-dollar's worth of other groceries. Isn't Monsieur Rotin just the shrewdest philanthropist the war has brought to the surface? Think it over.

To the indictment charging "big business" with paying for the war, the verdict is not guilty.

Passing to the great category of men working on a salary, certain facts spring into high relief. As with all Frenchmen, the most influential fact determining the salary earner's fate and the fate of his family, is age. Men above or below the military age—twenty to forty eight—are anchored in the snug harbour of safety. Each day they go as usual to their cages in the bank, their desks in the office, their counters in the store. The only change noticeable is more work. At the end of each week the pay envelope is forced upon them just as regularly as it was before the first of August, 1914.

An interruption occurred when the invader came thundering to the borders of the Marne, but when General Joffre's army hurled the enemy back upon his wagons, bank and business resumed operations. As soon as the general public became convinced the army was going to hold, and something more, trading and financial France bent every effort to back up fighting France. The salaried man excused from military duty for whatever reason is a cog in this dynamic effort, and except for the usual war economies, life moves with its wonted routine....

It is not in the cities behind the lines that we must seek the answer to the query "who pays for the war?" Nor should we seek it from the heads of the thousand industrial plants supplying the armies of France with guns, wagons, food, clothing. Nor yet from the millions who toil fifteen hours each day in those thousand industrial plants. If you would know who pays, pays, pays,—leave the feverish activities of the rear for the desperate dangers of the front. Leave the comfort of the cities for the torment of the trenches. There will you find your answer.

Omit from our record the fatal risks of loss of life, limb or eyesight, and examine the other calamities that overwhelm the French citizen-soldier upon his sudden transition to the battlefield. Instead of his salary which may vary from fifty to five hundred dollars a month, he receives five cents a day. He lives at the cost of the government. Yes, call it living if you wish, when a man "boards" in a mud and corruption-filled trench, when he fights each night with vermin for space to rest his reeking, weary body. Call it living when a man shares his crusts of bread, his soup, his stringy rancid stew and his cheap wine with those grim comrades—Disease, Disfigurement and Death.

Take the bank-teller, the bookkeeper, the salesman who is wrenched from his accustomed environment and thrust into the army, what is his plight? Stirred by the highest sense of duty, he takes his place in the ranks, willingly, proudly, never counting what a heavy share of the cost of war he pays. Kissing his wife and baby, he marches to that grim, mysterious region, the front.

Life for this man and this woman has changed in all its aspects. The wife, thinking of the fate that threatens her loved one, classifies want and her personal suffering as the minor calamities of the war. Somehow, she will provide. There is always her dot for which she thanks Heaven devoutly. The income from that dot has in many cases been a stop-gap against starvation. Luckily the sense of kinship so strong among the French people shows itself immediately. Mother and child find a new home with her own or her husband's folk. More plates are set at table, more *pot-au-feu* bubbles on the stove. For the wife the problem of living is solved.

But what of the husband? Supposing he is fortunate enough to come through the conflict unscathed, can he hope to find his old job after three, four, five, Heaven knows how many years of absence?

Today his place is filled. With the kindliest feelings in the world his old employer cannot put him back in his old position at his old salary. Even should this be possible, try to compute the financial loss these war years mean in a young Frenchman's life.

Here is the frightful injustice of war. Why should these men who bear all the burden of the fighting also pay the bills? Is it not enough that they give their arms, their legs, their eyes, perhaps their lives for France, but that they shall also give their wealth. In France at every turn you meet this bitter injustice. . . .

Down the busy Rue Bellefort two wounded soldiers are walking. Their uniforms are old and spotted with dirt ingrained on the shoulders, where the pack-straps cross. Their faces show no ruddy, weather-beaten glow. Instead, the skin is hospital bleached and waxen. One soldier, his right sleeve pinned to the side of his tunic, gives his left hand to the other, who wears a black half-mask across his eyes.

"Where are we now, Jean?"

It is the blind soldier who speaks.

"We pass Saint Saviour's Church."

A little way and the two soldiers are blocked by a crowd, hurrying in and out of a butcher shop. For a moment Butcher Grasse pauses in the press of his chopping and weighing as the crowd gives way before the soldiers. "*C'est la guerre*," he mutters when he catches Jean Dufour's bitter eyes. But his ruddy face takes on a deeper crimson and his cleaver bites viciously into the sirloin he carves, as the wounded soldiers pass.

Farther down the street the two derelicts pause before a storm-washed sign that reads:

*Jean Dufour*
*Bucherie.*

Blank, tight-drawn shutters close the shop, the ground-glass door is locked. Dirt and grime, the accumulation of two years of neglect reign over what once had been an altar of cleanliness.

"How does it look, Jean?"

Tears were in his voice as the one-armed soldier replied:

"Sadly, Paul, sadly."

The blind soldier pressed his comrade's hand in sympathy.

"Come, we shall go to your shop," was Jean's answer to the friendly hand-clasp.

On go the one-armed soldier and his blind comrade to the far corner of the Rue Bellefort. Here they stop before another slatternly shop.

*Bucherie Theobald*

.... appears in faded letters above the door. But again the tight drawn shutters, the broken-down air of neglect, tells the story of ruined business.

Moving his cane before him, the blind soldier approaches the door. He tries the knob. It is locked. He knew it would be so. Then he turns towards his comrade who stands on the curb studying the shop with dull eyes.

"How does it look, Jean?"

"Sadly, Paul, sadly."

The blind soldier turns. He feels with trembling fingers along the shuttered front, then wearily dropping his head against the boards, he sobs,

"God help us!" ...

From the trenches five million voices echo that prayer. From a million graves, a spirit sigh repeats,

"God help us!"

Chapter 10

# The Burden France Has Borne

France has taken war's foulest blows full on her breast. During the first two years of conflict German armies spread across her most productive provinces like a grey corroding acid, eating through farm, orchard, factory, home, destroying the most valuable property and most useful lives of the French nation.

But this scarification did not crush the spirit of France. Rather the enemy outrages—ruined cathedrals, ransacked homes, ravaged women—roused the French people to a terrible realisation of the German threat against the world.

For the French man and woman, love of France, under the scourge of war, became a religion—a religion where fathers, mothers, sons, daughters, claimed the highest privilege accorded the Crusader and the ultimate sacrifice that gained the martyr's crown.

The battle which checked the greatest expression of organised savagery the world has seen in three thousand years is often called the Miracle of the Marne. Surely it was a miracle. During three days lustful Uhlan outguards pointed their bloodstained lance tips at the Eiffel Tower, saying confidently, "Within the week and our flag will float from the highest pinnacle in France." But the God who weaves the world's destiny in mystery heard the prayers of France. The miracle was performed. Paris, the most beautiful achievement of man on earth, was saved from sack and rapine.

It is no easy task to try to interpret French patriotism to our home-staying Americans. Only sympathetic hands can inscribe the long, sad stories of sacrifice which mark the stations of the war in France. When one has lived in the sacred atmosphere of a people daily immolated on the altar of patriotism, one feels a certain unworthiness in sounding the depths of this feeling, of analysing its springs, of calculating its results.

When the earth's last judgment is given on this great war, France will be deemed to have saved the world from despotism. Diplomats, during many years, have prophesied the contest between democracy and despotism for the domination of the world. In the struggle that endures France is the true champion of democracy, and no better expression of this democratic spirit exists than the French Army.

When the French Army is mentioned today, the French people is implied, for the whole nation is bound by the most sacred ties to the trials and triumphs of the fighting section of the populace.

Contrasting the French with the German Army, we discover, though both are grounded on conscription, they are radically different in their inspiration of service. The French and the German Armies are completely separate in soul. History gives us the analogue of variance between the French and German military systems in the story of Greece and Rome. The Roman Armies were organised for conquest, with the aim of spreading Roman "*kultur*" to the southernmost boundaries of Carthage and the northernmost villages of Gaul. The Roman eagle, like his Prussian descendant, sank his beak into the breast of the world. Roman power, like Prussian power, sprang from the will of the emperor.

In Greece, in the age of Pericles, the *demos* was the fountain of power, and the army was the guardian of the freedom of the people. The ideals which inspired the Athenians, honour gained in serving the country, is today the ideal inspiring the soldiers of France.

In analysing the spirit of the French soldier, bear in mind this vital fact—fighting is an emotional act; and it is admitted that an emotion springing from an ideal is necessarily finer than one founded on a person. The German goes to battle with the *Kaiser's* sparkling figure in the back of his mind, while the Frenchman fights for all that is connoted in the one word—France.

Frankly, the German honours, reveres, sanctifies war; the Frenchman hates, despises, abhors war. I have seen the soldiers of both nations in battle. I have studied them and talked with them after battle. I have watched for some unconscious expression that would give the clue to the real feelings of the French and German soldier, and when some phrase of the lips or flare of the eye marked the true state of the inward soul, I have noted it.

In countless ways the German shows it is the *Kaiser* he fights for; that dominant, disdainful figure symbolizes the Teutonic system, inspiring the German race to the ultimate sacrifice in the effort to spread that system over the face of the earth.

Never has the French soldier given any indication other than that he fights for his country, his cities, his farms, his homes. Never does he give way to the lust of battle for battle's sake. He sees in this war an evil, a scourge laying waste his beloved country, and he conceives it to be his duty to his forefathers, himself, and his children to rid the earth of this plague. The cultivated Frenchman will take pains to explain to you how illogical, unintelligent, uncivilised is war; yet you will see this same cultivated Frenchman wearing the uniform of his motherland racing like fury to the muzzles of the machine-guns.

Will not the man who recognises the brutal side of war, still does not hesitate to pay its penalty, merit more the title of hero than he who fights to gratify ambition?

The paradox of the French way of thinking about war and acting in war is carried out in the organisation of the army. The wide, unbridgable chasm of caste which exists between the officer and the private in the German company is but the step of necessity in French battalions. French soldiers recognise the need for discipline, of the value of team-work, and the urgency of obeying in battle, as the very foundation of their worth as citizen soldiers. They know also that they of their own volition have created the authority behind the officer, and for this reason there can be nothing degrading in the surrender of personal privilege in the crisis of war.

Discipline is not maintained through fear, but by public opinion. Each private soldier recognises that his individual efficiency and effectiveness, and consequently the efficiency and effectiveness of the whole French army, is based on his prompt and intelligent obedience of orders delivered by military superiors.

He knows that his officers are trained specialists in war, and he puts himself freely in their hands, so that the nation's will in war may be accomplished. He understands the successive limitations of military authority—the private to the sergeant, the sergeant to the lieutenant, the lieutenant to the captain, the captain to the major, and so on through grade after grade, up to General Petain, who in turn is responsible to France. With this conception of his duty, the most difficult part of military instruction is readily instilled into the French recruit.

Thoroughly to appreciate the relations of officer to soldier in the French army, they must be seen together in the trenches. The captain watches over his men like a father. He shows a sympathetic under-

BEHIND THE BATTLE LINES
FIGHTING MEN BROUGHT BACK FOR A RESPITE FROM BATTLE FALL AT ONCE TO HOMELY ARTS AND PLEASURES

standing of their difficulties, while demanding in the common cause a rigorous adherence to their duties. The officer sets the highest standard of performance for himself and exacts the best each of his men can do.

But the soldier knows he can go to his officer with his private troubles and receive helpful advice. He knows he will never meet with intentional injustice. And what gives him supreme confidence is the knowledge that he will be led with intelligence and skill.

The French officer is constantly alert to take advantage of the enemy and safeguard his own men. The greatest crime in the officer's calendar is wantonly to waste the life of a subordinate. Circumstances may call for the last sacrifice at times, but short of this condition the French commander husbands the lives of his men as a miser his pieces of gold. In an attack he will plan how they must creep from shell-hole to shell-hole, keeping as safe as possible from the enemy's artillery fire. He will study the ground in front of his trench for every available bit of cover, and so manoeuvre his men that they will gain its every advantage. He will elaborate trench and sap until his men are as safe as the battle front permits, feeling his duty to his country demands not only that he defeat the enemy, but that he defeat him with the minimum expenditure of the lives under his command.

Men learn quickly to appreciate this quality in their officers, and this appreciation brings about a sense of loyalty which closely knits an army into an unbeatable whole.

The test of the trenches also brings out the indomitable spirit of France as could no other circumstance. I saw this spirit in its concrete cheerfulness during a visit to the battle line beyond the Somme.

It had rained for two weeks and it still rained. The battle ground, a great patch of black, desolate earth, looked as if for an age it had been submerged beneath the slimy waters of some flood. Gaunt and murky tree stumps marked the residue of woodlands. A thousand shell pits pocked the ground. Into these drained the top soil of the earth in flux.

The Germans kept up a sullen shelling of the French trenches, zigzagging across these fields of desolation. Depression hung like a lowering cloud over the scene. Yet as I passed along the communication trenches I heard a voice in blithe song issuing from the depths of a dugout. A sodden rain was falling, adding the last dismal touch to conditions, yet the singer chanted gaily:

*Elle a perdu son parapluie, tant pis pour elle.*

In a moment a mud-spattered soldier appeared from the dark of the cave.

"Good morning," he said, cheerily throwing the carcasses of two huge rats over the parapet "There goes the night's hunting."

The cheerfulness of this soldier personified the spirit of France.

In the proportion to her population, France has given more of her citizens to battle than any other nation. It would be valuable information to the enemy to give the exact figures of losses, so the French general staff publishes no record of the cost of victory. But from a study of such data as is available an estimate can be made. Counting the dead, the permanently disabled, and the prisoners, France's contribution to the holocaust of war is more than two millions.

The price France pays in flesh and blood is a greater sacrifice than has been yet demanded from any of the allied nations. In computing the value of this sacrifice, all the conditions of French population must be taken into account. Chief among these must be placed the abnormally low annual increase in the number of French citizens. Taking only the figures for native-born Americans during the last forty years, and the increase in population in the United States has been over thirty millions, while during the same period in France the increase has been less than three millions.

If the loss continues at the same rate, in another year France will lose the total surplus in citizens she has gained since the war of 1870. And it must be remembered that the death lists today are not compiled from the aged and sickly, but from the youth and health of the land.

Through the sacrifices in men lost during the early battles of the war France was able to check the German rush and gain time for England to prepare. The French Army met the German Army at its full strength and defeated it. The victory of the Marne was due to the tactics employed, and the blows struck by the French army. When the facts are finally revealed, history will grant France this honour. But it is an honour paid for in the best blood of the country.

Up to the present it has been the French Army, the French citizen soldier, who has saved the world from German conquest.

As an example of what France gives, let me quote the story of General Castleneau. He is a valiant, generous gentleman—a soldier with the soul of a Spartan.

He and his sons were among the first to draw their sabres in defence of their land. During the first year of the war, when he was pressed down with the cares of one of the most important commands in the French Army, news was brought to General Castleneau, first, that one of his sons had been killed; then in a few months a second died for his country.

The third son fought in the army commanded by his father. He was his father's favourite. Little more than a boy, in the first battles he had shown a courage that won him honour and rapid promotion. Then in one of those attacks, where regiment upon regiment charged through the fields of death, this third son was mortally wounded.

Upon the death of this boy, broken by his sorrows and the strain of war, General Castleneau thought to give up his high command and live out his last days on his home farm. Then his wife came to him. He told her his thought.

"No," said this French wife and mother, "you have given the best of yourself to your country. You have nothing left to give save these last years. We must keep up the fight." General Castleneau today, (as at time of first publication), is still at his post of duty.

Not only has France given the bodies of her sons in the sacrifice of battle, but she has also given the fruits of their brains. The trained professional officers of the French army have been the intelligence which directed the military operations of the Entente armies. These officers were instructors in the art of war to the allied forces and while acting in this capacity they evolved new tactics which so effectively thwarted German ambitions.

The new tactics were the outcome of trench warfare, which had brought into use weapons long since discarded in modern armies. When the war opened French battalions a thousand strong, had the organisation common to most armies, namely, four companies and a *mitrailleuse* section of two guns. The men were armed wholly with rifle and bayonet; but French ingenuity was quick to see the changes of organisation and armament made necessary by the new warfare.

Today, (as at time of first publication), half the battalion have discarded the rifle and carry grenades or one-man machine-guns. Three of the original companies are still infantry, while the fourth has been changed to a machine-gun company with eight *mitrailleuses*.

The infantry companies are subdivided into sections and armed with special weapons: first, the hand-grenade throwers; second, the rifle grenade soldiers, who, instead of throwing the grenade, fire it from their guns; third, the soldiers firing automatic rifles, and these are followed by the ordinary infantry, using rifle or bayonet.

The machine-guns as employed by the Germans were the great bugbear of the trenches. These weapons would mow down a whole company of advancing soldiers in the charge. French officers set themselves to solving this problem and devised the small cannon to be used in the assault. The gun 1½-inch calibre rapid fire, was dragged forward with the charging line. When brought into action it soon mastered the fire of any hidden machine- gun.

That ingenious weapon, the rifle grenade, merits special citation. It consists of an iron receptacle, clamped to the end of the regular rifle, in which a special type of grenade is placed, and the rifle fired. The explosion sends the grenade about 200 yards through the air, while the rifle bullet, piercing the centre of the bomb sets free the fulminate, which causes the grenade to explode on landing.

I have no intention of going into a technical discussion of the French infantry in attack, and only give the outline of tactical changes in order to indicate how the French people are fighting with their intellects. They have no belief in brute force in war; if they had, they long ago would have surrendered to the Germans. Their faith is pinned to their own finesse—a finesse which exasperates and thwarts the enemy.

As instructors, French officers have been of inestimable value to the English. In the beginning of the war the British army was deficient in artillery—a deficiency which was rapidly remedied in material, for England turned out guns for the army from the naval-gun foundries. But gunners, who are soldier specialists, were not available for the batteries.

In this dilemma England turned to France, the country that had developed the finest corps of artillerists the world has ever seen. French officers were detailed to the English batteries, and English officers also were taken into French artillery units and learned their art in the actual practice of war under the tutelage of the most competent teachers.

I have referred to French artillerists as the finest in the world. The statement is made without qualification; and were I seeking the factor of greatest single importance in the military strength of France, I should decide upon the artillery.

It was given me to see the French guns go into action in one of the early attacks of the war—the engagement at Dinant. Aside from its spectacular interest, the performance was one of the most perfect exhibitions of artillery technique I have ever witnessed. The guns were driven, wheeled, and unlimbered with the precision of parade-ground manoeuvres. The men dropped into their appointed places like the parts of a geared machine. Then guns were loaded, aimed, fired, reloaded, without an ounce of lost motion. When the projectiles exploded, and I could see the effect through my binoculars, I wanted to cheer for the gunners of France. They had scored four direct hits.

The guns of this battery were the *soisante quinze* calibre, since become the most famous cannon of the war.

The construction of this cannon was a jealously guarded military secret up until the time of the opening of hostilities. Other nations knew that France possessed a field gun of exceptional properties, and while they had hints of its effectiveness, as demonstrated in peace, it needed the brutal test of war to prove the superiority of this weapon above all similar makes of artillery.

It is readily understood that, with a cannon which shoots farther and faster than the enemy, the French army possessed an asset of great military advantage.

I have heard French artillerymen state that the superiority of their *soisante quinze* batteries made up for the German preponderance of numbers in the beginning of the war, and that the destructiveness of these guns was so great that they almost equalised the tactical value of the forces of France and Germany after several hours of actual fighting.

The gun is a marvel of fitted mechanism; breech- block, recoil cylinders, sighting apparatus, all the puzzling pieces of hardened steel which open and close the cartridge chamber, function with the smoothness of a dynamo.

In the process of loading and firing, it gives the impression of some sentient organism rather than a machine of turned steel. This impression is heightened by the short, dry sound of the explosion when the shell is fired—a sound that awes and electrifies when first heard, and which has come to be far more characteristic of battle than the conventional "*boom*" supposed to convey the noise of cannon.

As soon as the superiority of the French cannon was recognised, the great arms factories of France were enlarged and worked to the limit of capacity, not only to furnish new guns for the French Army, but also to supply the enormous demands of the Russian Army. Later Serbia and Roumania were also supplied with field batteries from

French foundries, and in these countries officers and men accompanied the guns to insure efficient handling.

From the above it is seen how generously France came to the support of her allies in the most important branch of military science; and when we reflect on the enormous amount of material destroyed during the two and one-half years of war, we begin to perceive what a drain this has been on the resources of France.

Reliance upon the decisive effect of artillery in battle has been a tradition with the French army since the victories of the first Napoleon. He it was who originally employed artillery in a massed formation. At Wagram, at Lutzen, at Hanau, this manoeuvre of concentrated artillery fire gave the victory to the armies of France. Napoleon III tried to continue the theories of his brilliant ancestor, but failed; yet the influence of the great master of tactics continued; so it is but natural that the use of artillery in war should reach its highest perfection through French development.

The French have relied for success in the fighting today on the ancient manoeuvre of the Napoleonic era—a mass of guns firing at a given point in the enemy line. At the same time they endeavoured to make the practice of concentrated fire more effective through increased speed and accuracy of fire.

Before the opening of the great war there were two schools of artillery tactics—the French, which believed in the above theory of rapid field-gun shelling, and the German, which pinned its faith to the effectiveness of huge guns having a greater range than the ordinary field gun and of course throwing a far more destructive exploding charge. The extreme of the German theory was the widely advertised 42-centimetre cannon, supposed to be able to reduce the strongest fortress to ruin with three well-directed shots.

The actual practice of war and the peculiarities of trench fighting developed the fact that neither of these schools were wholly right. The light French guns were ineffective against troops hidden in well-constructed trenches, while the difficulties of transportation involved in moving the giant German guns from point to point outbalanced their ultimate effectiveness.

French artillery experts began at once to experiment toward developing the most serviceable gun under actual conditions of war, and the result of this experiment can be gauged by the different calibre of cannon now used in the French Army. Here is the list given in metres and the approximate calibre in inches:

First the 75 m.m., the standard field gun, 3-inch calibre; the 95 m.m., 3½-inch; 105 m.m., 12-inch; 370 m.m., 15-inch; 400 m.m., 16-inch, and last the largest cannon in the world, 520 m.m., or 20 inches.

I give the list in full to impress upon my reader the extraordinary complication of industry involved in the casting, turning, and assembling of these various types of cannon. Special machinery must be employed in each instance where there is a variation in calibre. Complete foundries are given over to the manufacture of the separate parts of the gun and gun carriage. The industrial organisation for one size of gun alone is greater today than the total pre-war ordnance organisation.

From the failures of the Germans the French found that the problem of heavy artillery in the field was transportation; so French artillery experts began at once to try to solve this difficulty. They have succeeded in their task. Their triumph is the construction of a railroad truck upon which is mounted a 20-inch cannon, the heaviest piece of artillery in the world.

The marvellous manner in which the French have overcome the mechanical difficulties that hitherto confined heavy artillery to fortress or siege operations is a striking example of what French brains are doing in this war. Firing a 12-inch gun from a foundation built along a spur of railway was considered a mechanical impossibility before General Joffre's expert artillerists demonstrated the success of the idea.

It was not only in the construction of these guns that France showed her skill, but in their operation. French gunners first developed indirect fire—the art of hitting an unseen target—and in this war they have brought indirect fire to technical perfection and even applied its principles in new ways.

Undoubtedly, in accounts of present-day battles in Europe, the reader has met the phrase curtain or barrage fire. He may have guessed something of the nature of this artillery expedient.

The phrase means, in untechnical language, the art of aiming a mass of cannon in a manner that the projectiles from all of them fall in a given area in such a shower as to form a curtain or barrage of exploding iron.

This curtain may be dropped behind an enemy position so that reinforcements cannot come to his aid when attacked, or it may be used to check an advance.

Accurately to synchronize the action of fifty or one hundred batteries, two hundred or four hundred guns, so that while firing from widely separated positions at a target that is not in view the projectiles arrive simultaneously along a defined and predetermined line, is a matter of the highest technical skill and calculation. To the French belongs the honour of first employing this effective artillery principle.

I have seen these great pieces of ordnance, equal in size to the major guns of a battleship, moving from point to point along specially built lines of lateral railroads, running in rear of the trench position on the Somme. At the will of the commander they are brought into action wherever the press of battle warrants.

This development and operation of artillery is the most impressive manifestation of the colossal expansion of modern war. Consider the tons of metal moulded into each of these great cannon, and then reflect that wherever the trucks upon which they are mounted move, bridges, culverts, even the roadbed itself, of the railroad line must be strengthened to support the load.

Further, in order that the giant cannon shall have the mobility for effective use, new sections of railroad must be built whenever the army advances.

If you analyse the process of manufacture and the details of transportation involved in the creating and bringing of each one of the new heavy field guns to the front, you arrive at an understanding of the important part played in the war by the French industrial organisations.

I was witness to another phase of the effectiveness of this organisation, as shown in the munition industry in France. Taking the number of units produced daily as a standard, the greatest single business of the war is the making of shells. This comes about through the enormous disproportion in the time consumed in the production and the distribution of shells compared with the time needed to expend them.

Consider the making and the breaking of the shell. One is a tedious, toilsome, exacting, and complicated process, beginning with the digging of iron ore from the earth, its transportation to steel mills, its transfusion and casting into ingots.

These ingots are the raw material of the shell casing only. The production of the explosive that serves as the bursting charge is an industry in itself, while the construction of the mechanism of the fuses requires almost as much skill as watchmaking.

In the first year of the war, the critical period of the conflict, France led all the Entente nations in the production of shells. As was the case with guns, France had to supply her ally, Russia, with the munitions so necessary to the effectiveness of the armies fighting in Poland the Carpathians. To meet this drain the industries of the country were reorganised. The products of peace gave way before the demands of war.

The concrete example of this is the transformation of the plants of the Renault automobile works to the making of munitions. In one factory, formerly wholly concerned with the forging and fitting of motor machinery, fifteen thousand men and four thousand women are now employed twenty-four hours of each day grinding and filling high-explosive shells. The work divided into shifts, never halts, and from this one plant eleven thousand projectiles are daily sent forward to the front.

But during periods of heavy fighting, when the cannon is playing its important part in the tragedy of battle, the calculated average of expenditure of ammunition by one army corps is twenty-nine thousand shells per day. So the total effort of nineteen thousand workers employed during twenty- four hours furnishes somewhat more than one-third the ammunition used by a small part of the army.

The number of army corps holding the front in France is a military secret, and as the United States is now ranged on the side of France in the war, it would be injudicious to try and probe that secret. We violate no confidence when we state that it is more than thirty. This figure will give us a basis for calculating the number of shells produced by the munitions factories of France.

There are long periods when the expenditure of ammunition in no way approximates the figures given above, and it is during these periods when the guns are comparatively silent that production catches up with consumption.

It may be true that England is gradually approaching France, both in the manufacture of heavy guns and the production of munitions; but this condition appears after two and a half years of war. During those two and a half years it was the French cannon, French shells, French soldiers, and French brains that checked the military ambitions of Germany.

With all this effort applied to improve her killing power, France did not neglect the complement of war destruction—healing. The best surgical and medical minds of the country pondered long on the problem of saving all that was possible from the human wreckage of war.

The fruit of this thought is exemplified in the work of Doctor Carrel, whose achievements under the Rockefeller Foundation are well known in the United States, and Doctor Dakin.

These two men put all their efforts into curing the evil of infection. They had found in their work among the wounded that seventy-five *per cent*, of deaths, after the first twenty-four hours, were due to infection; that eighty *per cent*, of amputations were due to infection, and that ninety-five *per cent*, of secondary haemorrhage came through infection.

While the work incidental to healing the wounded was going on, Doctors Carrel and Dakin established a research laboratory in conjunction with their military hospital at Compiegne.

It is not necessary to give the details of the experiments of these two scientists. Today, (as at time of original publication), by the application of the Carrel-Dakin method of sterilising wounds, one amputation is performed where formerly twenty were necessary, and where there were ten deaths one now occurs, and the time of convalescence is reduced from three to six months to four or, at the most six weeks.

It has been found that the method of Doctor Carrel applied to the formula of Doctor Dakin has not only shortened convalescence, but in consequence reduced the strain on doctors and nurses and the cost of hospital maintenance; also it has minimised pain. But more than all this, it has resulted in a great saving of limbs and lives to France.

Turning from the purely military side of war to the economic side, we find another picture of French sacrifice. In this picture the Frenchwoman holds the foreground.

In the time of war every physically fit male in France can be called upon to shoulder rifle and fight the battles of his country. When this call sounds, it might be thought that the agricultural and industrial structure of the nation would be reduced to chaos.

But for the sturdy heroism of the women of France such might have been the case. When the men were called to the colours, the women came forward to fill the gaps in the farming and manufacturing armies.

French women, aided by their children, ploughed the fields, sowed the seed, harvested the crops that during two years have fed the soldiers of France. Frenchwomen tended the vines, gathered the grapes, and pressed the wine which France exports throughout the world. Frenchwomen became conductors, motor operators, ticket-sellers on the subways of Paris; they took the positions vacated by men in the post-office department; they were employed in the street-cleaning and other municipal departments.

In all industries, public or private, women replaced the men called to the front, and, what is much more to the point, they made good in their new work.

As farmers, as vintners, as labourers, as munition workers, Frenchwomen toil without ceasing to save France and take some of the burden of war from the shoulders of the men. In their own field, as housewives who understand the importance of thrift, they have saved the economic situation.

The enormous financial burden which war has so unjustly thrown on France has been lightened by the thousand economies put into practice by Frenchwomen in their homes. All the little dainties of table, the little *coquetries* of dress, the little temptations of amusement, have been sternly put aside for the duration of the war.

Sugar means money spent abroad; therefore the Frenchwoman gives up pastries, sweets, and reduces the amount of sugar used in the household. Coal is needed to keep the munition factories up to the maximum of production, so the Frenchwoman reduces the amount of gas and electricity used in her home, as these are the products of coal.

Thus Frenchwomen, through practising direct and indirect economies, actually reduce the cost of the war to France; and, more than this, when any money is saved to them from these economies they invest the saving in government war loan, making every copper do double work in the defence of the country.

I have only outlined what France has done in the war. I have mentioned the work of the army which met and turned the heaviest blows the military power of Germany could muster. I have mentioned how the artillery, the product of French brains, bulwarked the efforts of the soldiers. I have referred to the work of the women of France and their splendid stand under the strain of war, and I have mentioned the spirit of France.

In conclusion, I must again allude to that spirit. French men and women know that the resources of their nation in property and lives are being consumed in the furnace of war. They know what the death of their soldiers means to the nation in the future. They realize the terrible consequences of German occupation. Yet in the face of all these bitter trials the people have never faltered.

Throughout the misery, the suffering, the brutal injustice of this war, France has fought valiantly for one ideal the ideal upon which that nation and our own is founded the right of the citizen to liberty.

Each day, (as at time of first publication), as the French Armies press the enemy back from the territory so long occupied, the sacrifices of France are proved with greater poignancy.

The band of blackened land now given over to desolation is the visual testimony of what the war has meant to France. But it is not only the losses of today, but what those losses mean in the future that must be reckoned as part of the burden France bears. This is a sacrifice no man can gauge.

When democracy rises triumphant from the struggle with despotism, and when the last page of war history is written, the world will gladly acknowledge its debt to France.

## ALSO FROM LEONAUR
### AVAILABLE IN SOFTCOVER OR HARDCOVER WITH DUST JACKET

**THE RELUCTANT REBEL** by *William G. Stevenson*—A young Kentuckian's experiences in the Confederate Infantry & Cavalry during the American Civil War..

**BOOTS AND SADDLES** by *Elizabeth B. Custer*—The experiences of General Custer's Wife on the Western Plains.

**FANNIE BEERS' CIVIL WAR** by *Fannie A. Beers*—A Confederate Lady's Experiences of Nursing During the Campaigns & Battles of the American Civil War.

**LADY SALE'S AFGHANISTAN** by *Florentia Sale*—An Indomitable Victorian Lady's Account of the Retreat from Kabul During the First Afghan War.

**THE TWO WARS OF MRS DUBERLY** by *Frances Isabella Duberly*—An Intrepid Victorian Lady's Experience of the Crimea and Indian Mutiny.

**THE REBELLIOUS DUCHESS** by *Paul F. S. Dermoncourt*—The Adventures of the Duchess of Berri and Her Attempt to Overthrow French Monarchy.

**LADIES OF WATERLOO** by *Charlotte A. Eaton, Magdalene de Lancey & Juana Smith*—The Experiences of Three Women During the Campaign of 1815: Waterloo Days by Charlotte A. Eaton, A Week at Waterloo by Magdalene de Lancey & Juana's Story by Juana Smith.

**TWO YEARS BEFORE THE MAST** by *Richard Henry Dana. Jr.*—The account of one young man's experiences serving on board a sailing brig—the Penelope—bound for California, between the years 1834-36.

**A SAILOR OF KING GEORGE** by *Frederick Hoffman*—From Midshipman to Captain—Recollections of War at Sea in the Napoleonic Age 1793-1815.

**LORDS OF THE SEA** by *A. T. Mahan*—Great Captains of the Royal Navy During the Age of Sail.

**COGGESHALL'S VOYAGES: VOLUME 1** by *George Coggeshall*—The Recollections of an American Schooner Captain.

**COGGESHALL'S VOYAGES: VOLUME 2** by *George Coggeshall*—The Recollections of an American Schooner Captain.

**TWILIGHT OF EMPIRE** by *Sir Thomas Ussher & Sir George Cockburn*—Two accounts of Napoleon's Journeys in Exile to Elba and St. Helena: Narrative of Events by Sir Thomas Ussher & Napoleon's Last Voyage: Extract of a diary by Sir George Cockburn.

AVAILABLE ONLINE AT www.leonaur.com
AND FROM ALL GOOD BOOK STORES

## ALSO FROM LEONAUR
### AVAILABLE IN SOFTCOVER OR HARDCOVER WITH DUST JACKET

**THE 9TH—THE KING'S (LIVERPOOL REGIMENT) IN THE GREAT WAR 1914 - 1918** by Enos H. G. Roberts—Mersey to mud—war and Liverpool men.

**THE GAMBARDIER** by Mark Severn—The experiences of a battery of Heavy artillery on the Western Front during the First World War.

**FROM MESSINES TO THIRD YPRES** by Thomas Floyd—A personal account of the First World War on the Western front by a 2/5th Lancashire Fusilier.

**THE IRISH GUARDS IN THE GREAT WAR - VOLUME 1** by Rudyard Kipling—Edited and Compiled from Their Diaries and Papers—The First Battalion.

**THE IRISH GUARDS IN THE GREAT WAR - VOLUME 1** by Rudyard Kipling—Edited and Compiled from Their Diaries and Papers—The Second Battalion.

**ARMOURED CARS IN EDEN** by K. Roosevelt—An American President's son serving in Rolls Royce armoured cars with the British in Mesopatamia & with the American Artillery in France during the First World War.

**CHASSEUR OF 1914** by Marcel Dupont—Experiences of the twilight of the French Light Cavalry by a young officer during the early battles of the great war in Europe.

**TROOP HORSE & TRENCH** by R.A. Lloyd—The experiences of a British Lifeguardsman of the household cavalry fighting on the western front during the First World War 1914-18.

**THE EAST AFRICAN MOUNTED RIFLES** by C.J. Wilson—Experiences of the campaign in the East African bush during the First World War.

**THE LONG PATROL** by George Berrie—A Novel of Light Horsemen from Gallipoli to the Palestine campaign of the First World War.

**THE FIGHTING CAMELIERS** by Frank Reid—The exploits of the Imperial Camel Corps in the desert and Palestine campaigns of the First World War.

**STEEL CHARIOTS IN THE DESERT** by S. C. Rolls—The first world war experiences of a Rolls Royce armoured car driver with the Duke of Westminster in Libya and in Arabia with T.E. Lawrence.

**WITH THE IMPERIAL CAMEL CORPS IN THE GREAT WAR** by Geoffrey Inchbald—The story of a serving officer with the British 2nd battalion against the Senussi and during the Palestine campaign.

---

AVAILABLE ONLINE AT **www.leonaur.com**
AND FROM ALL GOOD BOOK STORES

www.ingramcontent.com/pod-product-compliance
Lightning Source LLC
Chambersburg PA
CBHW031621160426
43196CB00006B/220